GERMANY
POLAND
BELGIUM
Liège, EXHIBITED 1449
CZECHOSLOVAKIA
Paris, 1307
FRANCE
Lirey, 1357–1418
Montfort 1418
St.-Hippolyte-sur-Doubs, 1418–1449
Germolles, EXHIBITED SEPT. 13, 1452
AUSTRIA
HUNGARY
SWITZERLAND
Geneva, 1453
Chambéry, 1502–1537; 1561–1578
Bourg-en-Bresse EXHIBITED APR. 14, 1503
Milan, EXHIBITED 1536
Turin, 1578–1939 1946–PRESENT
Vercelli, 1537–1561 EXHIBITED GOOD FRIDAY 1494
YUGOSLAVIA
Marseilles
Nice, EXHIBITED MAR. 29, 1537
ITALY
Avellino, 1939–1946
ALGERIA
TUNISIA
N
W E
S
MILES 0 200
KM 0 200
MEDITERRANEAN SEA
National Boundaries as of Today

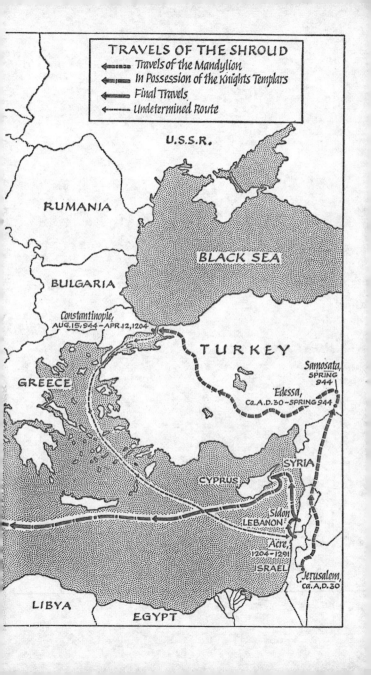

THE SHROUD
OF TURIN

The Burial Cloth
of Jesus Christ?

By IAN WILSON

REVISED EDITION

IMAGE BOOKS

A Division of Doubleday & Company, Inc.
Garden City, New York
1979

TO THE MEMORY OF
THE LATE DR. DAVID WILLIS
of Litton, near Bath, England,
without whose selfless
inspiration this book
would not have been written

Image Book Edition published September 1979 by special arrangement with Doubleday & Company, Inc.

Biblical excerpts unless otherwise noted from *The Jerusalem Bible*, copyright © 1966 by Darton, Longman & Todd, Ltd., and Doubleday & Company, Inc. Used by permission of the publishers.

Grateful acknowledgment is given for permission to quote material from the following sources:

Conquest of Constantinople by Robert de Clari, translated by E. H. McNeal, Records of Civilization Series, Columbia University Press, 1936, by permission of the publisher; *Edessa: The Blessed City* by J. B. Segal, © Oxford University Press 1970, by permission of the Oxford University Press; "The Holy Shroud and the Verdict of History" by Rev. Herbert Thurston, *The Month* CI 1903, pp. 17–29, by permission of *The Month*.

PREFACE

I am indebted to the excellence of several previous books on the Shroud, most notably John Walsh's *The Shroud* (Random House, 1963). The depth of Walsh's coverage of the early discoveries of Pia, Enrie, Vignon, and Barbet is such that these aspects have been only summarized in the present work.

Where I have sought to break new ground is in encompassing within a single volume much new research on the Shroud—the recently published findings of the Italian Commission of 1973, the remarkable pollen analysis by Swiss criminologist Dr. Max Frei, my own work on the problems relating to the Shroud's history before the fourteenth century, and the most recent research by U.S. space-project scientists inspired and co-ordinated by Drs. John Jackson and Eric Jumper of the USAF Academy, Colorado Springs.

I cannot speak too highly of the unstinting help and encouragement I received from people in many countries during the course of writing. It was through an enquiry made in 1966 to Fr. Adam Otterbein of the U. S. Holy Shroud Guild that I first met British medical practitioner Dr. David Willis, then of Guildford, England. During years of patient correspondence Dr. Willis transformed my early agnostic skepticism into total commitment both to the authentication of the Shroud and the essential truth of the Christian faith. Tragically Dr. Willis died of a heart attack during a BBC radio interview at my home just as news was being released of the most recent findings on the Shroud. No man could have assisted me more, and I have dedicated this book to him as a memorial to his selfless inspiration.

Among other colleagues in England my thanks are due especially to Fr. Maurus Green, who generously made available to me his copious notes and gave much valuable advice in the early stages of the manuscript; to Miss Vera Barclay of

Seaview, Isle of Wight, to Group Captain Leonard Cheshire, V.C., to Fr. Christopher Kelley of Canterbury (now of Richardson, Texas), to Dr. Henry Osmaston of Bristol, to the Reverend Robert Jones and the Reverend Jesse Sage of Templecombe, to Susan Hopkins of Oxford, and to London film producer David Rolfe, who made possible a valuable research trip to Turkey and Israel. The spirit of ecumenism is very much alive in the study of the Shroud, and I owe particular thanks to the Episcopalian Fr. David Sox of the American School in London and to the Anglican Right Reverend Dr. John A. T. (*Honest to God*) Robinson of Trinity College, Cambridge, who read the final manuscript and corrected several errors.

In the United States I am deeply indebted to Fr. Peter Rinaldi of the U. S. Holy Shroud Guild, who gave me an unforgettable opportunity to study the Shroud at first hand in Turin in 1973; through him I am also grateful to Mr. and Mrs. Leo Haiblum, who generously helped with my hotel expenses on that occasion. I would also like to thank Dr. John Jackson and Dr. Eric Jumper of Colorado Springs for inviting me to their 1977 conference on the Shroud in Albuquerque; also, for their subsequent help, Dr. Walter McCrone, Donald Lynn, Donald Janney, and other scientists who attended the conference.

When in 1976 the findings of the Turin Commission on the Shroud were published in Italian, the highly technical nature of the reports would have presented a virtually insurmountable translation problem but for some dedicated teamwork by Italian linguists in England, and I am indebted to Miss Valeria Ossola, Fr. Eric Doyle, Fr. Maurus Green, and most particularly Mrs. Maria Jepps, who checked and edited the entire work. My thanks are also due to Bernard Slater, the Reverend John Jackson, and the 1968 sixth-form boys of Bradford Grammar School for translating from the original Greek the entire text of the tenth-century "Story of the Image of Edessa." For Biblical translation I have in general used the Jerusalem version for its clarity and modern English.

In Shroud studies the field of history has proved one of the most implacable, and I hope the reader will forgive me that in Parts III and IV of this work I have dealt with this at perhaps disproportionate length in an attempt to throw new light on the problem. Undoubtedly future writers will correct and modify some of the more pioneering conclusions drawn, but in the meantime I have greatly valued the assistance of the following people: Professor J. B. Segal of the School of Oriental and African Studies, London, author of *Edessa the Blessed City*, who gave much helpful advice prior to my visit to Turkey; Dr. Timothy Ware, Spalding Lecturer in Eastern Orthodox Studies, Oxford, who assisted on Byzantine attitudes; Mrs. Pauline Johnstone, who helped correct dating of the Celestine III *umbella;* Miss Vivien Godfrey-White, who gave me the benefit of her prodigious unpublished research on the Knights Templars; and Miss Elizabeth Crowfoot, who provided much sound information on early textiles. I am also grateful for constructive criticism from Professor Kurt Weitzmann of the Department of Art and Archaeology, Princeton University, and from Sir Steven Runciman of Cambridge, England.

The story of the Shroud is scattered widely across Europe and the Near East, and I am indebted to the following individuals for assistance that saved much wearisome travel: FRANCE: Monsieur R. de Rouville, Père Jacques Le Roy, the Abbé Pierre Boufflers, and Mrs. Barbara Cornell; BELGIUM: Monsieur J. Leysen, Professor Gilbert Raes; SWITZERLAND: Dr. Max Frei; ITALY: Fr. Guiseppe Baracca, Don Piero Coero Borga, the brothers Dutto, and Dr. Alberto Zina; ISRAEL: Fr. Jacob Barclay; CYPRUS: Mr. A. Papageorghiou.

None of the research would have been possible without libraries, and I am particularly grateful to the British Museum Library, London, where the whole project began, and to the university and city libraries in Bristol; also to the Musée de Cluny, Paris, the Centre d'Entr'aide Généalogique, Paris, the Ufficia Stampa dell'Archivescovado, Turin, the Centro Internazionale di Sindonologia, Turin, and the Lord Chamberlain's Office, London.

The book itself would not have been possible without a publisher, and I am deeply grateful to those at Doubleday who have so painstakingly worked on its production—in particular, Editorial Director Robert T. Heller, who commissioned me, his assistant Janet V. Waring, and copyeditor James E. Ricketson, to whose assiduousness in checking detail I would like to pay a very special tribute.

Lastly but by no means least, I would like to thank the "home" team who suffered not a few of the pangs of the book taking shape: Rex Conway and others at Bristol United Press for assistance with photographs; my office secretaries Barbara Weeks and Andrea Selmes for many favors; Mrs. Anna Evans, who typed much of the manuscript; and my wife, Judith, who helped with the typing, gave much valuable advice, and adjusted magnificently to her husband's many idiosyncrasies.

IAN WILSON

Bristol, England
May 1977

CONTENTS

INTRODUCTION

THE SHROUD—A QUIET REVOLUTION

On the face of it, the very idea that the linen cloth in which Jesus Christ was wrapped in the tomb should have survived to this day would seem incredible. It demands even more of human credulity that the cloth bears a photographic likeness which would seem to be that of Jesus as he lay in the tomb. Yet it is on the evidence for these two seemingly impossible facts that this book has been written.

The cloth in question is known by the Italians as the *Santa Sindone,* or Holy Shroud. It reposes within Turin's Cathedral of St. John the Baptist, in the circular, black marble Royal Chapel, designed by Guarino Guarini, which was once the place of private worship for the dukes of Savoy, former rulers of Italy. To reach this chapel, the visitor has to walk the length of the cathedral and ascend a steep flight of steps to the side of the main altar. He finds himself in a baroque chamber lined with white marble tombs and capped with a soaring cupola. In the center is an ornate black marble altar, set on a stepped platform and ringed by golden cherubs. This altar is surmounted by a second altar, and it is within this, behind iron grilles, in a locked cavity known as the "sepulcher," that the Shroud is kept.

It lies rolled around a velvet staff and wrapped in red silk within a four-foot-long wooden casket ornamented in silver with the emblems of the Passion. The casket is kept within an iron chest wrapped in asbestos and sealed by no fewer than three locks, for each of which a separate key is required. In turn the iron chest is within a wooden box with a painted cover. This cover is all that is visible behind the two iron grilles in the upper "sepulcher" section of the altar in which the Shroud is stored.

The Shroud has always attracted controversy. Of mysteri-

ous origins, when it first appeared in the West a fourteenth-
century French bishop dismissed it as merely "cunningly
painted," and created "falsely and deceitfully."[1] In the early
years of our own century two learned Catholic historians,
Canon Ulysse Chevalier[2] and the Reverend Herbert Thurston[3] similarly condemned it as a fourteenth-century forgery.
More recently an internationally renowned art critic has described it as "notorious,"[4] and a clerical review as "a harmless piece of buffoonery."[5]

There have been, and still are, crankish claims about it. A
forceful German writer, Kurt Berna, has sought worldwide
publicity for his view that the Shroud "proves" Christ did
not die on the cross, the resurrection having been a mere revival in the tomb.[6] Conversely, a sincere Italian monsignor,
Giulio Ricci, has "seen" on the Shroud the most intricate reconstruction of Christ's Passion, unfortunately deriving more
from the imagination than observation.[7]

Such speculation about the Shroud has been allowed to
flourish all too easily because of the relic's inaccessibility.
Until very recently Turin's cardinals have been notoriously
resistant to pleas for expositions. In normal circumstances not
even the most privileged visitor is allowed to see it. Since the
time of Napoleon the Shroud has been seen publicly on no
more than a handful of occasions, always attracting vast
crowds of pilgrims, who have queued for hours just to file
past it as it hung in the cathedral, or catch a glimpse of an
exposition on the cathedral steps. An elaborate procedure
must be followed for any exposition. Permission has to be obtained from the pope, from the cardinal of Turin, and from
the ex-king of Italy, Umberto II of Savoy. Although Umberto
is technically still the cloth's owner, even he has not seen it
since 1933 because of his fall from power.

One man, who as an altar boy in Turin saw the exposition
of the Shroud in 1933, has fought ever since for the Shroud
to be more accessible. He is Fr. Peter Rinaldi, pastor for
more than twenty-five years of Corpus Christi Church, Port
Chester, New York.[8] Back in the 1960s Pope John XXIII in
his homely, forthright manner told Rinaldi that it would need
"a lot of pushing and shoving to move those people in
Turin." But the American pastor, undeterred, kept writing

articles pressing for an exposition, and traveled to Europe to call on Pope Paul VI, Cardinal Pellegrino of Turin, and ex-King Umberto in Portugal to plead his case in person.

It was forty years after the 1933 exposition before Rinaldi's efforts were rewarded. In November 1973 Cardinal Pellegrino agreed not to a traditional exposition but to something in many ways far better. The Shroud would be shown for the first time on television, in a thirty-minute RAI-TV program. Through the Eurovision network it would be seen throughout Italy, Spain, France, Portugal, Belgium, and even as far as Brazil. The pope would speak about the Shroud for eight minutes as part of the program, and the Shroud would also be shown at a special press conference for an international group of correspondents the day before the television program.

A few days after the cardinal's announcement, three men boarded a flight from London to Turin who represented almost the entire body of active British research on the Shroud. One was the author. Another was a Benedictine priest, Fr. Maurus Green, who had inherited a passion for research on historical aspects of the Shroud[9] from his father, a former army officer who wrote under the name "B. G. Sandhurst." The third was a devout Catholic, Dr. David Willis, the last of a veritable dynasty of English physicians named Willis stretching back to the time of King Charles II. In the seventeenth century Dr. Thomas Willis had discovered diabetes and the "circle of Willis" area of the brain. In the eighteenth century Drs. Francis and Robert Willis had been physicians to King George III. The present-day Dr. David Willis had kept interest in the Shroud alive in England by scholarly articles[10] and seemingly tireless correspondence during the long years when the Italians had turned deaf ears to pleas for expositions and scientific examination. His own work in analyzing the research that had so far been possible on the Shroud was meticulous, work which he carried on until his sudden death in 1976.

At noon on Thursday, November 22, having joined Father Rinaldi and his colleague Father Otterbein, president of the U. S. Holy Shroud Guild, we entered the gates of the former royal palace of Turin and made our way to the dimly lit salon in which the conference was to be held. It seemed like any other press conference the world over. Many of those present were casually dressed journalists and photographers; others were Italian scientists and clergy. There was a disarming air of informality.

In part the informality reflected the new attitudes alive in the Piedmontese region of Italy in which Turin stands. Since the war and the fall of the monarchy, Turin has grown into a prosperous, aggressively commercial city, very conscious of its importance as the manufacturing center for Fiat, Italy's biggest selling motorcar. It is the name Fiat, not that of the *Santa Sindone*, that greets the visitor on every kilometer of the *autostrada* approaching the city. Such casualness would not have been permitted further south.

In part the relaxed atmosphere reflected new attitudes on the part of Turin's clergy, some of whom undoubtedly found it difficult to adjust. One who had put up polite but continued resistance to Father Rinaldi was Monsignor Cottino, the cardinal's press officer, a man visibly uncomfortable with the responsibilities the arrangements for the conference and exposition imposed upon him. Rumor had it that he did not even trust the specially appointed security guards but stayed with the Shroud all through the night to be sure of its safety. Altogether more receptive to the new developments was Don Piero Coero Borga, the bustling curator of the quaint Museum of the Holy Shroud on Turin's Via San Domenico, and editor of *Sindon*, the international journal for Shroud studies. In touch with those interested in the Shroud from all over the world, Don Coero, like Father Rinaldi, had for years been pressing for an exposition and now rejoiced that at last his efforts were coming to fruition.

The man upon whom all eyes came to rest was the cardinal, Michele Pellegrino, quietly seated by a microphone at a round antique table in one corner of the conference room. His very clothes reflected the deep change that had come about in ecclesiastical attitudes since Vatican II. He wore no ceremonial vestments, traditionally associated with Shroud expositions, but simply the black habit of a working priest. He brushed aside attempts to address him with the customary "Your Eminence." In his dignity, his pallid countenance, and his classic profile, he reminded one of the old Roman emperors, from whom he was no doubt descended.

As he addressed the gathering, quietly and seemingly unemotionally, he made it plain why he had hitherto steadfastly refused the innumerable requests for the Shroud to be shown. He had no wish for it to be submitted to the hurlyburly of the traditional expositions of the past, with all their logistical problems of millions of pilgrims flooding into Turin. This was why, he explained, he had chosen television, "the eye of modern man," as the most satisfactory vehicle for a modern viewing of the cloth. Television would enable millions more people to see the Shroud in detail with far less risk than would a traditional exposition.

For him the Shroud's significance and value were "so lofty as to rise above every legitimate doubt and the debated question of authenticity." One sensed in him a great reluctance that the Shroud should at last be submitted to public spectacle and scrutiny. Yet one sensed also that in agreeing to the exposition he tacitly acknowledged a real twentieth-century need—the need to find an antidote to doubt, the need for some tangible evidence of Christ in an age that demands proof of everything.

He did not have to look far for precedents. Even at the time of the Gospels, even among those who were closest to the man Jesus, there had been doubters. One of the most human and intensely credible episodes was the outburst of Thomas: "Unless I see the holes that the nails made in his hands and can put my finger into the holes they made, and unless I can put my hand into his side, I refuse to believe" (Jn. 20:25). Thomas was given the opportunity. But what about us, living nearly two thousand years later?

That the Shroud might be the twentieth-century equivalent of the proof-giving body of Christ into which Thomas thrust his hand was suggested at the conference not by the cardinal but by the RAI-TV commentator, Fortunato Pasqualino, who spoke after him. Pasqualino found the Shroud deeply mysterious, but of one thing he was convinced—that it needed to be approached from the point of view of the doubter.

This very press conference was to open a whole new chapter in attitudes toward the Shroud, bringing in, from precisely the point of view of the doubter, men from many walks of life and many countries who have created a whole revolution concerning our knowledge of the Shroud—textile experts, forensic scientists, physicists, photographers, criminologists, hematologists, historians, theologians—all contributing new and intriguing information from their individual fields.

It has been essentially a quiet revolution, as yet largely unrecognized in academic circles, where the Shroud is still scarcely a respectable subject; as yet largely unknown by the public at large. Yet a whole new world has been opened, a world in which the mystery surrounding the Shroud has grown almost as fast as the case for the Shroud's authenticity.

This book is the story of the new discoveries about the Shroud. It is a story written not so much for those who already believe in Christ as for those who do not. Much of what is about to unfold will seem strange and often baffling. Much will seem new and unfamiliar. But all that is asked of the reader is that he approach it step by step with an open mind. For, if Jesus really did leave behind the cloth we now know as the Turin Shroud, it carries unique evidence for his existence, his Passion, perhaps even for his Resurrection. But equally it can scarcely be said that he made its authenticity obvious or the story it tells plain for all to see.

Part I
THE SHROUD
AS UNDERSTOOD
UP TO 1973

CHAPTER I

THE SHROUD ON VIEW

It was 12:55 P.M., Thursday, November 22, 1973. The press conference was over. At an unseen signal the gathering of some thirty or forty oddly assorted individuals began moving through a doorway and up impressive marble steps. Each person had been given a security label and was carefully scrutinized by guards as the group filed past marble statues of the dukes of Savoy and approached a huge palace doorway.

The great frescoed Hall of the Swiss, a former audience chamber, was ablaze with light. It had been converted into a television studio for the purposes of the RAI-TV exposition the next day, and the powerful lamps required for color cameras were full on. There, set against a huge ocher-colored screen, was the Shroud.

It was suspended in a plain, light oak frame, fastened at the top by a batten. Its fourteen-foot length hung loosely down, a break with the tradition of previous expositions, which always displayed the cloth horizontally.

Again, unlike the former traditional baroque splendor, the only ornament was a simple vase of fresh flowers in front of the cloth, a thoughtful reminder, perhaps, of the "lilies of the field." Amazingly, the Shroud was not protected by any glass.

For a moment the very vulnerability of the Shroud held everyone back. Then, hesitantly, some raised cameras. The guards and accompanying officials showed no reaction. While the more devout dropped to their knees in veneration, the photographers clicked away excitedly.

Since for many years one could only study the Shroud from black-and-white photos, it was a wonderful moment to be able to see the cloth in its natural color for the first time.

The linen, although ivory-colored with age, was still surprisingly clean looking, even to the extent of a damasklike surface sheen.

It was possible to study closely the herringbone weave of the linen. In the areas untouched by the ravages of history it was in remarkably good condition. Even when examined under a magnifying glass, the fiber showed no signs of disintegration. The texture was also surprising. Some writers have described it as "coarse." This is quite definitely not so. Although any handling was officially disapproved, the temptation was too great not to touch the linen gently when at close range. It was light and almost silky to the touch.

The dimensions of the cloth are impressive: 14 feet 3 inches long by 3 feet 7 inches wide. It was created in a single piece, apart from a strip approximately 3½ inches wide running the length of the left-hand side and joined by a single seam.

It is the imprint of the all-important "double image" that principally draws the eye. There, like a shadow cast on the cloth, is the faint imprint of the back and front of a powerfully built man with beard and long hair, laid out in the attitude of death.

To anyone who has not seen a photograph of the Shroud before, the two figures could only appear most curious, until one understands the manner in which the image seems to have been formed—that the body was first laid on one end of the cloth, with the remaining half of the cloth then drawn over the head and down to the feet.

The sixteenth-century Italian artist Clovio illustrated this beautifully in an aquatint of the Shroud in which, below the angel-borne cloth, he painted Joseph and Nicodemus wrapping Jesus in just such a manner after the descent from the cross.

The astonishing aspect of seeing the Shroud itself rather than a photograph is discovering how pale and subtle the image appears. The color of the imprint can best be described as a pure sepia monochrome, and the closer one tries to examine it, the more it melts away like mist.

The subtlety is particularly important for anyone studying the Shroud from photographs to appreciate. Any pho-

tography—whether color stills, color television, or, more strikingly, black-and-white stills—seems to intensify the image,
making it far more apparent than it is to the naked eye. In
the case of color photography, this is because the reduction
in scale brings otherwise diffuse elements into greater focus.
In the case of black-and-white photography, by a quirk of
photographic chemistry, the pale sepia (akin to yellow) reg-
isters disproportionately strongly. The main point is that, except when viewed from a distance, the image is extremely
difficult to distinguish.

Similarly strange is the actual "form" or shape of the
image. The face on the frontal image has a masklike quality
about it, with owllike "eyes." It seems detached from the rest
of the body because of the apparent absence of shoulders.
While the crossing of the hands across the pelvis is quite well
defined, the legs fade away below the knees, the feet being
just a blur.

The image of the back is more consistent but similarly
indefinite throughout. In everyday terms, both images most
resemble the faint scorch marks typical of a well-used linen
ironing-board cover.

Anyone looking for evidence of artistic technique could,
therefore, only find the cloth baffling. Solid particles of coloring matter, as would be required by an early painting process, are to all appearances totally absent.

Part and parcel of the same curious phenomenon is the
lack of any visible outline. Throughout the history of art, virtually until Turner and the Impressionists of the nineteenth-
century, artists relied to a greater or lesser degree on outlines
to give shape to their work. The character of these and the
manner of modeling in any painting have always been reliable data from which the art historian can make a confident
judgment of dating and origin.

But in the case of the Shroud there is nothing on which to
base any judgment, no other work with which to compare it.
The more one considers the task of any artist *trying* to create
an image in these terms, the more it becomes absurd that
anyone should have done so.

The same lack of substance is also characteristic of the apparent bloodstains. On the upper forehead there are flows

from something which has caused the scalp to bleed in several places, and on the dorsal side are similar flows at the back of the head. More flows of blood exude from the wrists and feet. The side has been pierced and a copious quantity of blood flows from an elliptical-shaped wound, about two inches across. A further quantity of blood, visible on the dorsal image across the small of the back, seems likely to be from the same wound.

But both the color and character of this "blood" need careful appraisal. One might expect old blood to appear brown and crusted, but this is not the case. In a subdued light the wounds appear very much the same color and consistency as the body stains. Only under strong television lights does a quite separate color become apparent, which is particular to the areas mentioned. It seems to be a clear, pale carmine, very slightly mauve. Visually, it is unnervingly "clean" (for want of a better word) and all the more mysterious for it.

Even when viewed with a magnifying glass, the wound in the wrist, and the wound in the side bear no trace of the sort of surface matter one might expect from a cloth that has been in contact with a major injury. Equally inexplicably, they bear no visible trace of any pigment either. Their coloring—if coloring you could call it—is so thin and flat that they appear as "portraits" of blood rather than blood itself.

All this has suggested to many that the Shroud is visually unique—that it was created by some sort of miracle. This may be justifiably criticized as a subjective opinion because it relies on each individual's interpretation of what he "sees" on the cloth.

But one constructive demonstration is possible. The Shroud, as we know it today, has been frequently copied by artists since the fourteenth century. However, without exception, every artist has produced a copy that is grotesque and seemingly deformed, because of the anachronistically "Impressionist" character of the Shroud and the extreme difficulty of reproducing its subtlety. These copies are useful from one other point of view—recording the damage the cloth has sustained in various incidents, and enabling us to pinpoint particular stages in its career, and its identity, with certainty.

All the copies since the 1530s, for instance, show the figure image framed with the disfiguring array of burns and patches visible to this day. These were sustained in a known historical incident in which it came perilously close to destruction. On the night of December 4, 1532, fire broke out in the Sainte Chapelle, Chambéry, where the Shroud was then kept. Flames spread quickly through the chapel, engulfing rich furnishings and hangings in their path. A beautiful stained-glass window of the Shroud, completed only ten years earlier, melted in the heat, and the cloth itself was only saved by the quick intervention of one of the duke of Savoy's counselors, Philip Lambert, and two Franciscan priests. Together they managed to carry the already burning casket out of the building. But they were too late to prevent a drop of molten silver falling onto the linen inside. This set fire to one edge, scorching all forty-eight folds before the fire could be doused with water. When the reliquary was opened up, the Shroud presented a sorry picture of holes, scorch marks, and stains left by the water. Yet, seemingly miraculously, the image itself had scarcely been touched. As an eyewitness, Pingone, a baron of Savoy, said at the time: "Indeed, we all clearly saw it (for I was then present), and were amazed."[1]

For sixteen months the Shroud languished in a state quite unfit for exposition. Then, on April 15, 1534, Cardinal Louis de Gorrevod had it sent to the nearby convent of Poor Clares for repair. Four nuns worked on it under the direction of their abbess, Louise de Vargin. They were hampered by a constant stream of visitors, but on May 2 the cloth was returned, now backed by a simple piece of holland cloth of the same size to give it strength. Over the worst of the damage had been sewn fourteen large triangular-shaped patches and eight small ones, all made from altar cloth.

A century and a half later the Blessed Sebastian Valfré made other, more minor repairs, for the installation of the relic in the Guarino Guarini chapel, in which it is housed today. Finally, in 1868 a few further repairs were made by Princess Clotilde of Savoy, who also provided the present crimson silk lining cloth.[2]

The 1532 fire was not the only incident in which the

Shroud suffered fire damage. There was another, unquestionably earlier, but of otherwise unknown character and date.[3] Its occurrence is apparent from four sets of triple holes in the linen which can be identified in a painted copy of the Shroud dated 1516 and kept in the archives of the Church of St. Gommare, Lierre, Belgium. These obviously antedate the 1532 fire by at least sixteen years, and most likely considerably longer. The charring of the edges of the holes is considerably blacker than what is visible of the 1532 damage, and they gave the impression of having been created by something like a red-hot poker, there being, for instance, what seem to be irregular, ancillary burn marks as from stray sparks. If the Shroud were folded once lengthways and once widthways, the holes back each other exactly and appear in the dead center of the folding arrangement, seeming to have been caused by one heat source penetrating each fold to a decreasing degree, the back fold being only lightly scorched. The creation of the holes appears to have been deliberate rather than accidental, and it seems very likely that they are the scars of some primitive "trial by fire" ceremony, in which one can almost hear the incantation "in nomine patris et filii et spiritus sancti." But without actual historical corroboration this must remain conjectural.

What then is the character of this cloth, with all these curious features, some seeming to defy natural explanation? It bears no trademark, nothing to indicate its age save the figure itself. At first sight to the skeptic it could only appear too good to be true. In an objective study one cannot avoid pointing out some of the contradictions. It seems impossible that such a fragile piece of linen should survive so long in such relatively good condition. It seems impossible that we should have been left an entire picture of Jesus Christ, in all his wounds.

Yet this is merely the start of the mystery.

CHAPTER II

THE CAMERA REVEALS

In Don Piero Coero Borga's quaint Museum of the Holy Shroud, at 28 Via San Domenico, Turin, there is in one corner a huge wooden boxlike contraption, which is in fact an early camera with a Voigtländer precision lens. It has played an important part in the history of the Shroud.

In 1898 a special exposition of the Shroud was arranged to coincide with Turin's celebrations for the fiftieth anniversary of the Statuto, the Italian constitution. Someone, no one is quite sure who, made a request that the Holy Shroud be photographed. Several reasons were given for the request: to record its appearance for posterity, to make more widespread the information about it, and to forestall illicit photography by any of the million or so visitors expected to file past the cloth while it was on display.

At the royal palace, the Shroud's owner, King Umberto I, of the house of Savoy, received the request coldly. Photography was still a relatively new and little understood science at that time, and there was great hesitation about using it for objects of extreme religious veneration. Fortunately, Baron Manno, one of the organizers of the festival, persisted, and eventually the king relented. But he decided that the work should not be carried out by a professional photographer. The man appointed was a forty-three-year-old councilor and lawyer who had already won several awards as an amateur photographer. His name was Secondo Pia.

The assignment presented many difficulties, chiefly because of the comparatively primitive photographic techniques available at that time. Pia was allowed to photograph the cloth only as it hung above the altar in the cathedral. Because the natural lighting inside the cathedral was too dim, he had to bring in electric lighting, new and uncertain in 1898. He had to build a special temporary platform for himself and the camera in order to photograph the cloth from a suitable level. And, of course, color photography not having yet been invented, he had to work in black and white.

At first things did not go too well. On May 25, the first of the eight days of the exposition, Pia had the advantage of being able to photograph the Shroud without protective glass. But the screens of his flood lamps cracked under the heat generated, making them unusable.

Pia returned on the night of May 28, after the last visitor had been shut out of the cathedral. The Shroud was hung horizontally in a huge frame above the main altar, covered in plate glass. Again Pia's assistants had to build a platform to raise the camera to the necessary height, and at 11:00 P.M. he took a first exposure of fourteen minutes, followed by a second of twenty minutes. It was almost midnight when he hurried back to develop the plates in his darkroom.

According to his own account,[1] his first thoughts were of relief when he saw the negative image begin to appear under the developer. Seconds later, they were to turn to astonishment, then to a chilling awe. On the glass negative there slowly appeared before him, not a ghost of the shadowy figure visible on the cloth, as he had expected, but instead an unmistakable photographic likeness.

The double figures of the Shroud had undergone a dramatic change. Now there was natural light and dark shading, giving relief and depth. Bloodstains, showing white, could realistically be seen to flow from the hands and feet, from the right side, and from all around the crown of the head. Instead of having a masklike, almost grotesque appearance, the man of the Shroud could be seen to be well-proportioned and of impressive build. Most striking of all was the face, incredibly lifelike against the black background.

Pia found himself thinking that he was the first man for nearly 1,900 years to gaze on the actual appearance of the body of Christ as he had been laid in the tomb. He had discovered a real photograph, hitherto hidden in the cloth, until it could be revealed by the camera.

Throughout history, saints and holy men have claimed to see visions of Jesus. None has ever been able to provide material evidence. In archaeology, ancient tombs have been opened up to reveal, for a fleeting moment, the perfectly preserved remains of someone from the distant past—only for these immediately to crumble to dust. Yet, here, an ordinary man had an amazing "vision" on a photographic plate, a vision capable of endless reproduction. And, above all, a vision seemingly of none other than Jesus Christ.

Not unexpectedly, the revelation caused enormous interest. Within days dukes and bishops, duchesses and princesses crowded to Pia's studio to view the glass negative, backlit in a darkened room. Marquis Fillipo Crispolti, who wrote under the name Fuscolino for Genoa's *Il Cittadino*, was the first to make the news public. The issue of June 13 carried his story:

The picture makes an indelible impression . . . the long and thin face of Our Lord, the tortured body and the long thin hands are evident. They are revealed to us after centuries; nobody having seen them since the Ascension into Heaven . . . I do not want to delay a minute in giving this news.[2]

Today the Pia negative, which caused such excitement, is rarely reproduced. It is of the whole cloth, with the face a mere detail, and by modern standards it is of poor quality and seems distorted by the cloth having been under glass at the time. It has been totally superseded by far more professional photographs taken in 1931, when the Shroud was exhibited for twenty days in May to celebrate the marriage of Prince Umberto. This time a widely accredited professional photographer was appointed, Commander Giuseppe Enrie, who worked in the presence of some hundred scholars and other dignitaries, including the then septuagenarian Pia.

With the archbishop, Cardinal Maurilio Fossati, smoothing out creases in the linen, Enrie was able to photograph the Shroud without any covering glass. He also had the advantage of the enormous technical advances in photography that had been made since the last exposition.

In all he took a dozen photographs—four of the entire Shroud, the Shroud in three sections, the complete dorsal imprint, the face and bust, the face two-thirds the natural size of the original, the face the natural size of the original, and a direct sevenfold enlargement of the nail wound in the left wrist.

They are all of superb quality, and, with the exception of the latest color prints, remain the most definitive taken to this day. As Enrie was to recall:

> I will remember as one of the most beautiful moments of my life, certainly the most moving of my career, the instant in which I submitted my perfect plate to the avid look of the Archbishop and that select whole group of people.[3]

The glass plate is preserved today, along with duplicates and prints made from it, in Enrie's old studio in Turin, taken over after his death by the brothers Dutto. It speaks for itself.

There can be no question regarding the authenticity of the phenomenon reproduced on it. Among those who watched Enrie working was a specially appointed commission of expert photographers who checked every stage and issued a notarized statement that his work was free from any kind of retouching. Subsequently the cloth was photographed again by Giovanni Battista Judica-Cordiglia, son of the professor of forensic medicine, during a special check on its condition in 1969, and by many of those present during the 1973 showing. The result is always the same; the image is there whenever the Shroud is reversed by the camera.

Many authors have waxed eloquent about it. During the special address he gave to accompany the television exposition, Pope Paul VI described his emotions when he first saw it as a young priest in May 1931. It seemed to him "so true, so profound, so human and so divine, such as we have been unable to admire and venerate in any other image."[4]

The French writer Paul Claudel said of it, "Something so frightening and yet so beautiful lies in it that a man can only escape it by worship."[5]

It is important that we attempt to define what appears on the negative. On the Shroud, although the figures are very pale, against the ivory-colored cloth they appear dark on light. A photographic negative, therefore, shows them light or white, on the cloth which now appears dark or black, as one would expect. It can be seen how this reversal has happened in a perfectly straightforward way in the relatively dark bloodstains, which show up white on the negative. Also, there is a left-to-right reversal, as when looking in a mirror—i.e., the lance wound switches from the left to the right side, etc. But it is in the relief or tonal values that something different has happened.

In the case of a normal portrait photograph, we understand that the face, when reversed on the negative, will appear strange and grotesque because the areas that were in light show up as dark tones. When the negative is exposed in its turn to photographic paper, these light values are reversed to produce once again a lifelike picture.

In the case of the image on the Shroud there is one less stage to the process. The face and body *are not* lifelike on the cloth itself; they *become* lifelike when their light values are reversed by a photographic negative.

Not unreasonably, therefore, it has been claimed that the Shroud itself is in a sense a photographic negative—a negative that, as we have seen, can unquestionably be traced at least as far back as the Middle Ages, many centuries before the invention of photography.

As in the last chapter, we are bound to ask again the question, Can it in some way have been made by the hand of man? Could, for instance, an artist have simply studied what marks were likely to be made on a cloth by a recumbent body, and then created the negative image by chance? This seems scarcely possible. Just how unlikely it is can be demonstrated by the instance of two artists, Reffo and Cussetti, employed at the time of the 1898 exposition to make copies of the Shroud. They were professional artists, using mechanical means to create a diffuse image. Yet the first impression given by their work is that it is very amateurish in the reproduction of the figure. Their reproduction of the burn marks is far more precise. When one sees the Shroud, it is easy to understand how anyone working close to it would have incredible difficulty trying to make sense of tones that are the reverse of all that he had been trained to create from nature. The problem is exacerbated by the image's faintness and subtlety. Small wonder, therefore, that negatives made of Reffo's and Cussetti's work totally lack the conviction of the original. And how much more absurd to contemplate the task of an early artist trying to reproduce tones that are the reverse of what he knows in nature without any means of checking his work, photography not having been invented. That the Shroud's negativity was created accidentally or deliberately by some early artist would seem impossible.

Could the image have *become* negative through age? Some hostile authors have pointed to certain old paintings in which the colors have undergone a reversal. One example cited is that of frescoes attributed to Cimabue in the upper church at Assisi. In these, the flesh tints have turned almost black, and dark beards have become completely white, a result of chemical changes in the plaster. As on the Shroud, they become more intelligible when seen in negative.[6]

But one must argue that such a parallel is not really applicable to the Shroud. If reversal had happened, that would mean that the original color of the cloth was black, with the figure depicted in white. Yet the Shroud is clearly the natural color of linen it has always been, merely yellowed with age. And we know that it has been that color at least as far back as 1516, as is evident from the Lierre copy made in that year.

Perhaps the most common argument is the suggestion made by a German writer, Blinzler, that the image was created by someone who procured a lifesize statue in the likeness of the dead Christ, or even an actual corpse.[7] According to this theory the "body" would then have been coated with a suitable substance to produce the image on the cloth, and the characteristic details of blood added in appropriate areas.

Plausible as this may seem in theory, in practice, neither among those who favor the cloth's authenticity nor among those who oppose it, has anyone been able to reproduce a comparable image on cloth by any means, natural or mechanical.

The French professor Clément tried, using for his purpose a bust of the artist Géricault.[8] Seen in positive or negative, the result was unimpressive and ugly. Even the lightest *con-*

tact impression produced totally unacceptable distortions, a problem that inevitably arises from trying to create, on a two-dimensional surface such as cloth, the impression of a three-dimensional object such as a human body.

One is bound to ask why some unknown "forger," for that is what he must have been, should have gone to such elaborate lengths to produce an image capable of being "seen" and properly comprehended only in the twentieth century. The argument is, in any case, a specious one. For as we shall see in the next chapter, the casual blood flows purportedly added for effect have nothing haphazard about them at all—they are physiologically convincing to some of the best medical minds of our time.

CHAPTER III

THE SHROUD AND MEDICAL OPINION

From the very discovery of Pia's photographic negative, the Shroud attracted the interest of medical men. This interest was nowhere more intense than at the Sorbonne, Paris, where early in the year 1900 a small team began to make a special study. They were led by Paul Vignon, then a young biologist, subsequently to become professor of biology at the Institut Catholique, Paris.

Considering the comparatively poor quality of the original Pia negative, it is quite remarkable to read in Vignon's first book, in 1902, the wealth of accurate data they were able to discover.[1] Before the book's publication, these findings were presented to the Paris Academy of Sciences by the most distinguished, and most unlikely, member of the group who had worked on the photographs. He was Yves Delage, the Sorbonne's professor of comparative anatomy. Then forty-eight years old and at the zenith of his career, he was well known for his agnosticism and for his aversion to anything that savored of the miraculous or supernatural.

He gave his lecture on April 21, 1902, in the very hall

where, only fifteen years before, Pasteur had announced his vaccine for rabies. He entitled it "The Image of Christ Visible on the Holy Shroud of Turin." Before an unusually crowded and hushed assembly he explained how, from a medical point of view, the wounds and other data were so anatomically flawless that it seemed impossible that they could be the work of any artist. He pointed out how difficult and pointless it would have been for anyone to work in negative, and how there was, in any case, no trace of known pigments on the cloth. He considered the Shroud image to be of Christ, created by a special physiochemical process while he had lain in the tomb.

The half-hour lecture caused an enormous furor. The British medical journal *The Lancet* and the London *Times* reviewed Delage's findings as well-reasoned and scientific. The Paris *Figaro* also voiced its support. But at the Academy of Sciences the reception was less effusive. The climate of the time was so dominated by rationalists and freethinkers that Marcelin Berthelot, the Academy secretary, refused to publish the full text of the lecture, and many of Delage's colleagues thought he had severely jeopardized an otherwise distinguished scientific reputation.

Upset by the fuss, and frustrated by the Turin authorities' refusal to allow him to make a definitive examination of the Shroud, Delage subsequently turned his interest to other fields, giving public vent to his feelings only in a letter to Charles Richet, editor of the *Revue Scientifique*:

When I paid you a visit in your laboratory several months ago to introduce you to M. Vignon . . . had you the presentiment of the impassioned quarrels which this question would arouse . . . ?

I willingly recognize that none of these given arguments offer the features of an irrefutable demonstration, but it must be recognized that their whole constitutes a bundle of imposing probabilities, some of which are very near being proven. . . . a religious question has been needlessly injected into a problem which in itself is purely scientific, with the result that feelings have run high, and reason has been led astray. If, instead of Christ, there were a question of some person like a Sargon, an Achilles or one of the Pharaohs, no one would have thought of making any objection. . . . I have been faithful to the true spirit of science in treating this question, intent only on the truth, not concerned in the least whether it would affect the interests of any religious party. . . . I recognize Christ as a historical personage and I see no reason why anyone should be scandalized that there still exist material traces of his earthly life.[2]

Since the time of Delage the situation has changed radically. While Pia's negative was the only source of reference, there was always a nagging doubt that some hoax might have been perpetrated. With the publication of the Enrie photographs, that slight doubt was dispelled. The Shroud found renewed and wide acceptance among medical men.

This acceptance began in the 1930s with enthusiastic research by Dr. Pierre Barbet, of St. Joseph's Hospital, Paris, who conducted numerous experiments on cadavers to build up an impressive body of evidence that the wounds visible on the Shroud are genuinely those of a crucifixion victim.[3]

He was followed by Professor Hermann Moedder, a Cologne radiologist who used experiments on living students suspended by their arms to determine the physical effects of a crucifixion of the kind visible on the Shroud.[4] In Italy at the same time Dr. Judica-Cordiglia, professor of forensic medicine at the University of Milan, began trying to reconstruct how the body and bloodstains visible on the Shroud might have been transferred from the body onto the cloth.[5]

In England during the early 1960s, Dr. David Willis, then a general practitioner in Guildford, Surrey, began to collate and evaluate all the research available up to that date. In 1969 he was foremost in the medical profession in refuting the sensationalist claims of German writer Kurt Berna that the Shroud "proves" Christ did not die on the cross.[6]

In the United States Dr. Anthony Sava of Brooklyn, New York, made a thorough study of the Shroud bloodstains, in particular the wound in the side.[7] Most of the present-day medical work on aspects of the Shroud centers on pathologist Dr. Robert Bucklin, formerly of Michigan, and now of California.[8]

In the main, the interest of all these men has derived from the anatomical accuracy of the image and the totally lifelike character of the bloodstains. They have, for instance, been able to build up remarkably precise data on the physical characteristics of the man of the Shroud, data drawn from careful measurements of what is visible of the bone structure on the image.

He would appear to have been of an impressive height, 181 centimeters (approximately 5 feet 11 inches), according to both Judica-Cordiglia and Vignon. This would certainly have been tall among Mediterranean peoples, but not unreasonably so. It is one of the most widespread fallacies that people of antiquity were significantly shorter than we are. He had a powerful and well-proportioned physique, the limbs being graceful and without obvious signs of a life given to undue physical labor. The only discrepancy to this is that several medical men have noted that the right shoulder appears lower than the left, a feature more evident in the dorsal than the frontal image. Some have suggested this may be an indication of the man of the Shroud's trade as a carpenter, bringing about a more powerful development of one shoulder than the other. An alternative explanation is that there was some dislocation of the arm during rough handling in the actual pinning of the victim to the cross. This would most likely have been intensified by the stiffening of the arm at the onset of rigor mortis.

We are able to deduce pleasing, well-delineated facial features. Using Shroud negatives in twin epidiascopes, a British photographer, Leo Vala, has been able to produce a life-size model of the head of the man of the Shroud,[9] reconstructing the profile. After studying photographs, one of the world's most distinguished ethnologists, former Harvard professor Carleton S. Coon has described the man of the Shroud as definitely "of a physical type found in modern times among Sephardic Jews and noble Arabs."[10] Age estimates are a subjective territory, but it would seem unlikely that he was younger than thirty or older than forty-five, judging by hair and beard development and general physique.

Not surprisingly the aspect that has most captured the imagination of medical men is the evidence that we are deal-

ing with a crucifixion victim, and one with considerable parallels to the most well-known of all crucifixion victims, Jesus
Christ. In this context the extent to which the whole character of the blood flows is convincing to medical men cannot be
emphasized enough. The comments of Dr. Bucklin are
typical:

> Each of the different wounds acted in characteristic fash-
> ion. Each bled in a manner which corresponded to the na-
> ture of the injury. The blood followed the flow of gravity
> in every instance.[11]

We will therefore consider each group of wounds both from
the medical viewpoint and in its relevance to the gospel
story.

First there are what we may define as the superficial facial
wounds, perhaps the least obvious to a layman, but readily
discernible to the eye of a qualified physician. Dr. Willis
listed these wounds as follows: (1) swelling of both eyebrows, (2) torn right eyelid, (3) large swelling below right
eye, (4) swollen nose, (5) triangular-shaped wound on right
cheek with apex pointing to nose, (6) swelling to left cheek,
(7) swelling to the left side of chin.[12] These injuries are
readily in harmony with the gospel accounts of Christ being
struck repeatedly on the face, both at the hands of the High
Priest's men and Pilate's soldiers, prior to the sentence of
crucifixion.

The first clear traces of spilled blood are again from a
group of wounds that we have no trouble in identifying. In
David Willis's precise medical terminology:

> On the back of the head, whose summit is not visible,
> there are dark irregular markings on the black-and-white
> photos. They could only be flows of blood and at least
> eight independent streams can be counted—some of which
> have divided. Only one has flowed almost vertically, at
> least seven have veered to the left and three to the right.
> They have been caused by independent puncture wounds
> of the scalp, which bleeds freely when injured, and they
> tend to expand as they descend. They have been halted on
> the nape of the neck along a line convex downwards

which, assuming them to have been caused by something like a cap of thorns, would seem to be at the level where the thorn-branches had been secured to the back of the head. The different directions of the flows would suggest a tilting of the head at various times during the wearing of the spiky cap. Turning to the front, there are similar puncture wounds with their counter-drawings of bloodflows but not so numerous as on the back. There are four or five that start from the top of the forehead moving down towards the eyes and the remainder are tangled in the masses of hair framing the face. The most striking of these flows is one in the shape of a reversed three and repays detailed study, so true to life is it. It starts just below the hairline to the left of the midline from a single wound; the flow then moves down to the medial part of the arch above the left eye following a meandering course obliquely and outwards. As the stream descends it broadens and alters course twice, finally building up and spreading out horizontally to the mesial line. Immediately below but separate is a "tear" of blood close to the eyebrow, which is presumably part of the same flow, or possibly from an independent wound. The reason for the meandering course of this vivid mark indicates that it met some obstruction in its downward course, and most likely this was due to the reflex contraction of the muscles of the brow from the pain of the wounds, furrowing the surface.[13]

As Dr. Willis found, it is quite impossible to talk sensibly about wounds such as these *except* in the context of a crown, or as it seems most likely to have been, a cap of thorns as described in the mockery of Christ as King of the Jews. Equally, as one reads such a description from a qualified physician, one cannot fail to be caught up by his own conviction of the sheer physiological logic of these wounds. Willis was not alone in this regard. Vignon too was fascinated by the thorn wounds, particularly the one shaped like a numeral three, which he too found entirely faithful to scientific and physiological detail. As he remarked, "No painter, in his most elaborate work, has ever risen to such exactitude."[14]

The next group of wounds that call for our attention, although not blood flows as such, offer not the slightest cause for questioning the credibility built up so far. These consist of numerous small marks, clearly visible on the photographic negative, peppering both the back and front of the body from the shoulders downward, excluding only the head, forearms, and feet. Each is about 1½ inches long, they are more numerous on the dorsal image, and their number, because some are so indistinct, has been variously estimated from 90 to 120.

It takes little deduction to identify what these marks are. Close inspection of both positive and negative reveals that they are distinctly dumbbelled in shape and are grouped generally in threes, spreading out from a horizontal axis across the loins, fanning upward on the shoulders from either side, downward from the right on the legs. We are clearly dealing with a whipping, the thongs of the instrument in question being evidently studded with twin balls of metal designed to cause the maximum pain. Doctors define the wounds caused as contusions and again have noted that they are physiologically accurate. As even the layman is able to appreciate, the very pattern of these marks carries conviction of authenticity. We are able to see that all blows were delivered from behind. The wounds on the front of the body seem to have been caused by the weapon having been aimed to whip round onto the upper chest and the front of the thighs. We are able to deduce the height at which the executioner's hand was raised. We have good grounds for the speculation that because the center from which the blows radiate on the right side is a little higher than the corresponding center on the left, there were two men carrying out this flogging, the one on the right being a little taller than his companion and having the somewhat sadistic tendency to lash his victim's legs as well as the back.

Inexorably we find ourselves bound to follow the sequence of the Passion, as we study the next group of wounds visible on the Shroud, again described by Dr. Willis:

If we examine the dorsal image and study the part between the large scorch marks and repairs just below the top of the shoulders, there is a quadrangular shading measuring four inches by three and a half inches over the right shoulder; further down on the left side there is another area of excessive shading in the scapular region. This is rounded with a diameter of about five inches. These two areas represent broad excoriated wounds superimposed on the wounds from the scourging, which can be seen through them and have been widened and altered in form and perhaps in some cases obliterated compared with the marks alongside. These wounds could well have originated from the friction of some heavy object rubbing on an already damaged area of skin.[15]

It needs little imagination for us to identify these wounds as from the carrying of a cross. We know that it was a prescribed part of the crucifixion ritual for the victim to carry his cross through the streets to the place of execution, suffering on the way the taunts and jeers of passers-by. In general, it would seem, the whole cross was not carried but only the crossbeam, the upright or "stipes" remaining permanently in position.[16] An average crossbeam, weighing an estimated one hundred pounds, would alone have been enough of a burden for a man already severely weakened by the effects of the merciless scourging. The chafing of the shoulders observed by Dr. Willis in the case of the man of the Shroud, significantly appearing over the marks of the scourging, is entirely consistent with the carrying of such a heavy beam. The sufferings of the victim were further exacerbated by what would seem to have been heavy falls. Professor Judica-Cordiglia has identified heavy damage to the knees of the man of the Shroud, there being a large contusion to the left knee together with excoriations with jagged edges in the region of the patella or kneecap, and further, smaller contusion wounds to the right knee.[17] It hardly needs mentioning that Jesus' difficulty carrying the cross, specifically recorded in the Gospels, strongly implies repeated falls.

We are now drawn to the wounds of the crucifixion itself. First we must establish that we can be quite confident we are dealing with a crucifixion victim. The principal evidence for this lies in the flows of blood from the wound in the left wrist. One of the most important aspects is the angle of the two streams of blood closest to the hand, flowing toward the inner border of the forearm. Other, interrupted streams run along the length of the arm as far as the elbow, dripping toward the edge of the arm at angles similar to the original flows. The first two flows are about ten degrees apart, the somewhat thinner one at an angle of about fifty-five degrees from the axis of the arm and the broader one closer to the hand at about sixty-five degrees. This enables us to do two things: (1) to compute that at the time the blood flowed, the arms must have been raised at positions varying between fifty-five and sixty-five degrees from the vertical, i.e., clearly a crucifixion position; (2) to compute that because of the ten-degree difference the crucified man must have assumed two slightly different positions on the cross, that at sixty-five degrees representing full suspension of the body, that at fifty-five degrees a slightly more acute angle of the forearm produced by flexing the elbow to raise the body.

We are enabled to deduce then that the crucifixion forced on the victim an up-and-down or seesaw motion on the cross —perhaps, according to one school of thought, in order to breathe, the arms in that position taking a tension equal to nearly twice the weight of the body, inducing near-suffocation if there was no crutch support; perhaps, according to another school of thought, by the victim attempting to relieve himself of one unbearable agony, the pain in his wrists, by raising himself, at the price of yet more pain, on the living wounds in his feet.

The very thought is harrowing, but it is intensified by detailed study that has been made of the actual wrist-wound area itself. The great point of interest for medical men is that the nail seems to have pierced the wrist rather than, as traditionally depicted by artists, the palm of the hand. This was observed early on by both Vignon and Delage, who regarded it as one of the many features of the Shroud that carried absolute conviction. They knew that suspension of a body on a cross by nailing through the palms would have afforded no support, as the weight would simply have caused the nail to tear through the flesh.

Research in the 1930s revealed the full significance of wrist-nailing. The experiments were carried out by Dr. Pierre Barbet, then chief surgeon at St. Joseph's Hospital, Paris, one of the city's largest teaching hospitals. He had at his disposal excellent facilities for experimental work, both on corpses and amputated limbs. Barbet, aware of the complexity of the bones in the wrist, was concerned to establish the exact point, according to the Shroud, that the nail had penetrated. He felt that there was a likelihood that small wrist bones would have been broken in the process, and that was contrary to the Old Testament prophecy regarding the Messiah, that not a bone of his should be broken (Ps. 34:20 and Ex. 12:46; cf. Jn. 19:36).

Taking a freshly amputated arm, he held a nail at the point the Shroud seemed to indicate, the chief bending fold of the wrist, at the very junction of the hand and forearm. He gave the nail a firm blow. To his surprise it diverted slightly upward and, with renewed blows, passed cleanly through the wrist. It had found and enlarged a passageway that was already known by anatomists as "the space of Destot" but was thought too small for a nail to penetrate. It was clear to Barbet that the spot had been known and sought for by one of the obviously experienced men who had carried out the crucifixion.

What astounded him was a quite unexpected inward contraction of the thumb, which happened spontaneously at the very moment of driving the nail through the wrist. Careful probing with the scalpel revealed the reason. The median nerve, one of the great nerves of the body, had been touched by the nail, and this mechanical stimulus had "worked" the muscles, making the thumb snap, as by remote control, into the palm.[18]

He referred to the Shroud. No thumbs were visible to either hand. In life, the piercing by the nail had made this happen to the man of the Shroud. In his own words: "Could a forger have imagined this?"

Although this experiment was carried out forty years ago, it has been recognized by medical men even today as a brilliant piece of research, and one of the many which carry absolute conviction for the Shroud's authenticity.

The evidence for the nailing of the feet is less dramatic, but of the same order. Most are agreed that, from the visible attitude of the feet when laid in the Shroud, it would seem that they had been crossed when the victim was nailed to the cross, the left foot having been placed over the right. Dr. Robert Bucklin has given us an authoritative summary of the main findings:

> In examining the photograph of the right foot, we are able to make out an almost complete imprint. The border is slightly blurred in its middle part, but it still presents a very definite concavity corresponding to the plantar arch. More to the front the imprint is wider, and we can distinguish the imprint of five toes. The print is that which one might leave as he stepped on the flagstone with a wet foot.
>
> In the middle part of this footprint there is a small rectangular stain a little closer to the internal border than to the external border. This mark is quite definitely the mark of a nail and it can be seen that the nail has passed between the metatarsal bones at the base of the foot.[19]

Barbet, using freshly amputated feet, again experimented, driving a nail between the second and third metatarsal bones, directly below the so-called Lisfranc joint, as the Shroud seemed to indicate. The penetration was easy, with no need for the force that would have been required to go through the bones higher up.

It needed little deduction to realize that such an arrangement was ideal from the point of view of the method of carrying out a crucifixion. The body was literally supported by the single nail impaling the feet, its own weight, and the nailing in the wrists, making it quite secure and unable to pull free.

No amount of experimental work can recreate for us the agony all of this must have caused, an agony which in the case of Jewish victims went on until a little before sundown, when the legs were broken to hasten death if death had not already intervened. Doctors had differed on the actual medical reasons for the breaking of legs bringing on death, some suggesting that because the victim would be unable to raise himself he would no longer be able to breathe; others that again because he would be unable to raise himself, his blood would sink to the lower part of his body, and death would ensue from orthostatic collapse.

At all events it appears that for the man of the Shroud

death intervened, mercifully, at some earlier stage. There is no sign of breakage of the legs. Instead there is a clear wound in the side, which may be interpreted as the spear thrust specifically recorded in the Gospel of St. John as being administered to the body of Jesus Christ to check that he was actually dead (Jn. 19:34). Visible on the left-hand side of the Shroud image, and therefore, because of reversal, having been originally in the right side of the man of the Shroud, it is seen immediately adjacent to, but not actually covered by, one of the triangular-shaped pieces of cloth used for repairs by the Poor Clare nuns. The flow appears to have proceeded from an elliptical area measuring approximately 1¾ inches long by $7/16$ inch high, the shape conforming precisely to what one would expect of a spear wound.

David Willis has succinctly summarized the main medical observations:

It is generally agreed that this wound is in the space between the right fifth and sixth ribs. . . . The lower and inner extremity of the wound is at a level of about two-fifths of an inch below the tip of the sternum or breastbone, and just under two and a half inches from the midline. The blood flow from the wound spreads downward in an undulating and narrowing fashion for at least six inches and its inner edge is curiously cut about by some rounded indentations. It does not spread out in a homogeneous manner but is broken up by some clear areas, which are thought to indicate the mixture of a clear fluid with the blood. The indentations on the inner margin are probably due to the serrated muscular protrusion on the middle ribs, which correspond with these regular notchings. The body must have been erect when this chest wound was inflicted.

Turning to the dorsal image—again at the level of the repair patches of 1534—two meandering flows of blood extend horizontally across the loins but do not transgress the borders of the body image, except possibly to a very small extent on the left side, where it merges into the dark scorch marks. This blood has clearly come from the right chest, and, again, it appears to be mixed with a clear fluid. It would seem that this second flow came from the wound in the side after the body was taken from the cross and placed horizontally in the cloth or in the tomb. . . .[20]

With Dr. Willis's mention of the clear or watery areas mixed with the blood, one unavoidably recalls the vivid description of blood and water emerging from the side of Christ, as described by St. John. It is important to note that had the spear been thrust into the left side there would have been little if any flow, as the ventricle on this side is usually empty after death. But the right auricle fills with liquid blood that has drained from the superior and inferior venae cavae. And as it happens, the right auricle is a thin-walled chamber, about three inches from the surface, directly in line with the direction we would expect the spear to have taken if driven into the body at the point indicated on the Shroud. So the blood is thoroughly consistent with what medical men would expect from a spear thrust into Christ's right side after death.

What about the water? No less than three different and equally eminent medical men have formulated theories on this. Barbet, required by French law to experiment with corpses not less than twenty-four hours old—and badly hampered by this—thought the water to have been pericardial fluid, normally present in the body only in teaspoonful quantity but increased by the maltreatment and scourging the man of the Shroud had clearly undergone.

The German radiologist Moedder thought it was fluid from the pleural sac, again increased in quantity because of the rough handling.

But the most well-formulated theory—and the most recent —appears to be that of the American Dr. Anthony Sava. He has noted that in his surgical experience of cases of severe violence against the rib cage, without an open wound, there frequently results an accumulation of bloody fluid in the pleural cavity, this being a response of the bruised lung surface to the injury. The amount of fluid can be considerable. In an experiment Sava took samples that he noted did not coagulate but settled to the heavy dark red consistency, with clear light fluid above.

According to Sava, the presence of scourge marks on the

chest of the man of the Shroud, appearing to come from blows which rained over the shoulders onto the front of the body, could well have brought about such an accumulation of fluid in the pleural cavity. This fluid perhaps was one of the principal causes of death, the effects of crucifixion being secondary.

Assuming, if we take the circumstances of the Gospels, that some time elapsed before the body was taken down from the cross, separation into "water" and blood might well have taken place before the spear was thrust into the side. As Sava shows, at this point an incision between the fifth and sixth ribs, as indicated on the Shroud, would have brought about the immediate emergence first of the thick cellular "bloody" layer, followed, as the level fell, by the clear watery fluid, conforming precisely to St. John's words:

When they came to Jesus, they found he was already dead, and so instead of breaking his legs one of the soldiers pierced his side with a lance; and immediately there came out *blood and water*. This is the evidence of one who saw it—trustworthy evidence, and he knows he speaks the truth—and he gives it so that you may believe as well. [Jn. 19:33–36. Italics added.]

The whole sequence of crucifixion injuries is so convincing to those medical men who have studied the Shroud that when, during the 1930s, Dr. Barbet showed his findings to an agnostic colleague, Professor Hovelaque, the latter is said to have pondered it all carefully, and then exclaimed, "But then, mon vieux, Jesus Christ really did rise from the dead!"[21]

Doctors who have examined the Shroud have been unanimously convinced from the visual evidence that the cloth genuinely once contained a corpse, and that the corpse had suffered death by crucifixion. But as we shall see, this conviction is far from solving all the problems raised by the Shroud, not the least of these being its compatibility with the New Testament.

CHAPTER IV
THE SHROUD AND
NEW TESTAMENT ARCHAEOLOGY

It is well known that many thousands of Jews and Gentiles before and after the time of Christ went to their deaths by crucifixion. It was a form of execution practiced by the Scythians, Persians, Phoenicians, Carthaginians, all long before the Romans. Alexander the Great is known to have crucified no fewer than two thousand inhabitants of the city of Tyre. Among the Romans crucifixion was reserved for those of non-Roman citizenship, chiefly slaves and rebels. Following the uprising of Spartacus in 71 B.C., the Roman consul Marcius Licinius Crassus had six thousand of the slaves crucified on crosses set up all along the Via Appia, from Capua to Rome. It is important therefore that we consider carefully to what extent the crucifixion visible on the Shroud is compatible with that recorded of Jesus Christ; also to what extent the entire picture furnished by the Shroud and its image is compatible with what is known of everyday life in New Testament times.

When an ancient burial is discovered by archaeologists, there is usually some special feature about it that can be dated with reasonable accuracy. This is normally done by careful appraisal of accompanying coins or pottery, the styling of any jewelry worn by the deceased, the attitude of burial, and so on. The location in which the burial is discovered is also obviously of considerable relevance.

In the case of the Shroud, any immediate attempt to identify it with New Testament times is very difficult. We are dealing only with a picture of a burial, and a very elusive picture at that. We have no certain knowledge of the original location of the cloth. The body that it wrapped was clearly naked, so there is nothing we can tell from the styling of the clothing. Yet despite these difficulties, there are certain data from which important information can be gleaned.

We have, for instance, the general appearance of the victim, in particular the beard and long hair. While one cannot go so far as to say this is characteristically Jewish, it is a fact that, with few exceptions, the Romans tended to be clean-shaven, while the Jews on the other hand traced their long hair and beards as far back as the time of Moses. Aaron, Moses' brother, is specifically stated to have had a beard, and beards were only shaved off as the sign of deepest mourning. Perhaps the most strikingly Jewish feature, and one which has curiously gone unnoticed by previous writers, is a long streak of hair visible at the back of the head on the dorsal image of the Shroud, falling to about the lower level of the shoulder blades. This gives an unmistakable impression of an unbound pigtail. A pigtail is scarcely a form of hairdressing associated with Jesus through art history. Yet quite independently of the Shroud, a German scholar, H. Gressman, has shown that it was one of the commonest fashions for Jewish men in antiquity, in the simple form of long hair caught at the back of the neck.[1] A great modern Biblical scholar, Daniel-Rops, tells us that, except on public holidays, Jews wore this pigtail "plaited and rolled up under their headgear."[2] Exclusively in the pigtail area the image seems to have a grayish hue. It is tempting to surmise that this may have been from the original oil with which the pigtail was dressed.

There are, then, at least superficial indications that the man of the Shroud was a Jew. There are also important clues to the era in which the crucifixion was carried out, chiefly demonstrable from the significant shape of the extensive marks of the flogging, studied in the last chapter.

Only from the Middle Ages onward did artists come to depict the scourging of Jesus, and even the best artists tended to be vague about the details. The sixteenth-century engraver Martin Schongauer, for instance, illustrated no less than three scourge implements, all of doubtful historical accuracy. But the Shroud is quite specific. The basic constituent of each wound is a dumbbell shape, as from twin balls or pellets of metal. When the pattern of these is studied carefully, it becomes evident that these fell in groups of three, indicating that the whip which inflicted them was three-thonged. Consultation with the *Dictionary of Greek and Roman Antiquities*[3] confirms this weapon as readily identifiable with the Roman *flagrum*, frequently mentioned in the accounts of early Christian martyrdoms, and dreaded for its *plumbatae*, pellets of lead (or sometimes bone), with which the thongs were tipped. Examples are illustrated occasionally on Roman coins, and during the excavations at Herculaneum, the sister city to Pompeii, an actual specimen was discovered. It was sufficiently intact to be reconstructed and put on display in the local museum. As a flagrum in this form is not typical of any other culture, the scourge marks may be argued to be an identifiably Roman feature.

Another detail on the Shroud worthy of similar attention is the stain of the apparent lance wound. The area from which the "blood" is seen to issue is quite precise, a perfect ellipse 1¾ inches long by 7/16 inch wide (4.4 by 1.5 centimeters). It seems logical that this shape should tell us something of the weapon that created it and again we are not disappointed. From Roman art, and from actual examples excavated, we know that there were three main stabbing and hurling weapons used by regular soldiers.[4] There was the *hasta*, the earliest developed of the three, which took the form of a long, heavy spear with a point of various design. This had a lighter sister, the *hasta velitaris*, a forty-inch-long javelin distinguished by a very thin, long point. Then there was the *pilum*, also with a long thin point but otherwise much heavier, being twice as long as the hasta, and chiefly used by Roman infantry. None of these would have produced the type of wound visible on the Shroud.

Then we turn to the Roman *lancea*, in Greek *lonche*, the very weapon described in St. John's Gospel as having been used to check that Jesus was dead. This was a spear of varied length, with a long, leaflike tip, thickening and rounding off toward the shaft. Whereas the other versions were intended to break inside the body of the victim, making it impossible for the enemy to reuse them against the Romans, the lancea was designed for continuous use. As such it is quite typical of what we would expect to have been standard issue for the soldiers of the military garrisons guarding Jerusalem at the time of Christ. From excavated examples, the shape of the lancea's blade corresponds exactly to the shape of the elliptical wound visible on the Shroud. It is another strikingly authentic, and Roman, detail.

At this point we must consider the crucifixion itself as visible on the Shroud, and the extent to which this seems to conform to known crucifixions of New Testament times. This is more difficult to deal with to any degree of precision. As we know from historical records, crucifixions varied greatly one from another, even when carried out by the same execution squad. The arrangement of the victim on the cross, and crosses themselves could differ considerably according to individual whims. Sometimes ropes were used instead of nails. St. Peter is said to have requested to be crucified upside down. The most positive evidence about the possible variations has come recently from a unique find in Israel.

Up to 1968 no known victim of crucifixion had ever been discovered. The reason for this is almost certainly because the really telltale evidence, the presence of nails, seems to have invariably been denied us. The Romans believed that nails used in crucifixion were highly efficacious in curing epilepsy, fever, swellings, and stings; hence these rarely remained with the body of a crucifixion victim. In June 1968, a year after the capture of all Jerusalem by the Israelis, bulldozing to prepare for a new apartment block began on a rocky hillside just over a mile north of the Old City's Damascus Gate. Almost immediately the site, called Giv'at ha-Mivtar (the Hill of the Divide) was found to have been an extensive Jewish burial ground dating back to the New Testament period.

Archaeologist Vasilius Tzaferis of Israel's Department of Antiquities and Museums was called in to make a hasty excavation.[5] He concentrated his efforts on four tombs and found in these fifteen stone ossuaries (caskets for the collection of bones), containing the skeletons of some thirty-five Jews of the period preceding the revolt of A.D. 70—eleven men, twelve women, and twelve children. Forensic analysis of the remains gave a dramatic view of the violence of the age. Three children had died of starvation. A child of four had died after much suffering from an arrow wound in the skull. A youth of seventeen had been burned to death upon a rack.

A woman of nearly sixty had died from a shattering blow from a club or mace, and another woman from fire.

But of the greatest interest to Tzaferis was one skeleton on which he observed that the two heel bones were held together by a large iron nail. It was urgent that all the remains be given a swift reburial, but special permission was obtained for this particular skeleton to be examined at greater leisure. At Jerusalem's Hebrew University Dr. Nicu Haas, a Rumanian-born anatomist and anthropologist, began the task of assembling the entire skeleton. By anthropometric measurement and reconstruction he was able to build up an astonishingly detailed picture of a graceful young man between twenty-four and twenty-eight years old at his death, about 5 feet 7 inches tall. Because the bones showed no signs of manual labor, he was probably of upper-class origins. His features when reconstructed were found to be slightly marred by an asymmetric skull and cleft palate, evidence of difficulties experienced by his mother at the early stages of her pregnancy and while giving birth. His name, incised in almost illegible Aramaic on the stone ossuary, was Jehohanan. Examination of the joined heel bones and the seven-inch nail holding them together confirmed beyond doubt that he had suffered death by crucifixion.

Below the head of the nail, traces were found of a plaque of acacia or pistacia wood. Whereas in Jesus' case the plaque or *titulus* describing his "crime" was specifically recorded as set over his head, Jehohanan's plaque was evidently at his feet. To hang him on the cross Jehohanan's executioners viciously bent his legs, forcing him into a sort of sidesaddle position and then driving the nail in from the side straight through the heel bones. This was followed, no doubt after several hours of suffering, by fracturing of the calf bones, obviously the same "breaking of the legs" that the Gospels describe Jesus as being spared because of his premature death. Finally, when Jehohanan was dead, we know that his legs had to be sawn off before he could be brought down, due it would seem to the heel-bone nail having bent awkwardly into the wood of the cross.

These gruesome details clearly show that Jehohanan's was a different crucifixion from that carried out on Jesus, illustrating the variations in crucifixion procedure that we have already mentioned. There is, however, one feature that is of great interest because of its relevance to the unusual medical discovery of the wrist nailing of the man of the Shroud. When Haas examined the radius and ulna bones of Jehohanan's forearms, he found at the wrist end of the radius a distinct scratch mark, as from a nail. Examining the scratch more closely, he noted that in parts it had been worn smooth, indicating "gradual increasing . . . friction, grating and grinding between the radial bone and the nail towards the end of the crucifixion."[6] The location of this nail mark, at the wrist end of the forearm is not identical to that on the Shroud image, but close enough. It confirms archaeologically the evidence previously known only from the Shroud, that Christian artists have been wrong both historically and anatomically in depicting the nails through the palms; the flesh would simply have torn through with the weight. More poignantly, it is clear that the rubbing of nail and bone visible on Jehohanan's remains must have been from the same characteristic that Barbet deduced from his examination of the double flow of blood at the wrist wound—that the essential mechanism of crucifixion was a ghastly seesaw motion from one source of pain to another. Shroud image and scratched bones of the first century A.D. both tell the same harrowing story.

The evidence seems, then, to indicate that the man of the Shroud was very probably a Jew crucified under the Romans. This draws us to the inevitable question, Could it have been Jesus? To what extent does the image on the Shroud correspond to the crucifixion of Christ as recounted by the Gospels? Given the premise that the Shroud is from all other points of view genuine, this presents us with virtually no difficulty. The parallels are best set out in tabular form:

Gospel Evidence	Source	Evidence on the Shroud
1. Jesus was scourged.	Mt. 27:26, Mk. 15:15, Jn. 19:1	The body is literally covered with the wounds of a severe scourging.

Gospel Evidence	Source	Evidence on the Shroud
2. Jesus was struck a blow to the face.	Mt. 27:30, Mk. 15:19, Lk. 22:63, Jn. 19:3	There appear to be a severe swelling below the right eye and other superficial face wounds.
3. Jesus was crowned with thorns.	Mt. 27:29, Mk. 15:17, Jn. 19:2	Bleeding from the scalp indicates that some form of barbed "cap" has been thrust upon the head.
4. Jesus had to carry a heavy cross.	Jn. 19:17	Scourge wounds in the area of the shoulders appear to be blurred, as if by the chafing of some heavy burden.
5. Jesus' cross had to be carried for him, suggesting he repeatedly fell under the burden.	Mt. 27:32, Mk. 15:21, Lk. 23:26	The knees appear severely damaged, as if from repeated falls.
6. Jesus was crucified by nailing in hands and feet.	implication) Jn. 20:25 (by	There are clear blood flows as from nail wounds in the wrists and at the feet.
7. Jesus' legs were not broken, but a spear was thrust into his side as a check that he was dead.	Jn. 19:31–37	The legs are clearly not broken, and there is an elliptical wound in the right side.

Of these seven stages, it is possible that stages one, two, and four through seven could have occurred in the case of any crucifixion victim. But the third stage, the crowning with thorns, is virtually signatory.

It is not difficult to reconstruct the circumstances in which this altogether singular event occurred. We know from the account of St. Peter warming his hands by the fire that it was cold in Jerusalem at the time of the crucifixion. And as wood has always been scarce in the area it is most likely that Jesus' captors had instead bundles of thorn branches for their fire. When left to guard the "King of the Jews" how appropriate it would have seemed for them to "crown" him with a cap of these branches,[7] a macabre piece of headgear which has stood out through time as the signature of a likeness of Christ. If the Shroud itself is genuine, the case for it being actually Jesus' shroud is very strong, as even one of those most convinced of its fraudulence, the Jesuit historian Herbert Thurston, felt obliged to admit in 1903:

> As to the identity of the body whose image is seen on the Shroud, no question is possible. The five wounds, the cruel flagellation, the punctures encircling the head, can still be clearly distinguished. . . . If this is not the impression of the Christ, it was designed as the counterfeit of that impression. In no other person since the world began could these details be verified.[8]

CHAPTER V

THE SHROUD AND THE RECORDED

BURIAL OF JESUS

If genuine, the Shroud is a record of a burial, a Jewish burial that reputedly took place nearly two thousand years ago of none other than Jesus Christ. Among the key questions therefore to be considered are the extent to which it is compatible with known Jewish burial customs of the time and, above all, the specifically recorded burial of Jesus Christ.

In entering this field, we come upon one of the most difficult areas of Shroud studies. From the rise of the Herodian dynasty to the first half of the second century A.D., Jewish burial custom would seem to have been first to wash the body, a practice normal in most cultures. Then it was dressed in clean linen clothes, generally the white garment worn by the deceased for festivals, and bound at the chin, wrists, and feet. Such a custom would seem to be quite explicit from the description of the raising of Lazarus in which we are told, "The dead man came out, his feet and hands bound with bands of stuff and a cloth round his face. Jesus said to them, 'Unbind him, let him go free'" (Jn. 11:44). So far this seems reasonable enough. Had Lazarus been swathed in bands, mummy fashion, it would have been impossible for him to move at all. Instead he appears to have been at least able to shuffle forward at the command "Come out," requiring only the chin, hand, and foot bindings to be severed for him to resume normal life.

Nor can there be much argument about the type of burial place. In the case of a reasonably well-to-do individual, the body would be laid out on a shelf within a rock-cut tomb, examples of which are still evident around Jerusalem. The body would be strewn in some manner with spices, and months or even years later, after sufficient decomposition had taken place, the bones would be placed in an ossuary, a small stone or wooden chest, such as we know to have been used for Jehohanan. In this way many members of the same family could occupy one tomb, each first being laid out full-length, and the remains then being gathered up and placed in the ossuary to make room for the next member. Small side chambers were commonly carved in the walls of each tomb to accommodate ossuaries as they accumulated, this practice explaining the point behind the gospel remark that Joseph of Arimathea's tomb was a new one "in which no one had yet been laid" (Lk. 23:54; Jn. 19:41).

Some of the details visible on the Shroud are consistent with such practices. As in Jewish custom we can be reasonably sure that the man of the Shroud was laid out flat and intact in some sort of prepared tomb. While this might seem obvious, it should be borne in mind that the Romans cremated their dead, and the Egyptians disemboweled and pickled them before swathing them in bandages. The position of the body with the hands across the pelvis is also identical with Jewish burials of the Essene sect, as excavated by Père de Vaux in the area of Qumran.[1]

We can also detect that, as in Jewish custom, the man of the Shroud seems to have been bound at head, hands, and feet. On the Shroud there is a distinct gap between the frontal and dorsal images of the head, almost certainly indicating the presence of a chin band tied around the face. At the region of the wrists we may perceive that there is an apparent break in the blood flow immediately to the left of the covering hand. A binding cloth or cord at this point would almost certainly have been functionally necessary to counteract the effects of rigor mortis, which according to some medical opinion would have tended to return the arms to the original crucifixion position. In the area of the feet, the possible presence of a similar cord or binding cloth is less obvious, but there is a blank in the image at precisely the most likely position.

From this point on, the going becomes more difficult. If we are dealing with a Jewish burial, there has clearly been departure from normal procedure, particularly relating to the proper preparation and enwrapping of the body. For instance, the body visible on the Shroud has not been washed, even though this was standard practice. We are immediately bound to ask what evidence there is for Jesus being denied such washing.

Here we enter a particularly thorny field of scholastic controversy. Tradition says that Jesus *was* washed. In the Church of the Holy Sepulcher, Jerusalem, the faithful revere to this day a reddish-colored stone on which he is said to have been laid to be washed and anointed prior to burial. The stone, which has been known since Byzantine times, is specifically called the "Stone of Unction."

Many scriptural scholars also insist that Jesus was washed,[2] quoting the gospel reference to the burial having been "following the Jewish burial custom" (Jn. 19:40) as positive proof that the proper rites were carried out.

But the real issue is, was Jesus in fact washed, or do Christians merely like to believe that he was? The St. John quotation is, after all, only an inference, not a direct statement. Nowhere in the Gospels are we specifically told that the washing was carried out, and conversely there are certain specific indications that it may simply never have taken place.

If we look back to the details of the recorded circumstances, according to all three synoptic Gospels Jesus died about three P.M., after a mysterious darkness that lasted some three hours. The immediate circle of followers seem to have been too shocked or frightened even to begin to consider making arrangements for a decent burial, and it was left for Joseph of Arimathea to step into the limelight and take charge. We are given too little information about this

...lthy and influential secret disciple of Jesus, but it is clear that it was already late when he appeared on the scene (Mt. 27:57; Mk. 15:42). The relevance of this is that the day in question was the eve of the Passover sabbath, as St. John tells us, a day of special solemnity (Jn. 19:15). On this day of all days not only did the body have to be removed by sundown, but by six P.M. all work had to cease. The staccato phrases of the Gospels indicate Joseph's haste. From Golgotha he had to go to the Antonia Fortress to ask Pilate for the body. If the streets of Jerusalem then were anything like those of the Old City today, it would have been at least a ten-minute journey, probably more because of the crowds of pilgrims gathered for the Passover. There may well have been a delay in gaining an audience. On Pilate's insistence a centurion had to be dispatched to check that Jesus was indeed dead. On his return no doubt some form of document had to be drawn up granting Joseph the body, after all of which Joseph had to wend his way back to Golgotha, joined by Nicodemus, purchasing the linen and spices on the way. The body then had to be removed from the cross and transported to Joseph's nearby tomb. Describing this, Luke tells us emphatically "the sabbath was imminent" (Lk. 23:54).

Some have argued that washing was a prescribed ritual that would have been permissible to carry out irrespective of the sabbath. Some eminent New Testament scholars do not share such a view. Even among the best exegetes there seems little major objection to the concept that there simply was no time for Jesus' body to be washed before the sabbath, particularly in view of the various Jewish requirements relating to this rite.[3] When, as events proved, it was also impossible to carry out this rite after the sabbath, one can understand a certain reluctance on the part of gospel writers to admit this directly. Only on the view that Jesus was not washed can the authenticity of the Turin Shroud be upheld.

What of the spices? St. John tells us that Nicodemus, assisting Joseph of Arimathea, brought a mixture of myrrh and aloes weighing about a hundred pounds. He also tells us that these were wrapped with the body in the burial linen (Jn. 19:39, 40). Had such spices been used for anointing, it would have been requisite in Jewish ritual and indeed in that of any other culture to wash the body first. As it is quite evident from the Shroud that the body was not washed, and as the weight of spices described would be vastly excessive even for the most lavish anointing, the most likely explanation would seem to be that they were dry blocks of aromatics packed around the body as antiputrefacients.

Indeed the presence of these preservatives packed around the body might well account for the lack of distortion of the body image, which has always been one of the Shroud's mysteries. They may well have enabled the cloth to hang over the body almost as flat as a photographic plate.

We have similar problems relating to the clothing of the body. As we have already mentioned, it was normal for Jews to be buried in clothing, more specifically the white garments they wore for festivals. In the case of Jesus we would not necessarily expect this, as we know his clothing was taken from him at the time of crucifixion. But many authors have pointed out that we would certainly not expect the fourteen-foot sheet that we find preserved in Turin.

Here again we are in a hornets' nest of controversy over gospel interpretation that exists quite independently of the Shroud. It all stems from apparent conflicts of information between the synoptic writers and St. John. The synoptics speak only of the *sindon* purchased by Joseph of Arimathea (Mt. 7:59; Mk. 15:46; Lk. 23:53). This is often translated as shroud, although it should be pointed out that it does not have a specifically sepulchral meaning. St. Mark, for instance, used the same word to describe the garment lost by the young man at Gethsemane who fled at the arrest of Jesus (Mk. 14:51, 52). St. John, on the other hand, does not use the word *sindon*, but instead says the body of Jesus was wrapped in *othonia*. And in his account of the discovery of the linens in the empty tomb again he uses the word *othonia* (which he describes as lying at the scene), and refers also cryptically to a mysterious *soudarion*, rolled up and lying in a place by itself (Jn. 20:7).

The precise meanings of *othonia* and *sindon* in their gospel context have been hotly debated. Some have contended that *othonia* (which is a plural form) means linen bands and that Joseph must have torn up the sindon into strips to wind Jesus mummy-style. Quite neutral exegetes such as Père Benoit have pointed out that it would surely have been easier for Joseph to purchase ready-made bandages rather than tearing up a large sheet for this purpose.[4] The most balanced modern view is that *othonia* means cloths in general, which could incorporate shroud and bands.

What of the *soudarion*, literally a "sweat cloth"? Some have thought of this as simply the headcloth or chin band—which is clearly what the soudarion mentioned in the story of Lazarus as "round his face" (Jn. 11:44) was. Others have argued that it may have been our Shroud, on the grounds that the description of it as having been "over his head" (Jn. 20:7) could well refer to the manner in which we know the Turin Shroud was used. In support of this argument we may note that in the Lazarus account St. John uses the word *peri* ("round" or "about"), in contrast to *epi* ("over"), in the case of Jesus, leaving open the possibility that a different arrangement (and different size of cloth) is being described. St. John makes special mention of Jesus' soudarion being "not with the othonia but rolled up in a place by itself," which certainly might suggest a cloth larger and more important than a mere chin band; but as many maintain adamantly that a soudarion could not be anything larger than a handkerchief-sized piece of cloth, it seems unwise to be dogmatic.

The conclusion to be drawn is that from exegetical studies alone we can be sure of nothing, that of themselves they can neither prove nor disprove that the Shroud is genuine. It does seem worthwhile at least to consider the various possibilities raised by the gospel accounts for what the Shroud might have been among the linens Peter and John found in the empty tomb on the first Easter Sunday.

Regrettably, we know very little about the appearance of the tomb itself. In the Gospels we are simply told that it was hewn in rock (Mk. 15:46), in a garden close to Golgotha (Jn. 19:41, 42) and near to the city (Jn. 19:20). Modern research has tended to confirm the authenticity of the traditional site, that marked today by the twelfth-century Church of the Holy Sepulcher in Jerusalem. Although this is now well within the city walls, excavations made in the vicinity by archaeologist Kathleen Kenyon have shown that at the time of Christ it was almost certainly outside the walls.[5] It has also been convincingly shown that this location in Jesus' time most likely had the appearance of a terraced quarry into which tombs had been cut, the area, as befitting the rich Jews who could afford such tombs, enhanced by gardens.[6] The real problem is that any semblance of the original appearance has today been lost, partly because of episodes of deliberate destruction by non-Christians, such as the total obliteration of the site by pickax and hammer ordered by Caliph Hakim in 1009. The destruction was also partially caused by excessive bouts of piety by Christians themselves, such as that of the first Christian Roman emperor, Constantine the Great, who shortly after A.D. 325 ordered most of the surrounding rock of the tomb cut away in order to build a magnificent basilica embracing the site of Golgotha at one end and the sepulcher at the other.

Tombs of roughly the same period, however, do still survive in Jerusalem. One of these is the so-called "Garden Tomb," popularized by General Gordon as an alternative to the traditional site. This and most other examples feature the low entrance described by St. John (Jn. 20:5), and several also have the large boulder described by all the Evangelists as used to seal the entrance to Jesus' tomb. From the weight of one example, one can well imagine the difficulty the women anticipated rolling it away on the first Easter Sunday.

What would have been inside? Christian authors often reconstruct an elaborate antechamber before the tomb itself—an idea usually gleaned from Jerusalem's Tombs of the Kings. It is doubtful that the tomb was this grand. There may well have been a small forecourt before the entranceway, possibly preceded by steps leading down from the garden. Inside, the gospel accounts themselves seem to suggest only one chamber, featuring at the right-hand side (Mk. 16:5) the *arcosolium*, or stone mortuary couch commonly spanned by an arch.

It is here that on the first Easter morning the momentous discovery was made:

It was very early on the first day of the week, and still dark, when Mary of Magdala came to the tomb. She saw that the stone had been moved away from the tomb and came running to Simon Peter and the other disciple, the one Jesus loved. "They have taken the Lord out of the tomb," she said, "and we don't know where they have put him." So Peter set out with the other disciple to go to the tomb. They ran together, but the other disciple, running faster than Peter, reached the tomb first; he bent down and saw the othonia lying there, but did not go in. Simon Peter, who was following, now came up, went right into the tomb, saw the othonia lying there, and also the soudarion that had been over his head; this was not with the othonia but rolled up in a place by itself. Then the other disciple who had reached the tomb first also went in; he saw and he believed. Till this moment they had failed to understand the teaching of scripture, that he must rise from the dead. [Jn. 20:1–9.][7]

The women had leapt to the obvious conclusion. In poor light, all they had been able to make out was that the body of Jesus had gone: someone therefore must have taken him away. Peter and John (traditionally identified as the "other disciple") were more analytical. John seems to have hesitated to go inside the dark entranceway, but he was able to make out the othonia, which suggests that these may have been lying on the ground. The more forthright Peter went right in and at this point espied the soudarion. Something about the arrangement of all these, whatever it was, convinced Peter and John that the extraordinary had happened, that the body of Jesus had left the tomb by no natural means.

The question is, What in this group of cloths could have been the Shroud? If the othonia were linen bands, used to tie the wrists and feet, one possibility is that St. John saw these still knotted lying on the ground, apparently discarded. It was left for St. Peter, on actually going into the tomb, to find the soudarion rolled up in its own place. In this interpretation the soudarion must indeed have been the Shroud, understandably an amazing sight in the sense that it would have conveyed forcibly that the body had left the cloth of its own free will.

Another possibility is that all the cloths were lying flat on the bench exactly in the positions they would have assumed for the burial, but without the body. Only the soudarion, in this instance the chin band, was separate. This too would have been an awesome sight, conveying that the body had literally passed through the cloths to release itself from the bonds of death. Why the displaced soudarion? Perhaps it had been moved by one of the women, or by one of the mysterious young men in white described by all the Evangelists as receiving the startled tomb visitors. It is impossible to tell.

What is certain is that the Evangelists were quite convinced it could not have been tomb-robbers at work. It also seems clear that the source of their conviction was something about the linens. While we cannot be sure from the scriptural evidence alone that the Shroud was among those linens, it is worth considering an observation made by Dr. John Robinson, former Bishop of Woolwich, now Dean of Chapel at Trinity College, Cambridge, and one of Britain's foremost scriptural scholars. To him the Shroud has the ring of authenticity precisely because it is not what one would immediately expect from the Gospels, and hence not what one would expect a forger to create to ensure acceptance.

There are many more issues of the Shroud's relation to the Gospels that must remain for the present in the balance. There is, for instance, the issue of why the Gospels make no mention of any imprint having been left on the linens, surely an obvious addition to the list of Jesus' miracles. This we will come to when we consider the Shroud's history. But for our next review of the Shroud's claims to authenticity we must turn to some of the most recent work, the examination of actual samples of the Shroud by Italian scientists following the exposition of 1973.

Part II
THE SHROUD
UNDER THE
MICROSCOPE—
THE WORK OF THE 1973
COMMISSION

CHAPTER VI
THE SHROUD AND THE
TURIN COMMISSION

So far all the evidence that we have studied is what we might term superficial, i.e., derived from what study of the Shroud is possible from photographs rather than from the linen itself. One of the most frustrating aspects for serious scientists, from the days of Delage right up to the time of the late Dr. David Willis, was the steadfast refusal on the part of the Shroud's custodians to allow any scientific access to the cloth, least of all the removal of actual samples. This attitude seems to have been inherited from the dukes of Savoy by Turin's cardinals, and Cardinal Pellegrino for many years similarly turned a deaf ear to such requests, despite continual pressure from Father Rinaldi of the U. S. Holy Shroud Guild.

Then in June 1969 came a breakthrough.[1] On the sixteenth, at 8:30 in the morning a small group of people gathered before the high altar in the Royal Chapel while Cardinal Pellegrino celebrated the Mass of the Holy Shroud, a rite dating back to the days of the High Renaissance. One of the clergy climbed the steps to the rear of the altar, then ascended by a small stepladder to reach the grille behind which the Shroud is housed. Taking three keys from a small velvet bag, he carefully opened the grille, then the inner iron cage. Reaching in, he brought out the casket containing the Shroud, which was opened and the Shroud carefully unrolled and laid out on a special long table covered with a white cloth. The small group of people moved around the table fascinated. The first scientific examination of the Shroud, albeit a preliminary one, was about to begin.

The ten men and one woman who now began to examine the cloth had each been specially invited by the cardinal to check the current state of preservation of the Shroud, and to make recommendations on any suitable scientific tests they considered should be carried out. They formed what has since been loosely termed a commission. What principles guided Cardinal Pellegrino in his choice of members of this commission we shall probably never know. Had he but asked, he could undoubtedly have called in men of the highest international eminence. As it was, his thinking ranged little further than his own Piedmontese region.

Predictably, three of the commission members were priests: Monsignors Caramello (the Shroud's custodian below the cardinal), Cottino (the overly conscientious press officer), and Baldi. The exiled King Umberto had asked for a personal representative of his choosing to be included, and this was Professor Luigi Gedda.

Of the remainder, five were scientists: Professor Enzo Delorenzi, head of the radiological laboratory of the Mauriziano Hospital, Turin, there to check on the feasibility of radiological testing; Professor Giorgio Frache, director of the Institute of Forensic Medicine, University of Modena, an expert on the analysis of blood samples; Professor Giovanni Judica-Cordiglia, the already mentioned head of the Department of Forensic Medicine, University of Milan; and Professors Lenti and Medi.

Representing the field of history and early textiles was the distinguished curator of Turin's Egyptian Museum, Professor Silvio Curto. The one woman, a very eccentric and unpredictable personality, was the former director of the art galleries of Piedmont, Noemi Gabrielli.

In fairness it should be said that while the cardinal may be criticized for thinking in too geographically limited a way about his choice of experts, he cannot be accused of a lack of objectivity. Although most of the individuals chosen were Catholics, they were selected foremost for their particular academic expertise, without constraint to voice honest doubt. Professor Curto is an agnostic. Professor Frache is a Waldensian Protestant, the grandson of a moderator of this now exclusively Piedmontese sect, which since the twelfth century has been persecuted by church and state for its opposition to Catholic temporality.

In fact, the most unfortunate choice was the man deputed

to assist the experts by providing a photographic record, reproducing the Shroud in color for the first time, Giovanni Battista Judica-Cordiglia, son of the Professor Cordiglia of the commission. Although he used more advanced photographic equipment, his photographs turned out to be in many instances inferior to those taken by Enrie in 1931.

The most regrettable aspect of the cardinal's methodology was, however, the secret manner in which he gathered the commission. It seems absurd, yet the fact remains that it was not until 1976 that the names of the members of the commission were actually released. It was not even a well-kept secret. The first news of the commission's existence was leaked out in 1969 by Kurt Berna, the German ex-waiter who has made highly publicized claims that the Shroud "proves" that Christ did not die on the cross. Berna gleefully derided the Turin custodians for acting "like thieves in the night."

Be that as it may, in 1969 the job of the experts was to study and report. The Shroud was available to them during two days in June, the sixteenth and seventeenth, during which time it was examined with the unaided eye, and under the microscope, and viewed with Wood's light and infrared light. Lengthy discussions took place, several of the experts having very limited previous knowledge of the Shroud.

Late on June 17 a collective report was drawn up under Monsignor Caramello's chairmanship noting the excellent state of preservation of the Shroud, and recommending a series of tests for a future date, with the removal of "minimal samples." Then at ten o'clock on the morning of the eighteenth the cloth was rolled up and returned to its casket above the high altar, to slumber for a further four years.

Those four years were busy with diplomatic activity and preparation. Count Umberto di Provana di Collegno, a witness of the commission's deliberations, reported back to King Umberto the commission's recommendations. The exiled king was still the acknowledged owner of the Shroud, and there was no certainty that he would agree to the request by the experts for the removal of even the most minute samples for ultramicroscopic examination. In his elegantly lonely retreat in Cascais, Portugal, Umberto lives in a world where the aristocratic ways of the old Italian monarchy are still scrupulously preserved. Counts and generals come and go, and while it is clear that Umberto can never again visit the relic that he owns, he still maintains the right to decree what can and cannot be done with it. When it was requested at one stage that the holland cloth backing the Shroud be removed, Umberto insisted on paying for the provision of another. As to taking "minimal samples," yes, he agreed, providing these were subsequently returned to the Shroud's reliquary. Count Provana di Collegno conveyed the news personally to the cardinal on January 23, 1973.

So secretly were all the arrangements conducted that when, on the twenty-second and twenty-third of November of the same year, the principal British and Americans interested in the Shroud were in Turin for the television exposition, none of them knew that the taking of the samples was planned for the next day, the twenty-fourth.

After the television exposition, the international group of observers imagined only that the Shroud would very shortly be restored to the silvered reliquary lying empty in the adjoining Royal Chapel. Instead, members of the commission were waiting to superintend the removal of the samples that would submit the Shroud for the first time to twentieth-century science's most critical eye, the microscope. The commission had altered a little in composition since the 1969 examination. Professor Lenti had resigned and Professor Medi was dead. Professor Frache, the Waldensian forensic expert, was unable to be present due to ill health. He was represented instead by two deputed colleagues, Professors Eugenia Rizzati and Emilio Mari, also of Modena University's forensic department. Also new to the commission were a prominent Turin physicist, Professor Cesare Codegone, there to consider the feasibility of radiocarbon dating; Professor Guido Filogamo, a blood-analysis specialist from Turin University's Department of Human Anatomy; and a chemist, Professor Mario Milone, director of Turin University's Department of Chemistry. Professor Curto had recommended that Professor Gilbert Raes of the Ghent Institute of Textile Technology be added to the list of consultants.

The morning was spent chiefly in the careful removal of the Shroud from the Hall of the Swiss, and its transport, still in its frame, to a small room off the gallery at the rear of the cathedral. Here it was examined intently by the newcomers to the commission while discussion took place on the formulation of a special grid "map" of the Shroud whereby the location of all its features could be defined by precise points of reference.[2]

In the afternoon it was unfastened from its frame and laid out once again on the long, cloth-covered examination table. Four nuns of Turin's Institute of the Daughters of St. Joseph, all proficient in darning and embroidery, were deputed to carry out the experts' instructions. By 3:34 P.M. the first thread, 12 millimeters long, had been removed and consigned to its own plastic envelope, labeled for identification purposes. For a little over an hour the nuns, taking turns, continued removing a total of seventeen samples, chiefly threads, from different locations on the Shroud (see Appendix D). Each selected thread was carefully lifted with the aid of a fine needle, picked up with microscopy pincers, then cut with microscopy scissors, thus avoiding as far as possible any contamination from the person carrying out the work. None of the thread removals appears to have left any visible damage to the cloth.

For Professor Raes's use two relatively sizable portions, one 13 by 40 millimeters, the other 10 by 40 millimeters were cut from one side of the cloth, exposed edges on the Shroud then being meticulously darned by the nuns.

By 4:40 P.M. the last sample had been taken. One hour later the Shroud was back in its casket, its wrapping sealed with the cardinal's own seal and that of the Royal Chapel, and returned to its altar home. Now it was up to the microscope.

CHAPTER VII

THE SHROUD AS A TEXTILE

Back in Ghent, Belgium, Professor Raes removed from their plastic box the samples he had brought back with him from

Turin. A prosperous, good-humored individual of somewhat generous proportions, he has about him the air of a burgomaster. He kept the samples in their plastic envelopes incredibly casually among a somewhat chaotic assortment of papers.[1] Shortly after his return, he began the task of setting these samples up for study under the microscope.

In all, Raes had been given four samples, two individual threads, one weft of 12 millimeters, one warp 13 millimeters long from the corner of the cloth to the left of the feet of the frontal image, one irregular 13-by-40-millimeter portion from the same area, and one 10-by-40-millimeter parallelogram-shaped portion from the 8- to 9-centimeter side strip that runs the full length of the cloth.

From previous visual study of the Shroud weave, a certain amount of information had already been deduced. The overall style of the weave had been generally agreed to be a three-to-one herringbone twill—each weft thread passing alternately under three warp threads and over one, producing diagonal lines, which reverse direction at regular intervals to create the herringbone pattern. That was in itself interesting, as most known Palestinian, Roman, and Egyptian linens of around the time of Christ tend to "plain weave"—i.e., a simple "one over, one under" style. The more complex three-to-one twill of the Shroud is certainly known from the period, but in silks rather than linen. Silk examples, thought to be of Syrian manufacture, have been found at Palmyra (dated before A.D. 276), and in a child's coffin (ca. A.D. 250) excavated at Holborough, Kent, England.[2] The lack of linen samples by no means invalidates the authenticity of the Shroud, merely suggesting a somewhat costly manufacture, as indeed one would expect of a purchase of the wealthy Joseph of Arimathea. The weave certainly offered no particular difficulty to Professor Raes, who merely saw it as too commonly used at different times and locations to be positively identifiable as coming from first-century Palestine.

Setting up fibers from various portions of his samples under the microscope, then viewing them under polarized lights for the best possible contrast, Raes was able to satisfy himself beyond doubt that the substance of both the Shroud itself and its side strip is linen. In his own words "the X- and

V-shaped structures examined are very typical and leave absolutely no doubt about the raw material."[3] He also satisfied himself that the sewing thread used for the seam joining the side strip was of linen as well.

But as he studied the fibers more closely, he made a hitherto unsuspected discovery. In the slides he had prepared from warp and weft threads of the main fabric he found minute but unmistakable traces of cotton. The consistency of these was sufficient for him to be sure that wherever the weaving of the Shroud had been done, it was done on equipment used also for weaving cotton.

Cotton is known to have been in use as early as the Indus civilization of Mohenjo-Daro, circa 2000 B.C. It is also known to have been introduced to the Middle East by the Assyrian monarch Sennacherib during the seventh century B.C. By the time of Christ it would certainly have been established in the environs of Palestine, and therefore offers no difficulty to the authenticity of the Shroud.

Cotton fibers are characterized by twists or reversals which vary according to the particular species of cotton. The fibers Raes found in the Shroud correspond to the species *Gossypium herbaceum*, which is characteristic of the Middle East and has as few as eight reversals per centimeter. (By contrast, *G. barbadense* averages eighteen to twenty reversals per centimeter, and *G. hirsutum* twenty to thirty reversals per centimeter. Of course, it would have been surprising indeed to find either of these species, as they are both native to America.) What is significant, however, is that cotton should be found at all, its very presence determining conclusively that the fabric of the Shroud came from the Middle East since cotton is not grown in Europe. Of course, it is possible that a fourteenth-century Western forger might have obtained a piece of genuine Middle Eastern cloth for his purpose, East-West trade being reasonably well developed at the time. To suppose that he did so intentionally, however, would be to credit him with an improbably advanced degree of sophistication, to say the least. Raes in his report to the commission published in 1976 was not inclined to push the issue this far.

But this was not the end of Raes's discoveries. As already mentioned, he had two samples of reasonable size, one from the main body of the Shroud, and one from the mysterious side strip. Methodically, Raes decided to analyze the characteristics of each to determine whether or not they were woven at the same period, and on the same loom. His table of the essential characteristics is reproduced below:

	Piece I		Piece II	
	Warp	Weft	Warp	Weft
Number of threads per cm.	38.6	25.7	—	25.7
Size of thread in tex.[4]	16.3	53.6	18	73.1
Direction of twist.[5]	Z	Z	Z	Z

Piece I is that from the main body of the Shroud; piece II that from the side strip. The type of weave used for both is absolutely identical—i.e., the three-to-one twill. But, as Raes observed, the size of the threads in piece II certainly seems to be different from that of those in piece I. He qualified this by saying that due to the very short length of the threads examined it would be impossible to be sure that they are from fabrics of different manufacture. But the inference is undoubtedly there. And it is strengthened by the fact that Raes was unable to find in piece II any of the cotton traces of the main body of the cloth.

The significance of this is not immediately obvious. Certainly it did not greatly trouble Raes. But as we shall see in Part III of this work, it may well be of considerable importance to us. For one fact is certain. Only by the addition of the side strip are the images of the face and body made central on the cloth; without them the body would appear too much to one side. This much at least was realized by Professor Silvio Curto of the commission. The question that immediately springs to mind is, did someone, *after* the formation of the image on the main sections of the Shroud carefully sew on the side strip in order to balance the image on the cloth? Certainly it is the only logical explanation for the presence of the side strip. And what is intriguing is that if this is what happened, whoever did it seems to have worked very close to the time of the original manufacture of the Shroud in order to be able to obtain such a closely compatible strip of linen. Also—again, only if our initial premise is right—

whoever added the strip does not seem to have been concerned that it was not quite as long as the Shroud itself, there being a short piece missing at either end which, so far as one can tell, was not merely cut off but never there in the first place. Could it be that for whatever cosmetic purpose the side strip was intended, it required the display of only a section of the Shroud, not the full-length image?

This possibility must be kept firmly in mind when we consider one question of the Shroud's early history in Chapter XV. In the meantime, one footnote to Professor Raes's cotton discovery deserves mention. Fr. Jacob Barclay of Bethany near Jerusalem expressed great relief that the substance Raes found mixed with the linen was cotton not wool. According to Father Jacob, wool added to the Shroud would have been the historic proof that it had never had any link with anyone Jewish. The Mishnah is quite positive that cotton may be added to linen without being a transgression of what is termed the "mixing of kinds."[6] But even shoelaces containing a wool mixture would be intolerable, particularly on the Sabbath. According to Jerusalem radio the ultraobservant have even been seen going to prayers at the Wailing Wall with no shoelaces in order not to transgress this particular requirement!

CHAPTER VIII

IS THERE ACTUAL BLOOD
ON THE SHROUD?

Due to its wide uses in combating crime, the science of the analysis of blood and bloodstains is a very advanced one. A bloodstain may be invisible to the naked eye, as when it has been spattered onto a shoe, then wiped away, leaving only the tiniest traces, perhaps in a minute crack of the leather. Modern forensic-science laboratories have the means of bringing to light such invisible stains, and showing that these, and more visible examples are unquestionably blood.

The methods employed are varied, depending on the material in question, but the peroxidase method is one of the most common. To a given area of suspected bloodstaining the scientist will apply a chemical mixture containing a special compound specifically devised to react to the presence of any hemoglobin—the substance that gives blood its red coloring. If benzidine is the compound used in the mixture, it will turn a very strong blue in the presence of hemoglobin. If phenolphthalein is the compound, the mixture will turn a bright pink. Having established that there is most likely blood present, the scientist can then turn to more specific tests, such as those used to determine blood-grouping, species, etc. So sensitive are these tests that they will produce a reaction from even the most minute traces.

It is important to understand this as background information when we turn to the work on apparently blood-bearing threads of the Shroud by two independent Italian scientific laboratories, that of Professor Frache at Modena[1] and that of Professor Filogamo at the University of Turin.[2]

Frache's laboratory, which is specifically equipped for forensic science, received by far the largest selection of samples, a total of eleven threads of lengths between 4 and 28 millimeters, all but one of which (a control) appeared to bear the image of blood. The areas from which these were taken are of considerable interest. Apart from the control, all were from the dorsal image, presumably the area considered marginally the less sacrosanct. Three were from one of the scourge marks on the left buttock. One 19.5 millimeters long, was from the blood flows that appear to extend across the small of the back. One, 13 millimeters long, was from the image of the bloodstained right foot. But the blood flow that seems to have been singled out for maximum attention was that of the rill from the foot, which has every appearance of having flowed onto the cloth at the time the body was actually laid on the Shroud. No fewer than five threads were extracted from the area bearing this stain. The reason for this selection is obvious. The rest of the stains seem to have flowed onto the body at various stages of the Passion, and subsequently to have been transferred to the cloth after death. But the flow from the foot should have been from fresh blood falling directly onto the cloth, and post-mortem blood at that.

From the sheer quantity of samples and their apparent characteristics positive results should have been easily obtained. Yet this was an area in which once again the Shroud showed its elusiveness.

Something of the nature of what was to follow made itself apparent even at the time of the actual extraction of the threads by the St. Joseph nuns. As one of the scourge-image threads was being removed, it accidentally broke into two pieces. At the moment of snapping, even though there was only a relatively minor amount of fraying, it could be observed with the unaided eye that the reddish tint of the thread was limited to the surface while the inside appeared to be perfectly white. In other words, whatever had caused the image had not penetrated it to any significant degree. This seemed to rule out actual blood. It also seemed to rule out immediately the equally obvious alternative of a conventional coloring agent. Bound by their instructions, the Italians on the commission went on carrying out the routine tests for the presence of blood, tests that in this light were not likely to be the most informative. Even so, what they were able to reveal was fascinating.

In Frache's laboratory in Modena the fibers of each thread to be examined were opened out with the aid of a histological needle in order to show more clearly the character of the substance forming the "blood" image. Under conventional microscopes the visibility of each thread was increased first by 63 and then by 285 diameters, so that the numerous vegetable fibers comprising each fragment of thread showed up clearly. The first thing the scientists noted was the absence of any encrustations of heterogeneous material, as would have been expected from the use of any artificial pigment. Instead it could be seen that forming the image were fine yellow-red to orange granules ranged in diagonal bands that corresponded to the warp/weft pattern of the original weave. There were two very significant characteristics about these granules. As had been observed with the unaided eye when one of the threads had broken on extraction, the granules were found only on the surface fibers of the thread, leaving the fibers below quite clean. And, most intriguingly, no granules were to be found in the spaces between the fibers.

The significance of this should in fact have been reinforced for the scientists by an independent discovery made during their study of the Shroud on November 24, 1973. King Umberto had given permission for the unstitching of a small area of the holland cloth used to back the Shroud in 1973 in order for at least a peripheral study to be made to determine if the image had penetrated both sides of the Shroud. Of all the members of the commission, the only one to note that this particular operation was carried out was the Egyptologist, Professor Curto. And what he noted reinforces perfectly the independent observations made under the microscope. For he was able to confirm quite positively that, despite the fineness of the linen, the image had not penetrated to the under side.[3]

Following their instructions, Frache's team, Professors Mari and Rizzati, pressed on with the standard forensic tests for detecting the presence of blood. As we have already noted, red blood cells contain a peroxidase which, if subjected to mixtures containing benzidine, will make the benzidine, normally colorless, turn blue. The peroxidase in blood is known to have a great resistance through many centuries. And it is an extremely sensitive test. Whether isolating only the surface granules or testing the whole of a fiber, the scientists obtained no blue reaction from the Shroud samples. Had the Shroud samples turned blue, this would not necessarily have proven the presence of blood—further tests have to be made, for blood-grouping, etc. in order to be absolutely specific. But the fact that the samples did not turn blue was a very, very strong indicator that there is no blood on the Shroud. And as it happened, the more specific tests then carried out produced similarly negative results. Attempts to dissolve the granules during chemical treatment with acetic acid, oxygenated water, and glycerin of potassium were all unsuccessful.

All this evidence might seem a death knell to the Shroud's authenticity, but in making their observations the Italians made no attempt to rationalize the implications, although clear implications there are. It is in the nature of any normal

fluid substance, whether blood, paint, or dye, to seep, to penetrate any absorbent material such as cloth, thereby affecting
subsurface as well as surface fibers and, of course, filling in
the spaces between the fibers. It is also in the nature of such
substances, after drying, to go back into solution if subjected
to contact with fresh fluids, chemicals, etc.

Yet these seemingly obvious processes appear not to have
taken place on the Shroud. Instead, whatever created the
image would seem to have had no actual substance of its
own. It would seem to have been a "dry" process as from
some physical force reacting with the surface fibers of the
Shroud threads, the granules thereby being formed, as it
were, from the fibers themselves. This process would of
course account for the "clean" and precise character of the
image. But what character of force could it have been? And
what could have happened to the blood that should by any
normal, natural process have been left on the cloth? The matter is the Shroud's greatest mystery and these are questions
we will consider later, in Part V of this work.

For the present, it remains to record the work of Professor
Filogamo's laboratory at the University of Turin, where, as a
control to the Modena investigation, two threads from the
Shroud, taken from the area of the apparently bloodstained
right foot, were studied under the intensely powerful electron microscope. This is a microscope that has a much
greater resolving power than the conventional optical microscope. Instead of light, a parallel beam of electrons is passed
through the object under study, the beam then being re-
processed to register as an optical image on a fluorescent
viewing screen. By this process objects invisible to the naked
eye can be shown in clear detail.

In the case of the Shroud threads, the standard procedure
was followed of putting the samples in resin and then cutting
them into slivers 500 to 1,000 angstroms thick. Very thin
cross sections of mere fibers of the thread were thus obtained, and viewed at between 17,000 and 50,000 x
magnification.

At this intensity individual fibers of a Shroud thread could
be seen clearly under the microscope, composed in their turn
of microfilaments of a few tens of angstroms. On these, mi-

nute bacterial spores and other odd minuscule organic bodies showed up in places, consistent with the sort of extraneous matter the Shroud could be expected to have accumulated in the course of centuries. The small yellow-red electron-dense granules that seem to compose the Shroud blood image were also apparent, but still defied identification.

From his laboratory in Turin, Filogamo, like Frache, turned in a negative report, merely remarking in a not very convinced way that from the point of view of his tests time could well have destroyed the vital traces of the presence of hematic substances. When the report was published in 1976, from the public point of view the fact that no blood had been detected on the Shroud was at least balanced by the fact that no fraudulent substance had been identified either.

In any case interest had been diverted by apparently more dramatic revelations about the Shroud by a scientist from Switzerland.

CHAPTER IX

A CRIMINOLOGIST AND THE SHROUD

A few weeks before the Shroud was shown on television in 1973, three experts had been invited by Monsignor Caramello to study the photographs of the Shroud taken by Judica-Cordiglia in 1969 and to give their opinion on whether the photographs were true pictures of the structure of the linen and the markings on it. One of these was Dr. Max Frei, a noted Swiss criminologist, chosen because he had published an article on the faking of photographs in 1955.[1]

Today a sprightly sixty-four-year-old living in the smart suburb of Thalwil, a few miles to the south of Zurich, Frei may be described as the Sherlock Holmes of the Shroud. Just as Sir Arthur Conan Doyle's Holmes managed to solve his crime mysteries by analysis of dust on a suspect's shoes and clothing, so Frei has established an international reputation for himself by the analysis of microscopic substances. From 1948 until his retirement in 1972, Frei was head of the Zurich Police Scientific Laboratory and worked on the analysis of many important crimes and accidents, including the air crash of U.N. Secretary General Dag Hammarskjöld. Although retired, Frei is still consulted on crimes by police forces of many nations.

It was on October 4, 1973, during his work notarizing the photographs of the Shroud taken by Cordiglia in 1969, that Frei noticed that the surface of the cloth was covered with minute dust particles. He therefore asked for permission to remove some of the particles for analysis, and Cardinal Pellegrino gave his permission. On the night of November 23, with the Shroud still hanging vertically in the frame used for the television exposition, Frei took his samples from the bottom zone to the left and right, and from the side strip. His method was absurdly simple: He pressed small pieces of clean adhesive tape onto the surface of the linen, then sealed these into plastic envelopes and put them into the modest satchel that he carries constantly with him. Frei was assisted in the work by Professor Aurelio Ghio of Turin, another member of the commission responsible for authenticating the photographs.

Back in his laboratory in Zurich, Frei surveyed the dust he had collected under the microscope. His trained eye immediately identified mineral particles, fragments from hairs and fibers of plants, spores from bacteria and nonflowering plants such as mosses and fungi, and pollen grains from flowering plants—all consistent with the sort of microscopic debris the Shroud could be expected to have accumulated over the centuries. Being chiefly a botanist by training, Frei found the pollen to be of the greatest interest. As he was aware, pollen grains have an extremely resistant outer wall, the exine. Although so small as to be virtually invisible to the naked eye, these grains can and do retain their physical characteristics for literally hundreds of millions of years, being immune to almost any form of destruction. As Frei was also aware, when viewed under the electron microscope pollen grains vary so considerably in physical characteristics that, thanks to careful classification of the different types over the years, it is possible to identify with certainty the precise genus of plant from which any grain has been derived. Frei realized that identification of the plants from which the pollen on the Shroud had been derived could lead to important deductions about the geographical regions in which the Shroud had been. On the one hand, it might confirm that the Shroud had never been outside the western Mediterranean region in which it is known to have been kept since the fourteenth century. On the other, it might reveal that the Shroud had at some stage been in other regions, the identification of such regions obviously providing important pointers to the Shroud's early history.

During 1974 and 1975, when he was not on call for freelance criminological work, Frei carefully examined each pollen grain he had removed from the Shroud, and crossmatched it against his files of known varieties. It was an incredibly delicate task. Each grain has a different appearance according to the aspect from which it is viewed, there being an equator and poles just like the earth, and the manipulation of such minute samples requires great dexterity even with special instruments.

The task was not made easier by the fact that Frei was using palynology, the science of pollen analysis, in a particularly unusual way. Normally a core is taken from some sedimentary deposit, and by simple analysis of the pollens at different levels, a picture can be built up of changes of flora in one region over a given period. By contrast Frei was trying to use the method to determine through which geographical regions one given object, the Shroud, had moved, the significant clues being the identification on the object of pollen from plants of specifically limited geographical distribution.

One of the complications of the method is that many plants are common to virtually all areas in which the Shroud might have been kept in the course of its history. Another complication is that plants that originally had one specific regional derivation are today found all over the globe. A typical example of this is the famous cedar of Lebanon (*Cedrus libani*). Frei actually found pollen from this on the Shroud, theoretically most valuable evidence for the Shroud's provenance in Palestine. But it cannot be regarded as specific. The same species of cedar has been planted in parks and gardens throughout the whole Mediterranean area during the last few centuries.

Fortunately, Frei had a breakthrough. As he analyzed the grains one by one, he came upon some that he could identify with certainty and that he realized *had* to be significant. They were from typical halophytes, plants common to the desert regions around the Jordan Valley and unique in one respect: They are specifically adapted to live in a soil with a high content of sodium chloride, such as is found almost exclusively around the Dead Sea. Among these were desert varieties of *Tamarix, Suaeda,* and *Artemisia.* In Frei's own words:

> These plants are of great diagnostic value for our geographical studies as identical desert plants are missing in all the other countries where the Shroud is believed to have been exposed to the open air. Consequently, a forgery, produced somewhere in France during the Middle Ages, in a country lacking these typical halophytes, could not contain such characteristic pollen grains from the desert regions of Palestine.[2]

Max Frei, a well-trained scientist, is a cautious individual, very conscious that a great deal rests on his findings. When in March 1976 he issued an interim statement concerning his research to date, he was widely reported, quite inaccurately, as having been able to date the Palestinian pollen to the first century A.D. Frei makes no such claims. But today his early skepticism about the authenticity of the Shroud is gone, a fact that he admits not without emotion. His upbringing was Zwinglian Protestant, and he is far removed from Catholic leanings.

What he has very recently completed is a full report of his work on the samples taken in 1973, a report which in his view "permits the definite conclusion that the Holy Shroud is not an adulteration."[3]

Altogether he has now identified forty-nine species of plants whose pollens are represented on the Shroud. A complete list of these is appended at the rear of this book, but in summary it may be said that they represent these main groups:

i. Halophyte type desert plants "very typical" of the Palestine area around the Dead Sea and the Negev.
ii. Steppic plants characteristic of the area of Anatolian steppe defined by Frei as including Bitlis, Diyarbakir, Mardim, Urfa, and Malatya. This is the dry zone where no natural pollen can grow on account of inadequate summer rainfall.
iii. A small group of plants characteristic of the environs of Istanbul.
iv. Northern European plants consistent with the Shroud's known history in France and Italy.

The significance of this list is very substantial, and it is ironic that Max Frei should have been able to deduce so much from material literally as humble as dust.

Essentially we can be certain that the Shroud was at one stage in its history in Palestine, the very area it *had* to have once been in to be genuinely that of Christ.

While it is of course still theoretically possible to argue that a fourteenth-century forger may have obtained a genuine Palestinian cloth for his purpose, in view of the accumulated independent medical and photographic evidence, this argument must be considered somewhat thin.

But in addition the list defines specific Turkish regions where similarly the Shroud must have been, very important as it could only have been in these places during the unknown period of the Shroud's history preceding the fourteenth century.

Of particularly strong interest is the pinpointing of the Anatolian steppe region, whose relevance we shall shortly discover.

Armed with these new clues we can therefore look afresh at any means by which the Shroud's historical existence can be determined during the seemingly silent period before the fourteenth century.

As we are about to discover, this is one of the most implacable of the Shroud's mysteries.

Part III
INVESTIGATING THE SHROUD'S HISTORY— THE SEARCH FOR CLUES

CHAPTER X

WHERE WAS THE SHROUD BEFORE THE
FOURTEENTH CENTURY?—THE DILEMMA

As is well known to everyone with some knowledge of archaeology, there is one scientific test, now almost routine, that could at a stroke determine whether the Shroud dates from the fourteenth century, or is indeed much older. This is what is now popularly known as the carbon-14 test. Carbon 14 is a radioactive isotope produced by cosmic-ray bombardment of the earth's atmosphere, and all living things take it in. When they die, this intake ceases, and radioactive decay sets in, the carbon 14 changing into other atoms at a precisely measurable rate.[1] In an object that has once lived, whether bone or the flax of linen or the reed of papyrus, half the carbon 14 decays and disappears in about 5,600 years, this being known as the half life of carbon 14. By measuring the amount of carbon 14 present in any organic object of unknown antiquity, it is possible to determine with a remarkable degree of accuracy the date when it "died." In the case of the Shroud this would be when the flax of the linen was cut down.

The technique has been applied successfully to materials very close in composition to the Shroud, most notably to a linen wrapping to the Dead Sea Scrolls. This was dated by the pioneer of carbon 14, Willard F. Libby of Chicago, to between 167 B.C. and A.D. 233, the sort of accuracy that, although not ideal, would at least give an unquestioned antiquity to the Shroud.

Among the various possible testings of the Shroud considered by Cardinal Pellegrino's commission, carbon-14 testing was high on the agenda. Dr. Cesare Codegone, director of the Technical Physics Institute of Turin Polytechnic, was actually set the task of preparing a feasibility study for carbon-dating the Shroud. When Codegone made his recommendations,[2] it became obvious that this was one test that would have to wait for future technical refinements. The test —at least in the form then understood by the Italians[3]— demanded a sample of linen thirty centimeters square, which would need to be totally destroyed in the process of isolating the carbon 14. For cross-checking purposes, thought particularly necessary in view of the various contaminations (fire and water-splashing) the Shroud was known to have undergone in its history, the destruction of a further three or four samples of similar size was considered desirable. And it was known that even in the most ideal conditions carbon-14 experts were at loggerheads among themselves as to the precise half-life dating. Dendrochronology, or tree-ring dating, for instance, had shown certain flaws in Libby's theories for carbon 14, namely that as a result of various environmental vicissitudes the rate of carbon-14 decay has not been absolutely consistent through time. For very understandable reasons the commission therefore decided that the carbon-14 test would have to wait.

Deprived of this independent means of dating, we are thrust upon the greatest dilemma of Shroud studies, what and where could the Shroud have been in history.

By far the greatest work on the Shroud's history was done in the early part of this century by two Catholic historians, the medieval specialist Canon Ulysse Chevalier in France and the very erudite Jesuit scholar Herbert Thurston in England. Their views may be regarded as identical. Eminent Catholics, even in the light of the findings of Pia and Delage they were unwaveringly certain that the Shroud was a fourteenth-century forgery. From the standpoint of Chevalier's and Thurston's hard documentary evidence it was virtually impossible to see how the Shroud could be genuine.

Without dispute the Shroud's history could be traced back to the year 1453, when it came into the possession of the Savoy family, the ancestors of King Umberto. Its owners then were Duke Louis of Savoy and his wife, Anne de Lusignan, a pious couple constantly accompanied, it was said by a retinue of Franciscan friars. Chevalier's documents showed how in that year Anne and Louis had acquired the Shroud after somewhat obscure negotiations with an intrepid French widow, Margaret de Charny. The records also showed how the Shroud could then be traced in the possession of the de Charny family back to the mid-1350s.

How did the de Charny family acquire the Shroud? Here one comes to the core of the mystery. Margaret de Charny inherited the cloth from her father, Geoffrey II de Charny, a distinguished *bailli* of France, who died in 1398. He in turn had inherited it from his father, Geoffrey I de Charny, who had died in 1356. Very little was known about the Shroud at the time of Geoffrey I de Charny. But from the year 1389 there exists a formidable memorandum[4] which seems to provide all the relevant details. Its author, Pierre d'Arcis, Bishop of Troyes, had had his attention drawn to a grave scandal which was going on at the de Charny family seat at Lirey, about twelve miles from Troyes, and in the bishop's diocese. The canons of the collegiate church there, founded thirty-six years earlier by Geoffrey I de Charny, were, it was said, exposing for veneration a cloth carefully described, with papal authorization, as a "likeness or representation" of the "sudarium of Christ."

There can be no doubt that this was the Shroud. It was being shown on a lofty platform flanked with torches and with great ceremony. And while they were describing it only as a likeness, the canons were making it known privately that it was the actual Shroud in which Christ had been wrapped in the tomb, a claim that was attracting multitudes of pilgrims.

It was a cause of annoyance to Bishop d'Arcis that Geoffrey II de Charny had bypassed him and obtained permission for the expositions from Cardinal de Thury, the papal legate. It was also a time notorious for abuses relating to relics, and d'Arcis, a thoroughly honest and upright churchman, was concerned that something of this kind should not be perpetrated on his doorstep.

He made enquiries and discovered that this was not the first time that the de Charnys had shown the cloth. There had been a burst of similar expositions thirty-four years earlier, about the time of Geoffrey I, when the same cloth was claimed quite openly to be the true Shroud by the canons of

Lirey. The then Bishop of Troyes, Henry of Poitiers, had similarly investigated the matter. In the words of a forthright memorandum d'Arcis drew up for the pope, Bishop Henry back in the 1350s had been told by "many theologians and other wise persons . . . that this could not be the real shroud of our Lord having the Saviour's likeness thus imprinted upon it, since the holy Gospel made no mention of such imprint, while, if it had been true, it was quite unlikely that the holy Evangelists would have omitted to record it, or that the fact should have remained hidden until present time."[5]

D'Arcis went on with a sentence that to many has been the *coup de grâce* to the Shroud's authenticity. I again quote Herbert Thurston's translation:

Eventually, after diligent inquiry and examination, he [Henry of Poitiers] discovered the fraud and how the said cloth had been cunningly painted, the truth being attested by the artist who had painted it, to wit, that it was a work of human skill and not miraculously wrought or bestowed.[6]

It may be argued, however, that the passage about "the artist who had painted it" is not quite all it seems in Thurston's translation. Latin lacks the definite article, and we can legitimately replace Thurston's *"the artist"* by *"an artist."* Similarly, while *depingere* certainly means "to paint," it can also mean "to copy," the phrase therefore being translatable as "the truth being attested by an artist who had copied it." This could throw quite a different complexion on the whole passage.

Despite this, the de Charnys' guilt seemed to be independently demonstrated by various factors, not least of which is that they failed to make any attempt to explain how they acquired the cloth. If the Shroud was genuine, such an explanation would surely have put an end to the matter.

They were, it must be understood, not the sort of family who would be expected to have in their possession such a fabulous relic, bearing in mind that relics of the Passion were worth a king's ransom at that time. And their withdrawal of the cloth after the enquiry by Bishop Henry of Poitiers seemed clear evidence of their guilt. Also, from 1389 and for the next sixty years they described it in official documents only as a "likeness or representation" of the Shroud of Christ,[7] seemingly as if they too were not convinced of its genuineness.

To visit today the village of Lirey where these events took place can only reinforce the apparent absurdity of the whole affair. Tucked away in rolling French countryside south of Bouilly, it is a tiny hamlet notable only for the disrepair of a few ancient timbered dwellings. Long gone is Geoffrey de Charny's wooden collegiate church where the canons so controversially exhibited the Shroud. There never was any ducal chateau in which might have dwelt the sort of great magnate who might have acquired the genuine Shroud by some legitimate means. The logical explanation seemed to be that the de Charnys had indeed forged it.

The more one studies the affair, the more one is impressed that the case presented by Chevalier and Thurston is a totally reasonable one. There were, after all, some fifty documents that Chevalier had amassed and edited. These all corroborated each other, and there could be no doubting their authenticity. Nor, going back six hundred years, could one doubt the integrity of the two bishops of Troyes involved in the issue, Henry of Poitiers and Pierre d'Arcis. One peculiar aspect was that Geoffrey II actually married a niece of Henry of Poitiers some time after the fuss about the first spate of expositions had blown over. Pierre d'Arcis held the see of Troyes for some twelve years before the 1389 controversy, had previously had a perfectly reputable legal career, and possessed no apparent sinister motive for sticking his neck out in this case. Rather the reverse, as the pope appears to have been displeased with his attitude and even threatened him with excommunication. Yet, despite the plethora of documents, one cannot escape the feeling that there is something missing, something more to the affair than meets the eye.

For instance, why after all the fuss there had been in the 1350s did Geoffrey II bring out the Shroud again in 1389? By this time he was a well-respected official of the king. It would surely not have been avarice that led him to bring out a relic whose authenticity had already been challenged. Why also, before commencing the expositions, did he seek out the approval not of his local bishop but, via the papal legate, of Pope Clement VII, agreeing, without qualm it would seem, to call the Shroud merely a "likeness or representation." Why, if he genuinely believed the cloth was only a "likeness or representation," did he indulge in the most elaborate ceremonial for Shroud expositions, amounting to virtual idolatry?

Why, after having received Bishop d'Arcis's powerfully worded memorandum, did Pope Clement VII not suppress the expositions as d'Arcis requested? Clement is known to have upheld the expositions as long as the de Charnys continued to describe the cloth as only a "likeness or representation," and most intriguingly insisted on two occasions that Bishop d'Arcis should remain "perpetually silent" about the matter.

And why, during the early fifteenth century, did Margaret de Charny, who withdrew the Shroud from the canons of the Lirey church when the structure fell into disrepair, resist several determined legal appeals on their part for its restoration, only to go to enormous lengths then to find some suitable noble family (the Savoys) to take it over from her?[8]

Were these the actions of a family knowingly perpetrating a forgery? Or did the de Charnys know something about the origins of the Shroud that, for reasons unknown, they were unprepared at the time to reveal?

The whole crux of the affair seems to center on the personality of the Shroud's first known owner, Geoffrey I de Charny.

His background is obscure. Recorded by genealogists as only "probablement" the son of a Burgundian Jean de Charny,[9] he appears to have had no lands by family inheritance. Instead he acquired some modest estates by gifts from the king, and by two marriages, the first to a Jeanne de Toucy, and the second to Jeanne de Vergy, the mother of Geoffrey II.

In the historical record he is pictured as a self-made man, a professional soldier with the highest ideals of honor and chivalry, important in an age that set great store by them. There were several recorded incidents of his personal heroism, among them a gallant attempt to recapture Calais from the English which, foiled through treachery, resulted in his spending eighteen months in prison in England in 1350 and 1351. Poems most probably written by him during this period have been preserved, revealing a profound, almost melancholy religious piety.[10]

The most curious aspect, however, was his plan for building the collegiate church at Lirey, which he would seem to have formulated during his captivity. In itself this would not be unusual. It was quite common at that time for rich men to found churches and chantries. But Geoffrey was not a rich man. He would appear to have had no means of his own for such a luxury, and had for the purpose to obtain a "rent" from his king, granted in 1353. Even then he was able to afford only a modest wooden structure, which was to fall into disrepair in less than half a century.

There is a trap into which most Shroud writers except Bulst[11] seem to have fallen, and which clearly appeared of no significance to Chevalier or Thurston. Because Geoffrey is known to have founded the Lirey church in 1353, most investigators have assumed that he had the Shroud at that time and that his intentions of keeping it in the church were already obvious. The first premise is most likely correct, but study of the documents reveals that the second is definitely not.

Fortunately, the documents have been preserved for both the foundation of Geoffrey's church in 1353 and its completion and consecration on May 28, 1356. Despite every opportunity, there is no mention of the Shroud among otherwise very ordinary relics placed in the church. Furthermore, the man who presided at the 1356 consecration was Bishop Henry of Poitiers, the very bishop who according to d'Arcis discovered the great Shroud fraud. On May 28, 1356, Bishop Henry was eulogizing over what Geoffrey had done. Clearly the first expositions of the Shroud and the subsequent controversy had not yet taken place.

These facts throw an entirely different light on the whole story as related more than thirty years later by Bishop d'Arcis. For we know with certainty that within four months of Bishop Henry's consecration of the Lirey church Geoffrey I de Charny was dead, killed in battle. Shortly after having been appointed standard-bearer of France, on September 19, 1356, he was on the battlefield of Poitiers, facing the English army of Edward the Black Prince, at the side of his king, John the Good, in a gallant last stand. Froissart[12] records how bravely Geoffrey wielded the battle-ax, against hopeless odds. Then, seeing a lance being thrust at his king, Geoffrey fatally intercepted it with his own body. When fourteen years later France had returned to some normality after the crushing defeat, Geoffrey's remains were given a hero's tomb, at royal expense in the Eglise des Celestins, Paris.

Was this knight, who wore on his epaulets the words "Honor conquers all," the perpetrator of the hoax claimed by d'Arcis? It seems unlikely. Above all, how was there time in the three and a half months between the Lirey consecration and Geoffrey's death at Poitiers for the controversial Shroud expositions, said to have drawn crowds from foreign countries, to have taken place? In terms of medieval communications and transport this seems impossible, and fortunately on this point careful rereading of d'Arcis's memorandum reveals *his* hesitations about the timing. He said the expositions had taken place thirty-four years *"or thereabouts"* before the time he was writing, 1389. This put the year of the expositions at 1355. With a margin of error of only two years, admissible by the vagueness of "or thereabouts," the possible date of the expositions could have been 1357—a year *after* Geoffrey's death.

This possibility threw a different light on how the expositions suppressed by Bishop Henry of Poitiers may have come about. It seemed arguable that Geoffrey might have inherited the Shroud in circumstances that were difficult to divulge, requiring him to choose his moment carefully. He had therefore proceeded first with the building of the church to house the relic, and revealed perhaps only to his immediate family circle his true intentions. His premature death at Poitiers ended his plans, leaving his widow, Jeanne de Vergy, with six clergy and a young son to support in hopeless financial circumstances.

Did Jeanne de Vergy then decide to bring out the Shroud to fulfill her late husband's intentions, thus enabling the Lirey canons to be kept in business? Unable to say how her husband had acquired the cloth, did she bring upon herself the not unjustifiable incredulity of Bishop Henry of Poitiers?

These seemed to be possible explanations of an otherwise irreconcilable series of events. But they were, in themselves, totally inadequate to explain the whole historical mystery, and in particular to explain in what circumstances Geoffrey de Charny had acquired the Shroud. The whole matter needed the most thorough investigation. And quite aside from all these fourteenth-century activities at Lirey, there loomed thirteen hundred long years in which the Shroud's existence had not been accounted for.

CHAPTER XI

PRE-FOURTEENTH-CENTURY "SHROUDS"

THAT LED NOWHERE

The first investigations into the Shroud's pre-fourteenth-century history were not encouraging. In the absence of any pertinent information from the Gospels, Fr. Maurus Green, a quiet-spoken, Ampleforth-trained Benedictine priest, had patiently extracted from pre-fourteenth-century documents every possible reference to supposed "shrouds" of Christ.[1] Some of these were descriptions of actual preserved shrouds, others mere speculations of what might have been the fate of the sindon purchased by Joseph of Arimathea. The latter were by far the most numerous.

The earliest example was a quotation, preserved by St. Jerome, from the otherwise lost second-century "Gospel of the Hebrews." According to this, after his resurrection Jesus had given his shroud (*sindon*) to the "servant of the priest" before appearing to James.[2] The quotation merely raised its own problems without helping any of those of the Shroud. Who was the "servant of the priest?" Textual scholars had suggested that perhaps the passage contained a copyist's error, the word *puero* (servant) having been incorrectly transcribed in place of *Petro* (Peter)—someone then later identifying the *puero* with the priest's servant mentioned in Mark 14:47. The reference led nowhere.

Another tradition came from St. Nino, the fourth-century apostle of Georgia. Shortly before her death she recounted information she had learned about the instruments of the Passion during her youth in Jerusalem.[3] According to her, the burial linen was for a while in the possession of Pilate's wife, then it passed to St. Luke, "who put it in a place known only to himself." The soudarion had a separate fate. It was found by Peter, who "took it and kept it, but we know not if it was ever discovered." Again the tradition led nowhere.

A seventh-century letter by Bishop Braulio of Saragossa (A.D. 635–51) revealed that he had no idea what had happened to the burial linen. Referring to the days of the writing of the Gospels, he said:

> At that time many things were known to have happened which are not written down; for example concerning the linteaminibus and the sudarium in which the Lord's body was wrapped—we read that it was found but we do not read that it was preserved. Yet I do not think that the apostles neglected to preserve these and such-like relics for future times.[4]

As Father Maurus pointed out, the only faintly encouraging sign was that the same bishop's liturgy (the Mozarabic rite particular to Spain), contained in its *Illatio* for Easter Saturday the cryptic sentence: "Peter ran with John to the tomb and looked at the recent traces [*vestigia*] on the linens of the dead and risen man." Someone had suggested that this could be a memory that there had been some form of image on the linen found by Peter and John. But it was far too vague to tell.

Father Maurus's research into the actual preservation of reputed shrouds was little more enlightening. The earliest reference, dated about 570, was in an account of the pilgrimage of St. Antonius Martyr, which, in describing a cave convent on the banks of the Jordan, stated, "In the same place is said to be the *sudarium*, which was over the head of Jesus."[5]

Father Maurus thought this the most likely reference to the Shroud's preservation, but this seems doubtful. Not only was there no reference to an image; there was no certainty that, as a sudarium, this was anything more than a reputed face-cloth.

It was a century before another account of a reputed shroud found its way into the historical records. This time there was much more information. About 670, a Frankish bishop, Arculf of Perigueux, shipwrecked off the lonely island of Iona in the Scottish Hebrides, had been given shelter in the island's monastery by its abbot, St. Adamnan. In gratitude he related to his host the story of his recent pilgrimage and how he had actually seen in Jerusalem the reputed shroud of Jesus. He told how he had learned that not long before there had been a dispute about the shroud between Christians and Jews, and Jerusalem's Saracen ruler had subjected it to a trial by fire, the relic fortunately landing safely in the hands of the Christians. He himself saw it taken out of its shrine "and raised aloft, amid a multitude of people assembled in the church, who kissed it, and he himself kissed it. And it was about eight feet long."[6]

As was immediately obvious from the next reminiscence, which described a cloth with an embroidered image, the shroud seen by Arculf could have borne no image or he would undoubtedly have mentioned it. Furthermore, the length of the cloth, eight feet, was much shorter than that of the Turin Shroud. Father Maurus observed that the argument was in any case a specious one. A Jesuit scholar, J. Francez, had in 1935 put up a very convincing case for the shroud seen by Arculf having been a gift to Charlemagne about 797.[7] In 877 Charlemagne's grandson Charles the Bald gave it to the royal abbey of St. Cornelius, Compiègne, and there for over nine hundred years it enjoyed great esteem as the Holy Shroud of Compiègne, an eight-foot-long tissue of fine linen that was the object of huge pilgrimages and numerous state occasions. This shroud was destroyed in the French Revolution. Clearly it could not have been the same as the present-day Shroud of Turin.

Another shroud on which Father Maurus produced copious information was that of Cadouin, a cloth found by

Crusaders in 1098 while besieged in Antioch. Like that of Compiègne an unfigured shroud, it was subsequently brought back to France and kept alternately at Cadouin and Toulouse, enjoying great esteem. Unlike the Shroud of Compiègne, it survived the French Revolution and indeed has done so to the present day. Unfortunately, in 1935 Fr. Francez showed it conclusively to be of eleventh-century Fatimite origin, its ornamental bands being actually Kufic writing carrying Moslem blessings.[8]

Father Maurus produced more references to the preservation of reputed burial linens of Jesus, this time ones in the East, in Constantinople, where several twelfth-century pilgrims' accounts described a shroud of Christ among the priceless relic collection of the Byzantine emperors. The nature of this particular shroud was unclear. Because of the very holiness of the whole collection, very few if any of the pilgrims actually saw the relics they described, and accounts are confused. As again there was no mention of any image, it was improbable that this would have been the Shroud now in Turin.

In fact, in all the years from the death of Christ to the time of Geoffrey I de Charny, Father Maurus was able to produce only one reference that seemed, albeit vaguely, to answer the description of the Shroud of Turin. This was the account of an ordinary French soldier, Robert de Clari, who related something that he had seen exhibited in Constantinople in August 1203, shortly before hostilities between Crusaders and Byzantines began. There was in Constantinople, he said, a church,

> which they called My Lady St. Mary of Blachernae, where was kept the *sydoine* in which Our Lord had been wrapped, which stood up straight every Friday so that the *figure* of Our Lord could be plainly seen there.[9]

It is an intriguing passage, particularly as it seems to be an eyewitness account. There was some uncertainty as to whether in early thirteenth-century French parlance *figure* had its modern French meaning of "face," or whether it might actually have been intended to describe a full figure in the English sense of the word. Either was suggestive. But what happened to the *sydoine*? Intriguingly, de Clari added, "No one, either Greek or French, ever knew what became of this sydoine after the city was taken."

In this one lone account lay many possibilities. The setting was, after all, Constantinople in Turkey, one of the places where Frei's research actually suggested the Shroud had been at some stage in its history. The cloth was described as having an image. But on its own it was still worth very little. For instance, it had inconsistencies with other accounts. The burial linen, if this was indeed the sydoine, was described consistently elsewhere as preserved in the imperial chapel of the Pharos, within the Boucoleon Palace, not in the church of Blachernae. It was therefore quite impossible on this one reference to explain thirteen hundred missing years of the Shroud's history.

All appeared completely hopeless. How could such a fascinating piece of cloth as the Shroud of Turin, if genuine, have gone totally unrecorded over thirteen centuries, suddenly to turn up in fourteenth-century France?

Could it have been hidden away all the time, due to Jewish and Roman persecution of Christians, followed by the danger to all image-bearing objects during the period of the iconoclastic controversy (725–842)? This was most unlikely. There were four hundred years from the conversion of Constantine the Great to the onset of iconoclasm, during which many previously "hidden" relics came to light, including the entire True Cross, the crown of thorns, the nails, the purple cloak, the reed, the stone of the sepulcher, and many others. There was ample opportunity for such an important and unmistakable relic as the Turin Shroud to come to light. Yet there was no record of any such event. Could the vital records of its preservation have been lost due to the destruction of ancient libraries? This, too, was most unlikely. Most relics found their way to major centers such as Rome and Constantinople and were adequately recorded there. Anywhere that housed or displayed the Shroud would have attracted pilgrimage and could scarcely fail to be noted by early Christian travelers. As Jesuit historian Herbert Thurston dryly noted in 1903:

The huge seventeenth-century altar, designed by Guarino Guarini, within which the Shroud is stored. It is locked away behind the grille visible in the center of the picture. (*Dr. David Willis*)

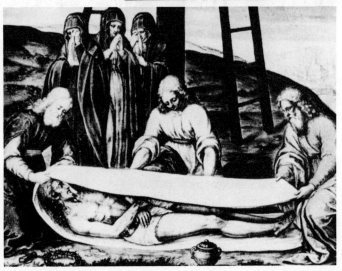

Reconstruction, by sixteenth-century artist Clovio, of how the body would have been laid in the cloth to create the double impression. (*Dom Bosco Filmstrips*)

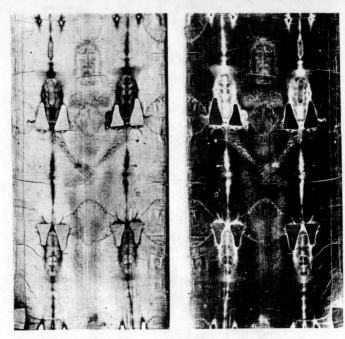

Enrie's photograph of the frontal image of the Shroud positive (left) and negative, 1931. (*British Society for the Turin Shroud*)

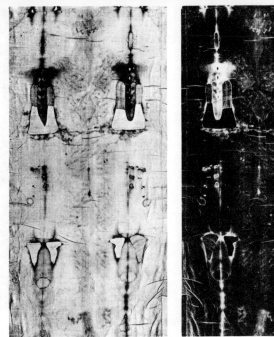

The dorsal image of the Shroud in positive (left) and negative.
(British Society for the Turin Shroud)

Above: Normal portrait photograph (right), with the masklike effect when seen in negative (left). *(Photo by the author)* Below: The Shroud face as it appears to the naked eye (left), with the altogether more harmonious appearance when the cloth is seen in negative (right). *(British Society for the Turin Shroud)* Deduction: That the Shroud is in some unexplained way itself a photographic negative, yet one that has been in existence since *at least* the fourteenth century.

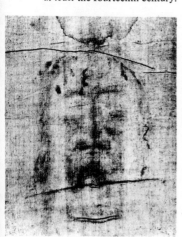

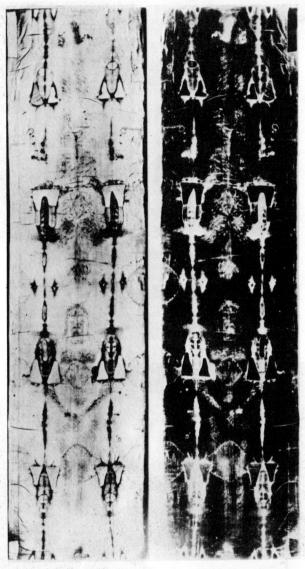

A full-length view of the Enrie negative (right) side-by-side with a positive print of the Shroud as it appears in black and white. From the Italian certificate of authenticity granted at the time of the 1931 exposition. (*British Society for the Turin Shroud*)

A. Paul Vignon, a young biologist at the time of the 1898 exposition, and subsequently professor of biology at the Institut Catholique, Paris. He researched prodigiously on the Shroud, venturing far outside his own field of specialty. (Sindon, *December 1970*)

B. Yves Delage, agnostic professor of comparative anatomy at the Sorbonne, Paris. In 1902 he astonished the French Académie des Sciences with a lecture claiming the Shroud's authenticity. (*John Walsh*)

Anthropometric Data on the Man of the Shroud:
Height (estimated by Cordiglia)   181 cm.
Cranial index (Cordiglia)   79.9 cm.
Nasal index   70.9 cm.
Estimated weight   170 lbs.
Racial type: classic Mediterranean

Reconstruction of the original appearance of the wounds from the crown of thorns (above), with the appearance of the wounds on the photographic negative (inset), and how they appear on the cloth itself (below). D is an enlargement of the arrowed area in C.

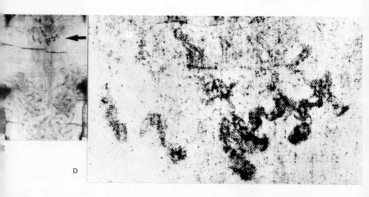

. . . it curiously happens that the history of the supposed relic for thirteen hundred years down to that precise date [the time of Geoffrey I de Charny] remains an absolute blank.[10]

And as he concluded elsewhere:

. . . the probability of an error in the verdict of history must be accounted, it seems to me, almost infinitesimal.[11]

What was the answer? If the Shroud of Turin was genuine, its history for some unknown reason had not been preserved in the documentary accounts of reputed "shrouds" before the fourteenth century. They led nowhere. The answer had to be elsewhere.

CHAPTER XII

THE SHROUD FACE AND THE

"FAMILIAR" CHRIST LIKENESS IN ART

The fact that Father Maurus's collection of "shroud" references failed to show up anything answering the description of that of Turin was troubling but not unduly so. If one forgot that the Shroud was a shroud, forgot about the relic's fourteen-foot length and its double-figure image, and concentrated only on the face, it took on a certain haunting familiarity, a certain "somewhere I've seen it before" quality.

The likeness on the Shroud, even though seen so imperfectly on the cloth itself, is unmistakably the same likeness that has come down through history as being *the* human appearance of Jesus. This likeness can be traced many centuries earlier than the era of Geoffrey de Charny. It is familiar also for another reason. One of the most vivid of Christian legends is the story of the "Veronica" cloth, the cloth on which, according to a very tangled tradition, Jesus' face was miraculously impressed as he toiled towards Calvary. As a tradition, whatever its truth, that cloth's ancestry also stretched back well before the fourteenth century. With such an unmistakable affinity between the Shroud face, the portrait of Christ in art, and artists' copies of the Veronica, there had to be a historical link among all three. Indeed, several authors of books about the Shroud had suggested the same, but had failed to follow the idea through.

The first consideration was the likeness of Christ that had come down to us in art. Even alone this raised intriguing questions. If the Shroud was a forgery, the compatibility was of no special significance because one could presume that the forger merely copied the conventional likeness. But if the Shroud was genuine, the fact that there was such a close similarity between its likeness and that in art suggested that somehow, somewhere its existence had been known in the early centuries, and if known, had most likely been documented.

Could one possibly tell by tracing the likeness back through the early centuries where and what the Shroud may have been? There was nothing to lose by giving the method a try.

It was important to establish certain first principles. For instance, if there were clear reliable descriptions of what Jesus looked like dating from his time, or if there was an unbroken artistic tradition dating from his time, the method would be a futile one. But neither was the case.

It comes as a surprise to many to learn that there is, in fact, no mention in the Gospels of what Christ looked like. The New Testament can be scoured from beginning to end without providing one morsel of information—whether he was tall or short, bearded or clean-shaven, handsome or ugly.

Nor is there any independent contemporary information. A letter is sometimes quoted that supposedly was written to the Senate of Rome by one Publius Lentulus (purportedly Pilate's predecessor as governor of Judea), describing Christ as "tall and comely, of reverent countenance . . . his hair the color of chestnut."

Agreeable as the description is, it has to be discounted. From the writings of the eleventh-century Anselm, Archbishop of Canterbury, it has been reliably shown to be of late composition. Its very title is its own condemnation, as no such person as Lentulus was "Proconsul in Judea" at the time to which the letter purports to refer.[1]

As early as the second century, writers were in fact obliged to resort to conjecture as to Christ's earthly appearance from the lack of any other reliable information. Justin Martyr and Clement of Alexandria thought he must have been ugly,[2] basing their ideas, in the absence of other information, on Isaiah's Old Testament prophecies on the appearance of the Savior:

> Without beauty, without majesty (we saw him), no looks to attract our eyes; a thing despised and rejected by men . . . a man to make people screen their faces; he was despised and we took no account of him. [Is. 53:2, 3.]

Many third- and fourth-century writers supported this view, among them Basil, Isidore of Pelusium, Theodoret, Cyril of Alexandria, Tertullian, and Cyprian. Others of the same period took an opposite view, not because of any greater historical knowledge but because they turned to a different passage in the Old Testament, the Forty-fifth Psalm: "Of all men you are the most handsome" (Ps. 45:2). St. Jerome (ca. 342–420) interpreted this as the correct prophecy for Jesus' human appearance. He argued that Isaiah's description of the suffering servant who was "without beauty" could only refer to the body of Christ when it had been disfigured by blows and spitting, not to his normal appearance:

> For unless he had possessed something starry in his face and eyes, the Apostles would never have followed him at once, nor would those who came to seize him have fallen to the ground. . . .[3]

In the apocryphal "Acts of John" it was as a handsome youth with a smiling face that Christ appeared at the grave of Drusiana. Similar descriptions could be found in the "Life and Passion of St. Caecilius," the "Passion of Saints Perpetua and Felicitas," and the "Actus Vercellensis."

This ignorance and confusion was similarly reflected in art, one reason being that it was most unlikely that there was ever a portrait of Jesus made in his lifetime because of the rigidity with which the Jews interpreted the second commandment, "You shall not make yourself a carved image or any likeness of anything in heaven or on earth beneath" (Ex. 20:4). There are various extant works said to have been painted by St. Luke, but these have no claim to authenticity.

In the earliest years of Christianity the Church appears to have followed Jewish thinking and shunned the idea of physical portraits of Jesus—a view that recurred many times in succeeding centuries. But as the faith percolated with increasing strength into a world where images were on coins, statues, ornaments, wall decorations, almost everywhere that the eye could look, it was inevitable that portrayals of the human likeness of Jesus would be sought. A somewhat heated correspondence in the early fourth century between the Empress Constantia Augusta and Bishop Eusebius of Caesarea indicates vividly the yearning for such portraits.[4]

Ironically, the earliest known example of a portrait of Jesus, albeit a poor one, occurs in a provincial Jewish setting, Dura-Europos on the Euphrates, where interpretations of the second commandment were clearly less severe. It is a fresco of the mid-third century and depicts Jesus young, beardless, and with short hair, in a scene of the healing of the paralytic. The same type of youthful, beardless likeness occurred in the fourth century in locations as far apart as Rome's cemetery of Massimus and St. Felicity, and the mosaic floor of a Roman country house excavated at Hinton St. Mary, Dorset, England, this latter being the earliest portrait of Christ found in Britain.

The same type was also found in the fifth century—in a Good Shepherd mosaic from Ravenna's Mausoleum of Galla Placidia, and in a well-known ivory diptych of the scenes from the miracles. There could be no doubt from these that in the centuries closest to Christ many of those in the civilized Roman world envisaged their Savior more as the Apollo of their forefathers than as a bearded Jew.

There were exceptions. A mid-third-century Christ as Shepherd from Rome's Hypogeum of the Aurelians certainly gave a vague impression of a bearded, long-haired man. A fourth-century Christ from the Catacomb of Commodilla, Rome, was similarly of the Semitic type—long, undulating hair, a long beard, large eyes and nose. These seemed to be attempts at representing what Jesus actually might have looked like, perhaps from some distant memory that he was a long-haired, long-nosed, bearded man.

All these different concepts were possible because of sheer ignorance of any authority for the human likeness of Jesus. As St. Augustine wrote in the early fifth century, the portraits in his time were "innumerable in concept and design," and for one very good reason: "We do not know of his external appearance, nor that of his mother."[5]

So how and when did knowledge of what we now recognize as the human likeness of Jesus occur? If one scours artbooks, one realizes that no one has really tackled the issue directly because no one has seriously considered that there might have been one specific source. It would be necessary to do the tracking from examples in art, scrupulously using the datings of modern art experts, and rejecting any work where later restoration might have altered the resemblance.

The best method of approach seems to be to track back rather than forward, and to use as a base the fifteenth century, i.e., within the period that the Shroud was known to have been preserved. In fact there was from this period an ideal work of art with which to compare the Shroud likeness, the "Rex Regum" of Jan van Eyck, which, although the original has not survived, is known to us from no less than four excellent copies made at the time. It is ideal because it has the same rigidly front-facing aspect as the Shroud face. One can therefore see how in each of the distinctive features— long hair parted in the middle and falling to the shoulders, a moderately long, forked beard, a long prominent nose, a thin mustache drooping to join the beard, a distinctive hairless gap beneath the lower lip—it matches the Shroud likeness virtually exactly. It might have been copied from the Shroud face, except that it is known from the work of art experts such as Pacht[6] that, in fact, Van Eyck derived it from Christ portraits of the East, from the world of Byzantium, in which artist after artist had copied from another the same likeness in a tradition going back many centuries. It is this tradition that is the path to the source of the likeness.

Looking back to the thirteenth century, the likeness can be found in a large and magnificent mosaic of Christ Enthroned in the gallery of Hagia Sophia, Constantinople. From the twelfth century there is an excellent example of the likeness in the huge, brooding Christ Pantocrator mosaic that dominates the apse of the Norman-Byzantine church of Cefalù, Sicily, a work described by British art critic John Beckwith as "one of the most sublime attempts to represent the Logos Incarnate."[7] The likeness is awe-inspiringly evident in the Christ Pantocrator from the eleventh-century dome of the church of Daphni, near Athens, a likeness called by writer Sacheverell Sitwell "a terrifying countenance that makes it credible that a man has lived beyond the grave."

There are two splendid tenth-century examples of the likeness, the Christ Enthroned fresco in the church of Sant'Angelo in Formis near Capua, Italy, and the majestic "Christ as Holy Wisdom" mosaic uncovered in this century high above the royal door in the narthex of Hagia Sophia, Constantinople.

Looking back to the eighth century, an epoch in which most eastern portraits of Christ were destroyed during the wave of image-smashing, or iconoclasm, the same likeness can be found, heavily influenced by Byzantium in a Pantocrator painting from the catacomb of St. Pontianus, Rome.

One can find the same likeness even as far back as the sixth century in several examples, but notably a mosaic Christ Enthroned at Ravenna's Sant'Apollinare Nuovo church, and a medallion portrait of Christ in the Byzantine manner on a silver vase discovered at Homs, the ancient Emesa, in Syria.

With these examples the trail back ends. Earlier, all that can be found is the vague and widely varied portraits of the time of St. Augustine and before. What seems clear is that at one given point, the sixth century, the features of Christ in art were brought into focus, as if by an invisible decree. The hair became long and center-parted, the beard established and decisively forked, the nose longer and more pronounced, the eyes deeper and their pupils larger, and the whole countenance set in a rigidly front-facing attitude. There is an au-

thority about it that seems to suggest that someone, somewhere suddenly knew what Jesus had looked like.

But how? Art historians merely attribute the phenomenon
to the Byzantine tendency at this period to create rigid artistic formulae that then became the pattern for future generations. But if this was so, it is surely a remarkable coincidence
that the Shroud likeness was followed so exactly.

Without probing further, one can only say that if the face
on the Shroud in some way introduced the likeness into art,
one thing is certain. It happened in the sixth century, not
later, and seemingly not before.

And one can also say that whatever the source of the likeness, it had some special relationship with the Christ
Enthroned portrayal of Christ, as if it were this type in particular, with its rigid front-facing aspect and tendency to be
given pride of place in church decoration, that embodied the
true likeness as it was then known.

Before probing deeper into what might have had such a
profound artistic influence in the sixth century, it is important to consider whether there is any way in which one could
be more positive that the Shroud likeness had been at work.

Fortunately, there is, in the form of some most unusual,
and so far largely unrecognized research on the part of
Frenchman Paul Vignon, the biologist colleague of Professor
Yves Delage. In the 1930s Vignon turned his interest away
from the scientific aspects of the Shroud, and began to study
some of the post-sixth-century Byzantine portraits looked at
earlier in this chapter, together with many similar pre-fourteenth-century portraits of Christ.[8]

He had noticed that in many of these portraits there were
certain oddities, certain peculiarities to the Christ face. One
painting to which he paid particular attention was the
eighth-century Christ Pantocrator from the catacomb of St.
Pontianus, Rome. On the forehead between the eyebrows of
this work a starkly geometrical ⎵ shape had caught his eye.
Artistically it did not seem to make sense. If it was intended
to be a furrowed brow, it was depicted most unnaturally in
comparison to the rest of the face.

It, therefore, intrigued him greatly that when he turned to
the equivalent point on the Shroud face, there was the same

feature, equally as geometric, and equally as unnatural because it appeared to have nothing to do with the image itself.

The significance of the Pontianus discovery was heightened when other Byzantine Christ portraits were found to exhibit the same marking. The eleventh-century Daphni Pantocrator, the tenth-century Sant'Angelo in Formis fresco, the tenth-century Hagia Sophia narthex mosaic, and an eleventh-century portable mosaic from Berlin are typical of many Byzantine works featuring the same peculiar-shaped brow, generally more stylized, but still suggestive of the same derivation.

Coincidence? Or could the Byzantine artist have been working from some blueprint likeness of Christ, faithfully reproducing this feature derived from the Shroud? Vignon, and after him the American scholar Edward Wuenschel,[9] began to search for other such peculiarities, and found some twenty in all, oddities originating from some accidental imperfection in the Shroud image or weave, and repeated time and again in paintings, frescoes, and mosaics of the Byzantine period, even though artistically they made no sense. By no means every work featured every peculiarity. Nor were the markings confined exclusively to front-facing portraits but were sometimes found three-quarter face. Occasionally some, such as the forehead markings, were given to saints, perhaps as a special mark of holiness. And some were seen reversed right to left, perhaps because of understanding of the reversing effect of an "impression."

Not all of the twenty markings deduced by Vignon and Wuenschel are acceptable. Because of the very imprecisions of the Shroud likeness, many seem too elusive to permit firm deductions. But even so, one could still make a reasonable case for the validity of some fifteen that a Byzantine artist might have "seen." These are:

1. A transverse streak across the forehead.
2. The three-sided "square" on the forehead.
3. A V shape at the bridge of the nose.
4. A second V shape inside feature 2.
5. A raised right eyebrow.
6. An accentuated left cheek.
7. An accentuated right cheek.

8. An enlarged left nostril.
9. An accentuated line between nose and upper lip.
10. A heavy line under the lower lip.
11. A hairless area between lip and beard.
12. The fork to the beard.
13. A transverse line across the throat.
14. Heavily accentuated, owlish eyes.
15. Two loose strands of hair falling from the apex of the forehead.

It is even possible to produce statistics for the presence of these features in works of art. Taking as an example the Pantocrator from the dome of the church of Daphni, no fewer than thirteen of the features can be identified, particularly noteworthy being the triangle or V shape at the bridge of the nose, the ⊔ shape, the V shape within this, and the streak across the forehead (these somewhat stylized in the hands of a very competent artist), together with heavy accentuation of the eyes and the raised right eyebrow. The Sant'Angelo in Formis fresco also features thirteen features, the Cefalù apse mosaic fourteen, and the Hagia Sophia mosaic nine, an average incidence of an impressive eighty per cent.

When all is said and done, the peculiarities are so distinctive and prevalent that it seems doubtful that they could be mere imagination or coincidence.

Then what does it all mean? It seems likely that some unknown artist carefully prepared from the Shroud face a drawing—as it were, from the life. He carefully studied each feature and composed it into a living face accumulating on the way many of the peculiarities of the Shroud image that he could not hope to understand. He would, for instance, have "seen" open eyes because this is how they indeed appear on the cloth itself, open and staring, even though as we know from the photographic negative they were in reality closed in death.

Copies of such a drawing circulated throughout the Christian world, wherever churches were being decorated, would have quickly established the new "true likeness" that emerged from the sixth century on.

Was it the cloth we now know as the Shroud of Turin that the artist worked from? If so, where was it at the time? The answer seems to be to track back, just as we have done with the portrait of Christ in art, the Veronica-type tradition of Christ impressing his face on cloth.

CHAPTER XIII

THE SHROUD AND THE TRADITION OF CHRIST'S FACE IMPRESSED ON CLOTH

In studying what we will for the present term the "Veronica" tradition, one enters a field quite different from that of art. With the latter, one treads on solid ground. For any given artistic work there are photographs that can be studied, locations that can be visited, expert works that can be consulted on datings and earlier influences. In the case of the Veronica there is little that is tangible. In general most books that deal with the subject are full of pious misconceptions; the few serious authors who refer to it rightly recognize so many problems and contradictions that they give it little more than cursory study.

The Veronica story in itself has a simplicity that totally belies the undercurrents. As everyone understood it in the High Middle Ages:

Veronica was in her house when she heard the shouting and wailing from a crowd surrounding the soldiers who were leading Jesus to Calvary. She rose hurriedly, put her head to the door, looked over the heads of the crowd, and saw our Redeemer. . . . Transported, beside herself, she seized her veil and threw herself into the street, oblivious to the insults and blows from the soldiers who pushed her back. Arriving in the presence of our Savior, whose face was pouring with sweat and blood, she wiped [his face] with her veil. . . . All honor to you, courageous woman. . . . The Savior granted you the most precious gift which he could make to a creature of this world, his portrait imprinted . . . on your veil.[1]

So widespread did this story become in Christian mythology that today it is rare to find a Catholic church that does not have somewhere a scene depicting Jesus, toiling on his way to Calvary, impressing the likeness of his face on Veronica's veil. The incident was made the sixth of the fourteen Stations of the Cross, and the guides in the Old City of Jerusalem today point out to the wanderer the site on the Via Dolorosa where it purportedly took place. There is an accompanying small, dark church where one can see an eighteenth-century icon of the veil, and many Catholics are under the impression that the story is recorded in the Gospels.

In attempting a brief but serious evaluation of the tradition, the first difficulty is the discovery that the original "veil" venerated by medieval pilgrims is no longer in existence. Modern enquiries meet with almost no information from Vatican custodians,[2] but according to the historical record the relic was one of those seized by the troops of Charles V who sacked Rome in 1527, and when last heard of, it was being sold by drunken soldiers in the city's taverns. While the square medieval silver reliquary is still preserved in the sacristy of St. Peter's and carries indeed the outlines of the face it originally framed, in 1907 this was opened up by art expert Monsignor Joseph Wilpert to reveal nothing of the cloth immortalized by medieval artists. In his own words, all that he saw upon removing the covering glass "was a square piece of light-colored material, somewhat faded through age, which bore two faint, irregular rust-brown stains, connected one to the other. . . ."[3]

Clearly this was not the cloth image of Christ that pilgrims had trampled upon each other to see in papal Jubilee Years such as 1300 and 1350. But when one examines contemporary descriptions and the artistic record, no one consistent picture of the Veronica's appearance emerges. For fifteenth- and sixteenth-century artists such as Quentin Massys, William of Cologne, and Albrecht Dürer, the Veronica depicted Christ as a disembodied head crowned with thorns and suffering, consistent of course with the saga of the Via Dolorosa. This is, however, only a late phase of Veronica portraits. Artists working only slightly earlier, such as Robert Campin, and illustrators of French and English manuscripts of the fourteenth century, again showed the disembodied head, as from an "impress" likeness, but now without crown of thorns or indeed any signs of suffering. Both of these show striking similarities to the face on the Shroud. But to confuse the issue, there is a still earlier phase in which illuminators of thirteenth-century manuscripts such as Matthew Paris's *Chronica majora* and the Westminster Psalter show the Veronica likeness with neck and indeed body. Puzzling as this is, it cannot easily be attributed to copyists' error. Independently, the early thirteenth-century author Gervase of Tilbury verbally described the Veronica as portraying Jesus "from the chest upwards."[4] It was hard to see how this could be equated with a reputedly "miraculous" impression of Christ's features.

Study of early records of the actual expositions of the cloth "called Veronica" throws little light on the issue. Something of the probably blackened and discolored character of the image in the fifteenth century can be gathered from the contemporary English mystic Juliana of Norwich's *Revelations*, in which she describes a vision of an empty human skin which:

> . . . with its many changes of color, brown and black, its pitiful and drawn look . . . made me think of the holy vernicle [Veronica] of Rome, upon which he imprinted his own blessed face, when he was in his hard Passion and going willingly to his death. Of this image many wondered . . . how it could be so discolored and so far from fairness?[5]

Given a cloth image of this character, it would perhaps have been relatively easy for artists to imagine traces of suffering where originally there had been none.

But as one tracks back further, the surprising fact emerges that a precisely determinable history for the cloth relic is not as ancient as might have been expected. One can read records that in the year 1207 Pope Innocent III instituted a procession of the Veronica from St. Peter's to the Hospital of Santo Spirito, Rome.[6] In the year 1191 it was recorded that Pope Celestine III had proudly shown to the visiting king of France, Philip Augustus:

the heads of the apostles Peter and Paul, and the Veronica, that is to say the very cloth on which Jesus Christ imprinted his countenance and upon which the impression is so clear that the face of Jesus Christ can be seen upon it even today.[7]

The earliest positive reference to the preservation of the cloth is a casual remark by a canon of St. Peter's, Benedict, in the year 1143: "Afterwards the Pope made his way to the *sudarium* of Christ which is called Veronica and incensed it."[8]

Pope Sergius IV is known to have consecrated an altar to the *sudarium* in Pope John VII's chapel in St. Peter's in 1011. Quite possibly this was a record of the coming of the cloth to Rome, as the relic certainly was kept above the altar of this chapel in subsequent years. Any earlier existence of the Veronica seems unlikely, as popes in early times tended to carry relics of the Veronica type in procession at moments of great trouble and in two such instances, during the pontificates of Stephen II (752) and Leo IV (847–55), it was a very different image of Christ, the Acheropita icon that we will shortly discuss, which was employed.

What does it all mean? What is the source of this likeness, ostensibly so reminiscent of the face on the Shroud? To gain yet another perspective on the subject, it is necessary to study the Veronica story as a tradition, and in like manner to trace it, too, back through the centuries.

The concept of Veronica as a woman of Jerusalem bursting through the crowds on the Via Dolorosa is a late medieval innovation, the invention of Parisian miracle-play writers to add drama to their stagings of the events of the Passion. When one looks back earlier, to the account of a canon of St. Peter's, Peter Mallius, ca. 1150, the whole scene is different. The cloth is still the possession of Veronica. But it is described as "the *sudarium* of Christ on which *before* his Passion he wiped his most sacred face . . . when his sweat became as drops of blood falling to the ground."[9] Mallius clearly had in mind the pre-Passion agony in Gethsemane and St. Luke's vivid description of the "hematodrosis" of Jesus, when "his sweat fell to the ground like great drops of blood" (Lk. 22:44). There is no Via Dolorosa dash, no suggestion even that Veronica herself was present at the time.

When one looks back further to before the records of the actual preservation of the relic in Rome, the stories of Veronica take on more primitive forms. There is the "Death of Pilate,"[10] a short Latin work undated but almost certainly of seventh- or eighth-century creation. In this account, Veronica, knowing that Jesus was about to leave her, decided to have his portrait painted. Meeting her on her way to the painter and learning her errand, Jesus asked for the canvas, pressed it to his face, and returned it to her with his image miraculously imprinted on it. About A.D. 600 another Latin work, the "Healing of Tiberius," together with an Anglo-Saxon variant, the "Avenging of the Savior,"[11] identifies Veronica as the "Hemorrhissa" of the Gospels, the woman with the issue of blood who sought to be cured by touching the hem of Christ's garment (Mt. 9:20–22; Mk. 5:25–34; Lk. 8:43–48). Again the possessor of a portrait of Christ, in this work she is described as using it to cure the Roman Emperor Tiberius of leprosy.

It is possible, in fact, to trace the name of the woman Veronica, at least in its Roman form of Berenice, back to the fourth century. When we get back this far—in, for instance the "Acts of Pilate" and the *Apocritus* of Macarius of Magnesia[12]—we no longer find her connected with the portrait. Instead she is firmly identified with the Hemorrhissa, and is described by Macarius and other authors of the time merely as having erected outside her house a bronze statue of Jesus in the act of healing her, in gratitude for her cure.

Only at this point does the story take on a credible historical character. Bishop Eusebius of Caesarea, writing about A.D. 325 in his highly authoritative *History of the Church*, actually mentions having seen this statue, a two-figure work comprising:

A woman, resting on one knee and resembling a suppliant with arms outstretched. Facing this . . . an upright figure of a man with a double cloak neatly draped over his shoulders and his hand outstretched to the woman. . . .[13]

The location of this statue was Paneas, better known as Caesarea Philippi, said to have been the Hemorrhissa's home town, where Eusebius himself had resided. The statue was probably not even that of Jesus. Some scholars have made a case for its having been merely a votive work erected by grateful citizens of Caesarea Philippi to their benefactor the Emperor Hadrian, this accounting for the reputed inscription "To the Savior, the Benefactor."[14] Whatever it was, it was destroyed about A.D. 600.

Was the whole saga of Veronica merely a totally distorted version of the story of the gospel Hemorrhissa? Were the Shroud-like face on the eventual cloth "relic" and the long tradition of the impression of Christ's features all pure fabrication? However much this might appear implicit from what has gone before, the answer is no. Those who wrote down traditions such as that of the Veronica were not charlatans or inventive geniuses who spun the stories out of nothing. Nor was the likeness on the Veronica cloth, as revered during the Middle Ages, the brainchild of one inspired eleventh-century Italian artist. As historians of the eminence of Sir Steven Runciman have recognized, the common source was a deeply rooted tradition of the East, the story of another immensely renowned cloth portrait of Christ, the image "not made by hands" of Edessa, or as the Byzantines were later to call it, the Mandylion.

This was a cloth image of Christ with an *early* historical existence, the parent both of the Veronica cloth itself and several of the post-sixth-century elements of the Veronica story.

In the collection of Queen Elizabeth II at Buckingham Palace is a seventeenth-century icon of the Mandylion that beautifully illustrates its appearance and, in surrounding painted panels, something of its long history as one of the foremost relics of the Eastern Orthodox Church.

Part of this history is semilegendary. As early as the first century A.D. it is supposed to have been sent to a King Abgar of Edessa to cure him of a disease. But most of the history is firmly historical—from its *sixth century* rediscovery in Edessa, to A.D. 944, when it was transferred to Constantinople, to

1204, when it disappeared without trace from Constantinople during the Fourth Crusade.

In considering the Mandylion and the Shroud, with their obvious common denominator of a mysteriously imprinted image of Jesus on cloth, there are many features of potential major significance. One is that the known locations of the Mandylion—Constantinople in western Turkey, and Edessa (present-day Urfa) in the eastern Anatolian steppeland—conform perfectly to what is known so far of the geographical origins of the Turkish pollen on the Shroud identified by Dr. Frei. Another is that the Mandylion's apparent rediscovery in the sixth century corresponds precisely to the starting point of the seemingly Shroud-inspired definitive likeness of Jesus that we have seen emerge in art. Yet another is the similarity of the sepia-colored face on artists' copies of the Mandylion to the sort of face one might reconstruct from that visible on the Shroud. This latter is reinforced by the powerful and consistent literary tradition that the Mandylion's image, like that of the Shroud, was *acheiropoietos,* a Greek word meaning "not made by hands." (Compare the remark of Pope Pius XI during the 1930s that the Shroud was "certainly not by the hand of man.") Last, and by no means least, is the fact that the period of the Mandylion's known history would fill in, with just a comparatively short gap, almost the entire missing period of the history of the Turin Shroud.

Clearly the nature, origins, and subsequent fate of the Mandylion demand the most intensive enquiry. . . .

CHAPTER XIV

WERE SHROUD AND MANDYLION
ONE AND THE SAME THING?

Could the Mandylion of the Eastern Orthodox Church have been one and the same as the cloth we know today as the Shroud of Turin?

It was not an easy question even to begin to tackle. On the

one hand, the Shroud of Turin is an existing fourteen-foot length of linen bearing the imprint of the front and back of a human body, and for all the world appears to have been a burial wrapping. On the other, the Mandylion is a now apparently lost cloth that from artists' copies made of it at the time of its known existence, and from contemporary descriptions, seems to have borne the image only of the face of Christ, and that apparently made when he was alive and well. One cloth has been known for certain only in the West, the other cloth for certain only in the East. The only reasonable grounds for suggesting common identity were the shared concept of the image having been "impressed" in some extraordinary manner upon cloth, and the strangely familiar Shroud-like look of the face on artists' copies of the Mandylion.

In embarking upon the subject, I found little encouragement from professional historians. Sir Steven Runciman of Cambridge, England,[1] and Professor Kurt Weitzmann of Princeton, New Jersey,[2] have each written scholarly articles on the Mandylion. I consulted both at an early stage, and, although they replied courteously to my letters, they failed to offer any support. Runciman wrote in 1929 that the Mandylion was "some old icon whose origins we cannot possibly hope to trace."[3] The French Professor André Grabar wrote of it during the same period, "In approaching this subject, new in historical circles, we must take into account the difficulties it presents, particularly due to the paucity of documentation. It has never been the subject of specialist research."[4] The most apposite remark was one made more recently by Victoria and Albert Museum art historian John Beckwith. "Its origins," he said, "are shrouded in mystery."[5]

One can only acknowledge a certain sound wisdom in these attitudes. The Mandylion was but one of dozens of relics preserved in Byzantium up to the time Constantinople was sacked by the Fourth Crusade of 1204. The manuscripts of the Dark Ages are littered with accounts of the miraculous happenings and phenomena the Byzantines attributed to such relics. Why should the Mandylion have been more important than any of the others?

The problem is made all the more difficult by the air of secrecy that has surrounded the Mandylion—secrecy while it was kept in Edessa up to 944, during which time there was not a single record of a viewing of the cloth, let alone an exposition; secrecy after its transfer to Constantinople, during which time only the privileged few were allowed to see it.

The most crucial aspect of study is therefore to determine what one can of the overall physical characteristics of the Mandylion vis-à-vis of the Shroud. There is a reasonable amount of artistic and documentary information available, but what rapidly becomes clear is the importance, as in an archaeological "dig," of placing each item in its chronological sequence. Only by this method do certain details make sense.

There is for instance a significant difference between copies of the image made after its disappearance from Constantinople and those made before. An exhaustive study made of copies of the Mandylion by Professor Grabar[6] showed that those made more than fifty years *after* the relic's disappearance were of what one may term the "suspended" type—i.e., they showed the cloth limp and hanging free. This style first appeared at Sopocani, one of the Eastern Empire's nearest points to the West, suggesting that it may well have come about because the Veronica cloth was beginning to appear in the West at this time.

Copies from the *earlier* period, rarer and chiefly dating from the eleventh to early thirteenth centuries, showed the cloth seemingly stretched taut, with a fringe, and frequently with a curious trellis pattern—features that seem to be important indications of its pre-1204 appearance.

An obvious but essential feature of all copies is the background color of the cloth, consistently an ivory white, the natural color of linen, just as on the Shroud. Many copies also bear some form of decoration, but these vary so much one from the other that these variations are obviously artistic whim.

Consistently on the copies the face is frontal and disembodied, an important characteristic. When seen in isolation, with the body image concealed, the real Shroud face has a similar appearance.

Then there is the color of the image. On artists' copies of the Mandylion, it ranges from a sepia monochrome to a rust-brown monochrome, slightly deeper but otherwise virtually identical to the coloring of the image on the Shroud. In the case of the Holy Face of Laon, one of the early period copies, a later artist obviously felt the need to relieve the monotony by adding small traces of color in certain areas, but Professor Grabar has made it clear that these were absent when the icon was originally executed.

In literary accounts of the Mandylion, the Shroud image's watery and blurry character can consistently be detected. This is implicit, for instance, in the very stories told during the Byzantine era about how Christ had formed the image.

According to one sixth-century version, Jesus had asked to wash his face and his image was found imprinted on the linen after he had dried himself with it.[7] According to another, that of an eighth-century patriarch of Constantinople, the image was "the impression of Christ's sweat-soaked face."[8] According to yet another, that of a tenth-century Byzantine writer, the image was "a moist secretion without coloring or painter's art" and elsewhere "due to sweat, not pigments."[9]

The blurry character is implicit too in the way the face of Christ on artists' copies of the Mandylion differed one from another. Some vary in the length of the beard and the degree to which it forks. The direction of the eyes is sometimes represented to the left, sometimes to the right, sometimes straight ahead, suggesting that the source of the copies is not explicit.

Although the majority of depictions are without a neck, two early manuscript illustrations, the Codex Rossianus and the Alexandria menologion, show a neck in a very truncated form.

In every version the portrait is bearded, but the stylings of the beard and the hair vary slightly, some showing the hair falling vertically to the neck, others showing it splayed out to the sides. In each case the variations could be explained by details in which the Shroud face itself is vague. The Shroud could even explain the "neck" on the manuscript illustrations, there being an old crease-line readily compatible with such misinterpretation at the appropriate point on the Shroud.

However, the most pertinent example of all of the Mandylion's image being identical to that of the Shroud belongs to the earliest firsthand account that we have of any "viewing" of the Mandylion in Byzantine times—that of the evening of August 15, 944, when the cloth first arrived in Constantinople after its long journey from Edessa. In the sacristy of the Church of St. Mary of Blachernae (the very church where 250 years later Robert de Clari was to describe having seen the "sydoine"), a small gathering of princes and clergy celebrated the Mass for the Assumption of the Virgin, then crowded around to see the casket containing the Mandylion opened up. Two somewhat ignorant sons of the reigning emperor, Romanus Lecapenus, were present. It is recorded that they found the Mandylion disappointing, being unable to distinguish Christ's features clearly because they found the Mandylion's image extremely blurred.[10] One could only interpret this as a classic reaction of anyone seeing the Shroud for the first time.

In fact there is one other way that the Mandylion image can be shown to be related closely to the Turin Shroud. Artists' copies feature the same Vignon markings that we saw on the related likenesses of Christ Enthroned. On one early copy of the Mandylion can be found thirteen of the features—particularly evident being the transverse streak across the forehead, the V at the bridge of the nose, the second V above this, the accentuated cheeks and enlarged left nostril. On another copy, that at Spas Nereditsa, a similar number of characteristics can be found, particularly noteworthy again being the forehead markings.

The logical deduction seems to be that whoever made the Mandylion copies appears to have been working from the Shroud. This raises the inevitable question, were Mandylion and Shroud actually one and the same thing? Here we arrive at the central point of the whole argument, the point at which historians such as Sir Steven Runciman very justifiably feel that they cannot back the concept of identity.

The problem relates primarily to one of the most important documentary sources for the Mandylion's character and history, the "Story of the Image of Edessa."[11] This was written by a man present at the court of Constantinople at the time the Mandylion arrived in the city, an unknown author specially commissioned by the emperor, Constantine Porphyrogenitus, to set down all that was known of the cloth to that date. Because of his assignment, he was probably allowed a special viewing of the cloth; if not, he certainly gleaned the pertinent details from those who had, among these being the emperor himself.

For any theory of Mandylion/Shroud identification what is seemingly shattering is this writer's attitude regarding the formation of the Mandylion image. He describes two alternative versions for how Christ might have performed the feat. The first is the sixth-century story that Christ asked to wash himself, and his image became imprinted on the cloth used to dry his face. The second—which he reports because, in his own words, "it would not be at all surprising if the facts had often been distorted in view of the time that has elapsed"— was that the image was formed during Jesus' agony in the garden of Gethsemane, when,

> according to the Evangelist, sweat dropped from him like drops of blood [see Lk. 22:44]. Then they say he took this piece of cloth which we see now . . . and wiped off the drops of sweat on it. At once the still-visible impression of that divine face was produced.[12]

This latter account, it may be noted in passing, is obviously the parent of the identical tradition relating to the Veronica (referred to in the preceding chapter) that became popular in Rome two centuries later.

The real dilemma of both versions is that they seem quite incompatible with the deductions of anyone looking at the cloth we now call the Turin Shroud. If one asks oneself whether there is the slightest suggestion in the writer's account that the Mandylion might have been the burial shroud of Christ, the answer must be an emphatic no.

If one asks oneself whether artists' copies of the Mandylion convey in any way the idea that the cloth was burial linen, the answer again must be no—Jesus' eyes are represented as open, as in life. This is supported by a tenth-century account, that of Symeon Magister, which actually describes having seen "eyes" on the Mandylion.[13]

In fact, wherever one looks for information on the Mandylion, the same conclusion must be drawn. The special days on which the Mandylion, sealed away in its casket, was carried in procession in Edessa were recorded. They were the Sunday before the first week in Lent and the Thursday of the middle week in Lent. Had the Mandylion been thought to be Christ's burial cloth, it would surely have been carried in procession not on these days but on Good Friday.

There are Byzantine depictions of the burial of Christ dating from the tenth century and before. In each case these show Jesus wrapped mummy-style, in swathing bands, without the slightest suggestion of the use of a large cloth such as the Shroud. Had the cloth we know as the Shroud been known then as the shroud, these portrayals would surely have been different.

The same deduction can be drawn from the very word *Mandylion* used to describe the Byzantine relic. It derives from the Arabic *mandil*, and is generally taken to mean a veil or handkerchief. The Arabic word in turn was derived from the Latin *mantile*, or mantle, and it was therefore possible for it to denote a relatively large cloth, but there was not the slightest suggestion of a sepulchral function to the word, as there is with our word "shroud." If there was, therefore, any case to be made for the Byzantine Mandylion being the same as our Turin Shroud, one fact must be faced—that those individuals who saw the cloth, at least from the sixth century to the tenth century, *thought* they were looking at a cloth representing Christ alive. They had not the faintest idea that they were looking at a burial shroud.

The question is, How is this possible? This problem is indeed a baffling one. But consider what is known of how the Mandylion was kept in the early centuries. Most of its time, as scholars have exhaustively pointed out, was spent locked away in its casket. What did it look like when it was taken out? What was its physical appearance at the time? This is an aspect on which both artistic and literary sources are able to furnish information. The tenth-century text of the "Story of the Image of Edessa" is quite explicit. The cloth has been "stretched on a wooden tablet and covered with gold," which, as far as the writer was aware, had been done by King Abgar many centuries before. This statement at least proves one thing—that those of the tenth century could have been quite innocent of the cloth's full nature as the shroud, if this had been disguised earlier.

The question is how could the Shroud have been arranged that such a deception, intended or otherwise, might have occurred? Here the copies of the Mandylion made before its 1204 disappearance turn out to be of considerable importance. For instance, one of their oddities is that on all with the exception of two icons the head was arranged in a landscape aspect rather than a portrait aspect—i.e., as shown in the sketch on the left rather than that on the right.

This is particularly marked in examples from Trebizond and from Gradac, Serbia.

What was so significant about this? The setting of the head on the cloth in this manner is totally at variance with a virtually universal artistic convention. That is, that throughout history, and in any country where artists created portraits, they have almost invariably chosen to set the face on the background of an upright rectangle rather than a horizontal rectangle, just as when creating a landscape they have done the reverse. There is no mystery about this—it is visually unappealing to set a head on a landscape-shaped background (particularly a totally plain one), and even more important, it is wasteful of available space. The consistent appearance of the head in this manner on artists' copies of the Mandylion therefore suggests one thing—that the artists were deliberately trying to reproduce a curiosity of the original. If the Shroud was the Mandylion, was this the manner in which it appeared in the early centuries?

This speculation takes on more credibility in the light of a piece of information gleaned from a text of the sixth century, the period when the Mandylion first came to light in Edessa. The text gives a description of how the image was thought by those of the time to have been created by Jesus on the linen of a cloth he had used to dry his face. This text, as translated in Roberts and Donaldson's voluminous *Writings of the Ante-Nicene Fathers,* at first sight seems totally uninformative:

> And he . . . asked to wash himself, and a towel was given to him; and when he had washed himself he wiped his face with it. And his image having been imprinted upon the linen . . .[14]

But, as a footnote reveals, one word in the passage gave the translators some difficulty. In order to convey the sense evident from the description, they used the word "towel." But they were careful to point out that this is not the literal meaning of the strange Greek word used in the original text.[15] The actual meaning is "doubled in four."[16]

The discovery is intriguing. Could the sixth-century writer have been trying to convey that the cloth he saw was literally "doubled in four"—i.e., that it was a substantially larger cloth, the folds perhaps being actually countable at the edges but otherwise inaccessible?

The only logical test is to try to "double in four" the Turin Shroud to see what effect is achieved. This is not a difficult task. One simply takes a full-length print of the cloth, doubles it, then doubles it twice again, producing a cloth "doubled in four" sections. The head of Christ appears on the uppermost section, curiously disembodied, exactly as on artists' copies of the Mandylion. Furthermore, it appears on the cloth in landscape aspect, again exactly as on artists' copies of the Mandylion. It takes little imagination or artistic license to visualize the cloth as it would have been without the burn marks of the 1532 fire. There lies the most convincing original of all the various artists' copies of the Mandylion, the true and only cloth "not made by hands."

At this point, the information in the tenth-century "Story of the Image of Edessa," that the Mandylion had been stretched on a wooden tablet, assumes a sudden importance. How was this effected? Could it have been done in such a way that the face on the Shroud was not only the sole area of the cloth visible but also the sole area accessible?

The artists' copies of the Mandylion provided the vital clue. In the majority of examples a fringe was illustrated, the copyists seeming to be in some doubt as to whether this was at the sides, at the bottom, or top and bottom. Three of the examples showed small circles at the end of each strand of the fringe, and from the taut manner in which the fringe was illustrated there could be little doubt that these circles were intended to represent nails hammered into a board backing the cloth, and around which each strand of the fringe had been carefully knotted in order to keep the cloth at an even stretch.

If it was the Shroud for which this arrangement was devised, nothing finer could have been provided for it. It would involve not the slightest damage to the linen itself.

One further piece of information provided by the "Story of the Image of Edessa" clarifies what had been done with the cloth—that it had been covered or "embellished" with gold.[17] It is difficult to determine what form that "embellishment" took until one studies the artists' copies. One of the oddities of examples from Alexandria, Spas Nereditsa, Gradac, and Laon is that the cloth itself seems to be decorated with a kind of trellis pattern. A first reaction to this might be to interpret it, as Professor Grabar does, as an attempt to convey in a very stylized way the weave of the material. But as one considers the matter more, it seems too insistent to be dismissed in such a manner. Instead what seems clear is that the trellis, actually picked out in gold in examples such as that of Laon, is the gold embellishment that the artists have faithfully reproduced in making their copies, and that presumably was placed over the cloth before the Byzantine period. A circular "halo," present in all the copies, may well have been formed by the absence of trelliswork around the face area.

The presence of such a trellis cover, coupled with the nailing of the edges of the Shroud by means of the fringe, would have had one far-reaching effect. Without a great deal of dismantling it would have been quite impossible to gain access to the invisible areas bearing the image of the body.

It is possible to reconstruct how people in the early centuries may have seen the Shroud and had no idea that they were seeing Christ's burial linen. The face on the cloth would certainly appear blurred, just as that of the Mandylion did to the emperor's sons in 944. The face on the Shroud when seen in isolation would look disembodied, failing to give any indication of shoulders.

But most importantly, without the knowledge of the "corpse" image hidden away in the folds, it would have looked *alive*, just as the early stories report. Today we know the eyes are closed in death from the Shroud negative (unavailable to the Byzantines) and from the fact that we can make out the image of a body laid out in death. But what would the reaction be if all we could see were the Shroud face? The white circles in the area of the eyes would have the very appearance of eyes open and staring, as in life. Many sixteenth- and seventeenth-century copyists of the Shroud reproduced the "eyes" in this manner even though, like us, they knew they were looking at the image of a corpse. Here then is the explanation of why the Byzantines believed the Mandylion image had been made while Christ was alive.

There is but one more problem. What about the blood from the crown of thorns that is visible on the Shroud face? Would this not lead anyone looking at the cloth to believe that the image had been formed during the Passion itself, rather than by water or sweat?

Not necessarily. As was noted in Part I of this work, the image of the blood flows on the Shroud has an unnervingly "clean" appearance, with none of the encrusted, dark-brown character that one would expect of dried blood from major wounds. Furthermore, as members of the Turin Commission noted, in even a moderately subdued light it is virtually impossible to distinguish a color difference between "body" and "blood" stains on the Shroud.[18]

Bearing these points in mind, it would certainly have been quite possible for viewers in the sixth century to make their deduction of "wet towel" image formation.

Those who saw the Shroud during the tenth-century clearly looked at the image very critically. They were able to observe the pale carmine-colored flows around the forehead that did not seem to be proper blood but did not seem to be purely sweat either. Steeped as they were in the New Testament, their deduction was intensely logical—the flows *had* to be the bloody sweat of Jesus' agony in Gethsemane, as recorded uniquely by St. Luke.

At last one arrives at what ostensibly seems to be the explanation of why the Shroud might have gone unrecorded in history—for the completely unforeseeable reason that no one at the time recognized it as a shroud.

It appears that someone at the very earliest stages of the Shroud's existence mounted and folded the Shroud in such a way that it no longer looked like a shroud. Furthermore, this was done in such a clever way that, either accidentally or deliberately, it deceived many generations.

Also, it will be recalled that Professor Raes, the commission's textile expert, deduced from careful study of the side strip sewn onto the Shroud that although this was of the same weave as the main body of the linen, certain characteristics suggested it had been made on a different loom and by a different hand. Its purpose seemed to be cosmetic—i.e., making the face appear central on the cloth where otherwise it would have appeared too much to one side. In the light of the deductions in this chapter, it seems more than likely that the side strip was added at the same time as the fringe and the gold covering, the overall purpose being to transform the cloth from a shroud into what seems to have been some form of "portrait."

One conclusion is inescapable. If the Shroud was indeed identical with the Mandylion, something very odd was done to it at the very earliest stage of its existence, seemingly by an expert. This mystery clearly could lie at the very heart of the absence of any mention of the Shroud's fate in the Gospels. Given the hypothesis that the Shroud *was* the Mandylion in the early centuries, the whole theory must now be tested in the light of a most searching inquiry into the Mandylion's history.

Part IV
TOWARDS A HISTORY
THE SHROUD AND THE
MANDYLION

CHAPTER XV

TO THE EARLIEST CHRISTIAN CITY—
A MYSTERIOUS "PORTRAIT"

Reconstructing what the Shroud's history might have been from what is known of the Mandylion's history is a long and complex task. As mentioned earlier, the Mandylion's history is certain only from the sixth century, when it was rediscovered in Edessa, and from which time it was recorded as a specific historical object. Its association with the first-century Abgar story is semilegendary, although the monarch referred to, Abgar V, was a definite historical personage. What happened to it after 1204 until its presumed reappearance as the Shroud is also a mystery.

If the identification of Mandylion with the Shroud is to be sustained, some satisfactory explanation for such gaps is necessary. The first task is to show how the Shroud found in the tomb of Jesus about A.D. 30 could have become the trelliscovered work, unrecognizable as the Shroud, which seems to be the form it had at the time of its rediscovery in Edessa in the sixth-century A.D.

Today Edessa scarcely looks like a likely place to which to bring such an important relic of Christ in the earliest centuries. Now named Urfa, it stands in the southeastern border country of Turkey, serving as the commercial center for a somewhat desolate region stretching to the Syrian boundary thirty miles to the south. It is a bustling, thoroughly Moslem town. Its board sidewalks are reminiscent of the Wild West, but there the resemblance ends. This is the world of the Orient, with insistent Eastern music blaring from cheap transistors, and every few hours the unforgettable sound of the faithful being called to prayer from a high minaret. Boys run from shop to shop with ornate trays of steaming Turkish coffee. Swarthy men stride the streets in baggy Persian-style trousers, while veiled women peep out from the doorways of primitive flat-roofed dwellings. The few visitors that come to the city stop only to see the *baliklar*, the myriads of carp preserved in Urfa's shady fishpools, then pass quickly on. As the guidebooks say, there are few historical remains of any note, and not a single surviving Christian church.

The fact is that the town's appearance is an accident of history, created in the twelfth century when Turkish Moslems took the city, dispersed the Christian population, and wiped out every feature of Christian civilization. For below the tightly packed houses and shops that comprise modern Urfa sleep the remains of an altogether different past, when Urfa, under the name Edessa, was one of the famed cities of Christendom. In those days it attracted Christian pilgrims from more than a thousand miles away. It bristled with some three hundred churches and monasteries. In its surrounding cave tombs, now dung-smelling and desolate, lived a population of thousands of hermits and monks, many shunning bread, meat, and wine and leading "so extraordinary a life that it can scarcely be described."[1]

The reason for Edessa's fame lies in a story that must be regarded as central to the whole transformation of the Shroud into the Mandylion, the story of the conversion to Christianity of the area's king, Abgar V, in the first century A.D.

In the first century, Edessa was an independent principality just outside the Roman Empire, ruled by kings or toparchs owing their allegiance to the mighty Parthian empire to the east. The city, controlling the surrounding region of Osrhoene, was prosperous, its citizens deeply involved in the trade in silks and spices brought by the caravans that passed through from east to west. They were able to afford rich mosaics that represent them in colorful Parthian-style costumes, the men in turbans and baggy trousers, the women in high headdresses. They spoke Syriac, the principal language of the Aramaic group, virtually identical to that spoken by Jesus and his disciples.[2]

About 325 Bishop Eusebius of Caesarea, in his *History of the Church*, recorded that Abgar V of Edessa, who reigned from A.D. 13 to 50, had suffered from an incurable disease and, hearing of the miracles of Jesus, sent a messenger to Jerusalem inviting Jesus to come to Edessa to cure him. Jesus declined but promised to send a disciple to cure Abgar. Eusebius, a very sound and scholarly writer, quoted the reputed correspondence between Jesus and Abgar, and carefully noted that his source was "the archives of Edessa, which was at that time ruled by its own kings," translated by Eusebius himself from the Syriac into Greek.[3]

More details to the story, with a greater ring of authenticity, emerged when whole caravanloads of manuscripts were rescued from the Nitrian monastery in the desert of Lower Egypt during the 1840s. Among the manuscripts early Syriac versions of the Abgar story came to light,[4] some very fragmented, others very anachronistic, but their very profusion indicated the memory of some real event.

With these manuscripts and the tenth-century "Story of the Image of Edessa," which also claimed original Syriac manuscripts among its sources, it has been possible to piece together a saga far more extensive than that quoted by Eusebius—an intriguing story of an early evangelization of Edessa in which the Mandylion was integrally involved. All accounts agree that after Jesus departed this world the disciples sent to Edessa an evangelist named in the Greek texts as Thaddaeus, in the Syriac as Addai. The more reliable versions are careful to point out that he was not the apostle Thaddaeus but merely "one of the seventy" (or seventy-two), the outer circle of disciples whom St. Luke described Jesus as having sent ahead of him to preach the gospel (Lk. 10:1). In origin he was said to hail from Paneas, the same town as the gospel Hemorrhissa.

In Edessa Thaddaeus stayed with Tobias, son of Tobias, a Jew whose father was originally from Palestine. Tobias was clearly one of a substantial Jewish community known from their tombs to have inhabited Edessa at this period. He was also, it would appear, well known to King Abgar. When Tobias reminded the king of the earlier correspondence, Thaddaeus was immediately summoned to the royal palace.

At this point an important incident took place. According to the tenth-century text, Thaddaeus took with him the Man-

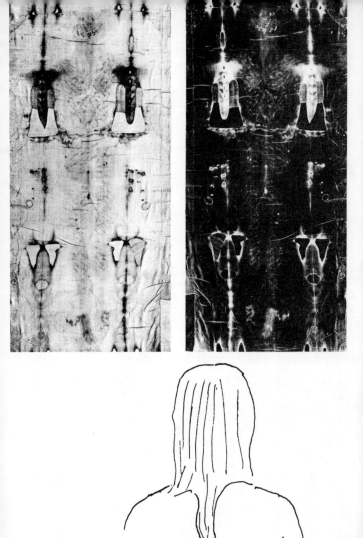

RECONSTRUCTION

Shroud dorsal image, showing apparent streak of hair at the back of the head, in the manner of an unbound pigtail. This was characteristic of Jewish hair fashion at the time of Christ.

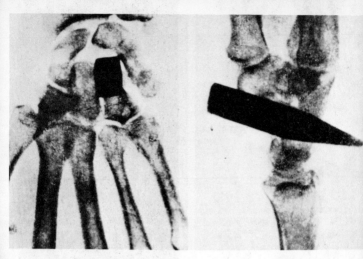

X-ray photographs of nail piercing human wrist at point indicated on the Shroud. *(Dr. David Willis)*

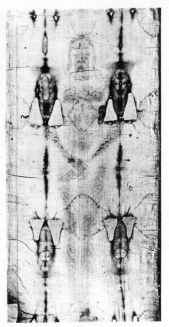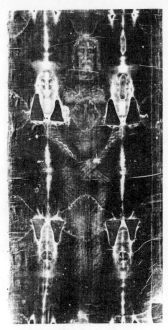

The angle of the arms at crucifixion, deducible from the Shroud by determining the path of the blood flows in following the course of gravity.

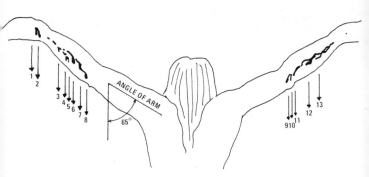

The main angle appears to have been 65 degrees, but there is evidence that at some stages the forearms were at 55 degrees, indicating that the man of the Shroud sought to raise himself, probably continually, during crucifixion.

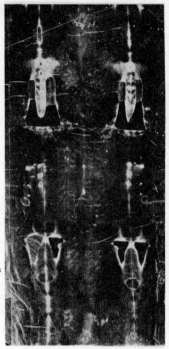

Reconstruction, after Ricci, of the way the whipping of the man of the Shroud appears to have been carried out (left), with the marks as they appear on the Shroud negative (top right), and the twin pellets with which the whip appears to have been tipped (below right).

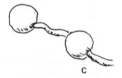

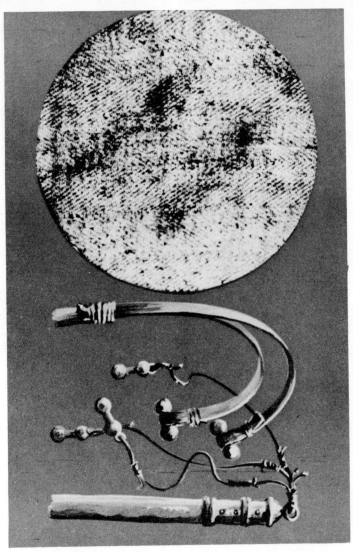

Scourge marks as seen on the cloth, and examples of Roman *flagra*. (*Dom Bosco Filmstrips*)

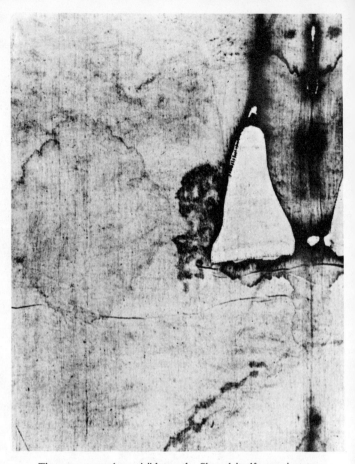

The spear wound, as visible on the Shroud itself, seen just to the left of a triangular-shaped patch sewn on by the Poor Clare nuns. By orthogonal projection medical men have calculated the spear to have penetrated between the fifth and sixth ribs.

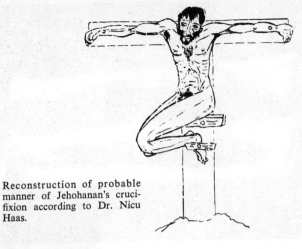

Reconstruction of probable manner of Jehohanan's crucifixion according to Dr. Nicu Haas.

head of nail

remains of plaque of acacia or pistacia

heel bone

grains of olive wood from upright of cross

Seven-inch nail found piercing calcaneus, or heel bone, in ossuary at Giv'at Ha-mivtar, Jerusalem. (*Photo by Mrs. E. A. Salomon, courtesy of the* Israel Exploration Journal)

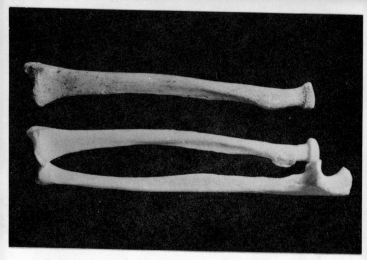

Radial bone of Jehohanan (top) in comparison with two other arm bones, a radius and an ulna, of the same length. Note the scratch on the lower edge near the wrist end (left) of Jehohanan's bone, produced by friction between the bone and nail. *(Photo by Mrs. E. A. Salomon, courtesy of the* Israel Exploration Journal*)*

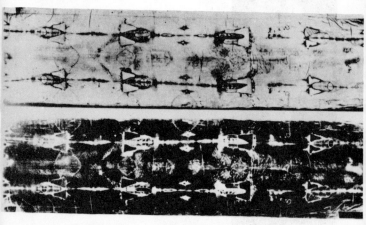

How the body was laid in the tomb (reconstruction).

dylion, and before entering Abgar's throne room "placed it on his forehead like a sign."

Abgar saw him coming from a distance, and thought he saw a light shining from his face which no eye could stand, which the portrait Thaddaeus was wearing produced.

Abgar was dumbfounded by the unbearable glow of the brightness, and, as though forgetting the ailments he had and the long paralysis of his legs, he at once got up from his bed and compelled himself to run. In making his paralyzed limbs go to meet Thaddaeus, he felt the same feeling, though in a different way, as those who saw that face flashing with lightning on Mount Tabor.

And so, receiving the likeness from the apostle . . . immediately he felt his leprosy cleansed and gone. Having been instructed then by the apostle more clearly of the doctrine of truth . . . he asked about the likeness portrayed on the linen cloth. For when he had carefully inspected it he saw that it did not consist of earthly colors, and he was astounded at its power. . . .

At this, Thaddaeus explained about the time of the agony, and that the likeness was due to sweat, not pigments. . . .[5]

Now, it should be made clear that while the tenth-century text specifically mentioned the Mandylion and described it, because at the time the relic was actually known and preserved at Constantinople, this was not the case with the documents dating before the sixth century, when the Mandylion's location was not known. Eusebius, writing in the fourth century knew only of some "wonderful vision" seen by Abgar at this time:

As he presented himself, with the king's grandees standing there, at the moment of his entry a wonderful vision appeared to Abgar on the face of Thaddaeus. On seeing it Abgar bowed low before the apostle, and astonishment seized all the bystanders, for they had not seen the vision, which appeared to Abgar alone.[6]

So confused was the memory in the early centuries that according to one fourth-century text of the "Doctrine of

Addai," as preserved in Leningrad, the Mandylion was merely a painted portrait, the work of the messenger Hannan (also known as Ananias), who ". . . took and painted a portrait of Jesus in choice paints, and brought it with him to his lord King Abgar. And when King Abgar saw that portrait he received it with great joy."[7]

Such confusions in the early texts can be explained by the degree of knowledge of the time in which they were written, it being sufficient that they at least contain some memory of the Mandylion, however confused or imperfect. They at least confirm that we are dealing with an object that once existed and then became lost, the memory then understandably growing dim. What is important is to establish the way that object could have become lost, and here the manuscript traditions provide the vital information.

All accounts agree that after curing Abgar, Thaddaeus also healed a certain Abdu, described as the second man of the kingdom.[8] The evangelist then asked to preach before the assembled citizens of Edessa, and a herald was sent out to summon everyone to a suitable spot, "the place which is called Beththabara, the wide open space of the house of Amida," a spot still identifiable today. Here Thaddaeus delivered Edessa's first Christian sermon.

According to the documents the sermon had a powerful effect. Many citizens of Edessa there and then renounced paganism, several altars being thrown down, but not (and here we have an interesting note of authenticity) "the great altar which was in the middle of the city."[9]

Under Abgar, and in the reign of his son, Christianity of a primitive kind was allowed. Thaddaeus became a sort of prototype bishop, aided by an individual by the name of Aggai, who "made the silks and headdresses of the king." Aggai was clearly an important man. Among the Edessans and in Parthian territories in general such headdresses were an important symbol of rank, those of the king being decorated with gold ornament, which sometimes included pagan symbols. On Thaddaeus' death Aggai took over responsibility for the infant Christian community, and it was at this point that Aggai's old craft brought him into direct conflict with royal authority.

According to the documents, on the death of Abgar's first son, a second son ascended the throne, hostile to the Christians. He ordered Aggai to return to the old practices. "Make me a headdress of gold, as you did for my fathers in former times." Aggai refused. "I will not give up the ministry of Christ, which was committed to me by the disciple of Christ, and make a headdress of wickedness."[10]

This act of lèse-majesté was fatal. With a savagery not uncommon at this period, the king's men burst in upon Aggai as he was preaching and broke both his legs, causing his death. The infant Christian community was snuffed out. Nothing is said in the early documents about the fate of the Mandylion, from which one can only infer that by the time they were written some while after the events described, it had already been lost and its whereabouts forgotten. Pilgrims and chroniclers writing about Edessa between the second and sixth centuries, were quite unaware that the Mandylion existed in the city. A typical example was Egeria, an indomitable lady pilgrim from Aquitaine, who visited Edessa as part of a tour of the holy places of Christendom about the year 383.[11] She described sights of the city in minute detail, among them the *baliklar*, the city's shady fishpools, famous even in her day. But she made no mention of the image-bearing cloth.

As historian Sir Steven Runciman commented:

> She was a sightseer of a thoroughness unrivalled even by the modern American; and, had so interesting a relic then existed, she would certainly have referred to it. . . .[12]

The so-called "harp" of the Syrian church, St. Ephraim, who lived in Edessa during the late fourth century and wrote reams of ecclesiastical verse, made no reference to the Mandylion. The monk-author of the "Chronicle of Joshua the Stylite," written at Edessa about 507, made no mention of it, nor did Jacob of Serug, another most prolific Edessan writer, who died about 521.

It is then, only from the circumstances of the cloth's rediscovery in the sixth century that we can deduce, as did the Byzantines, something of what seems to have happened to it.

According to the tenth-century "Story of the Image of

Edessa," the location of the rediscovery is described as a space above one of the city gates, carefully bricked up for concealment,[13] a location clearly illustrated in one of the pictorial scenes on the Buckingham Palace icon.

It is also described as having "the appearance of a semi-spherical cylinder," in other words, the shape of an arched vault. This is significant, for one of the four main gates of Edessa, that to the west, was specifically known in Syriac as the *Kappe* gate, which means gate of arches or vaults.[14] The vault was a characteristic feature of Parthian architecture.[15] It is a reasonable inference, therefore, that the original construction of this gate was during the Parthian period—i.e., roughly contemporary with the Abgar dynasty.

It was inside this that the Mandylion lay, but not alone. Found with it were two items. One was a face of Christ of identical appearance to the Mandylion but "imprinted" on a brick-red tile. The other was a lamp, described, in the fanciful way of the time, as still burning when found. The very ordinariness of such items gives a ring of authenticity to the account, and there is no question but that the tile was a genuine historical object. Subsequently known as the *Keramion*, it was preserved in Edessa's sister city of Hierapolis before being transferred to Constantinople in 969, and is actually depicted along with the Mandylion in the eleventh-century Rossianus codex. It needs little conjecture to determine what the Keramion originally was. It was common practice in the Parthian empire to display stone or clay heads of gods and gorgons over gateways. There are still examples to be seen at Parthian Hatra. Almost certainly the Keramion was one of these made in the likeness of the Christ head on the Mandylion and displayed on the city gate at the time that Christianity was tolerated by Abgar V. When persecution set in, it had to be removed. The real surprise is that, in stowing it away in a niche behind, the Mandylion was concealed there too. The lamp may be identified as a Jewish touch, it being a common practice at the period to bury lamps with the dead.[16]

From all this information the question that arises is how the Shroud, if indeed it was the Mandylion, might have come to Edessa in the first place, and become made up in the "portrait" form deduced in the last chapter. To answer this question, it is necessary to resort to a limited amount of conjecture, justifiable within the terms of the information that has been brought together.

One has to think back at this point to the religious scruples of the very disciples Jesus left behind, the disciples who would have been the discoverers and hence first owners of the burial linens Jesus left behind in the tomb. It is important to appreciate that they were first and foremost Jews and from this point of view, while it is difficult for us to comprehend today, they could not have regarded the image they discovered on the Shroud with anything but horror.

Its very existence would have violated two of their most deep-seated beliefs. As a cloth which had been in contact with a dead person, it would be regarded as unclean and should be destroyed, as it made ritually unclean anyone who handled it. As a cloth bearing an image, it broke the second commandment: "You shall not make yourself a carved image or any likeness of anything in heaven or on earth beneath" (Ex. 20:4).

From their knowledge of their Master, the disciples might have been able to reconcile themselves to the cloth's preservation, but they would have known that any acceptability of the cloth among their fellow Jews was out of the question. It would be regarded as a blasphemy, an abomination, and every effort would be made to ensure its destruction.

In this light we may perhaps speculate just a little on the ensuing course of events. As we have seen, although historians are by no means unanimous on the matter, it does seem possible that Abgar V of Edessa, a definite historical monarch, came to hear of the activities of Jesus and made friendly enquiries about him. Probably these reached the disciples too late—i.e., shortly after the crucifixion. The disciples could only have been flattered by such interest from a king beyond the borders of the Roman Empire. Since Jesus was no longer around to go to Edessa in person, they would have sought for the best possible substitute. Here Jesus' image on the Shroud might well have been seen as literally the heaven-sent answer.

They would have known that among pagans such as those

at Edessa images were not only permitted, they were most acceptable. Parthian art of the time was characterized by images presented frontally as was the Shroud.[17] Why not therefore send the Shroud to Abgar—the cloth's safety in the environment of Edessa being far more assured than in Jerusalem?

The one snag was the unseemliness of sending a reigning monarch a cloth that was the gravecloth of a man recently executed as a convicted criminal, in the most degrading circumstances possible. In any culture, including that of Edessa, the very idea of such an object was repellent.

Logically, bearing in mind the cloth's very nature and the fact that the face is the Shroud's most distinctive and comprehensible feature, the answer was to transform the cloth into a portrait.

Unfortunately, absolutely no information has survived on who decided to carry out this transformation and in what circumstances. Whether the "portrait" was intended to be a gift to Abgar or was merely to be shown to him must remain conjecture. But from the manner in which the Shroud seems to have been transformed into the Mandylion, it is irresistible to identify the hand of the maker of the king's headdresses, Aggai, in the actual makeup of the portrait.

The most telltale feature is the gold trelliswork, the cover laid over the folded Shroud which was illustrated in the early copies of the Mandylion. This work is typical of the rich trellis-style embellishment of the headdresses and costumes of Parthian monarchs, featured for instance on the Mosul Museum's statue of King Uthal of Hatra.

Aggai, we are told in the documents of the Abgar story, was a skilled worker in silks and gold. He fits exactly the expert hand for the work that we deduced in the last chapter, and for such a man to occur in the story in such a central role would seem to be far more than mere coincidence.

We may conjecture that it was in this manner that the Shroud in the guise of the Mandylion "portrait" came to be brought before Abgar V. Shown to him by Thaddaeus, we may guess that it impressed him, leading to at least toleration of Christians during his reign. There is an increasing body of scholarly opinion that such evangelizations did occur in the Semitic world in the early years,[18] evangelizations that, unlike the activities of Paul to the west, were swiftly forgotten.

The rest is easy to reconstruct. Proud of his new "god," Abgar ordered a likeness to be set up above the gate of the city, having it made in the style of the time in the form of a relief tile set into the arches of the Kappe gate.

Either on this or on the Mandylion itself, we are told, was put an inscription in gold "Christ the God—he who hopes in you will not be disappointed."[19]

Everything went well for a while; then Abgar V died, swiftly followed by his son Ma'nu V. In A.D. 57 Ma'nu VI ascended the throne, the monarch who reverted to paganism. Trouble loomed for the Christians, no doubt heralded by early outbreaks of persecution.

Someone saw the dangers to the safety of the Mandylion. Ordered, perhaps, to destroy the offending copy of the Mandylion from the gate, the rescuer resorted to a desperate expedient. Dislodging the tile from the surrounding brickwork, he opened up a niche that lay behind out of normal reach, an ideal place of safety.

For the Parthian and Mesopotamian mind there was, in fact, nothing strange in using a niche in this way. The dead were buried in a similar manner in the brickwork of the floors and walls of houses.[20]

Carefully the Mandylion was laid underneath the tile likeness for protection. As a mark of respect the lamp also was left. The niche was then sealed with plain bricks to render the surface once again neat and tidy. The person who hid the Mandylion seems not to have had the opportunity to return to the hiding place, or to pass the knowledge of it on to surviving Christians.

Whoever he was, he did his job well. He provided hermetically sealed conditions for the preservation of the Mandylion, something for which posterity would be more grateful than he could ever know. He had no way of knowing that it would be nearly five hundred years, in a totally different political and religious climate, before his place of concealment would come to light.

CHAPTER XVI

THE "PORTRAIT" IS FOUND—

"NOT MADE BY HANDS"

High on the western side of modern Urfa traces of the old city wall can still be found, and at one point, tucked among squalid present-day habitations is an old bricked-up entrance-way and the crumbled remains of a twelfth-century guard-room. These are all that have survived of the original west gate of Edessa.

If our reconstruction is correct, it was here that the Shroud, in the guise of the Mandylion, was sealed about A.D. 57—by most calculations, before a single Gospel had been written.[1] Through nearly five centuries, a quarter of its entire existence, it lay unknown and untouched.

The hiding place was a remarkably propitious one. It was remarkable first because there were no fewer than four severe floods in Edessa during this time, one in 201, one in 303, one in 413, and a final deluge in 525. Extensive damage was done to public buildings in these floods, palaces and churches alike being destroyed. Only if the Mandylion had been in a particularly special hiding place could it have survived. And the location above the west gate was just that. The land rises steeply at this point, and even in the worst flooding a cloth sealed above the gate would have remained safe and dry.

It was remarkable also for another reason. During the time that the cloth's existence was unknown at this spot, the gate nevertheless had a distinct fascination for Edessa's Christians, almost as if there was some memory of a special event associated with it, without anyone knowing exactly what.

When the woman pilgrim Egeria was shown around Edessa by Bishop Eulogios in 383, he pointed out the gate to her, describing it as the one through which Abgar's messenger had brought the reply to the king from Jesus. The bishop read a prayer at the gate and told her from the day when the messenger Hannan brought the Lord's letter through this gate until now, neither has anyone been allowed to pass through it who is unclean or in mourning, nor has any dead body been taken through it.

He also told her that an attack on Edessa by Persians had been repulsed by the reading of Jesus' letter from this gate.[2]

If this then was the site where the Mandylion and its companion objects lay unknown for five centuries, when did they come to light? While no account of the time describes this event exactly, certain guidelines can be laid down. For instance, the latest possible date is 544. In this year the Syrian-born historian Evagrius (527–600) described the cloth's having been used as a protective talisman or palladium to ward off a determined attack on Edessa by the Persian king Chosroes Nirhirvan.

In this incident Chosroes, in an all-out attack, ordered a huge mound of timber built, which was gradually pushed forward in order to enable his men to scale Edessa's high walls. As a counterattack the Edessans decided to tunnel under their walls in an attempt to set fire to the mound from below before it could be maneuvered into position. At this point the Mandylion was deployed. In Evagrius' words:

> The mine was completed; but they [the Edessans] failed in attempting to fire the wood, because the fire, having no exit whence it could obtain a supply of air, was unable to take hold of it. In this state of utter perplexity they brought out the divinely made image *not made by the hands of man*, which Christ our God sent to King Abgar when he desired to see him. Accordingly, having introduced this sacred likeness into the mine and washed it over with water, they sprinkled some upon the timber. . . . the timber immediately caught the flame, and being in an instant reduced to cinders, communicated with that above, and the fire spread in all directions.[3] [Italics added.]

This account, fanciful as it is, could be regarded as the entry of the Mandylion into history, the first description from which one can be sure that the cloth had been rediscovered after its long confinement, and was now a real historical object. It is important because it unhesitatingly identifies the Mandylion as having been involved in the Abgar story. The incident was so dramatic that the author of the tenth-century "Story of the Image of Edessa" assumed that it was the actual occasion of the rediscovery.

Had this been so, however, one would not expect Evagrius to have missed the opportunity of telling the story. The fact that he made no mention of it suggests that the discovery had taken place earlier—but not much earlier. For, as we have noted, neither of two Edessan authors, Joshua the Stylite, writing about 507, or Jacob of Serug, who died about 521, made any mention of the existence of the Mandylion, although they would surely have done so had it been known.

So one can be reasonably certain that this discovery took place sometime between 520 and 544. It is not too difficult to determine during which incident of Edessa's history in those years it might have taken place.

The year 525 was a particularly black one in Edessa's history. By this time a part of the Byzantine Empire, the city sported a wealth of Christian churches and imposing public buildings. There was the Church of St. Thomas, a three-naved structure enshrining the body of the apostle brought to Edessa from India. There were shrines to the physician martyrs St. Cosmas and St. Damian, both likewise buried in the city. There was the Church of St. John and St. Thaddaeus, containing the bodies of King Abgar and Thaddaeus. There was a fine cathedral built close to the site of the "Old Church," the original church of Edessa and reputedly the first proper church building anywhere in the world, recorded definitively as far back as A.D. 201. Through the city, and past some of these churches ran the river Daisan, normally an unspectacular stream. But every so often, as already noted, rains could cause it to rise dramatically and burst its banks, bringing about widespread destruction in the low-lying areas of the city. In 525 the scale of the damage was the most serious ever. Many of Edessa's citizens were asleep in their beds when the river

rose to an extraordinary height . . . levelled to the ground
a large part of the outworks and of the circuit-wall, and
covered practically the whole city, doing irreparable damage. . . . in a moment it wiped out completely some of
the finest buildings and caused the death of one third of
the population.[4]

In the wake of a disaster of this scale, such a far-flung out-
post of the Byzantine Empire would normally have been left
to sort out its own repairs. But at this time Edessa was fortu-
nate. At Constantinople, while the aged emperor Justin I
spent his last days in languor, the affairs of the empire were
in the hands of his nephew, the brilliant emperor-to-be Justinian, who subsequently reigned from 527 to 565.

Justinian hastily dispatched engineers to Edessa to begin
the work of reconstruction, reclaiming ruined parts of the
city, and even more importantly, diverting the river by
means of a still-extant dam, so that such a flood could never
happen again. But most significant among Justinian's engineers' activities was their work on the walls.

As recorded by the contemporary historian Procopius:

. . . it happened that the main walls of Edessa and its
outworks had suffered from the passage of time no less
than they had from the flood, and for the most part were
fit only to be called ruins. Therefore the Emperor rebuilt
both of them and made them new and much stronger than
they had been formerly. . . .[5]

In such circumstances we might expect the old Parthian
gateway containing the Mandylion to have been dismantled
and its intriguing contents brought to light.

The news of the discovery does not seem to have been received with rapture in Edessa. Quite apart from the flood,
which would have created its own problems, it was a troubled time with deep divisions between religious factions,
both in Edessa and elsewhere. Central to these divisions
were questions relating to the permissibility of representing
Christ. The Orthodox contended that Christ had two natures,
human and divine, his human appearance being representable in art. Opposing this view, the Monophysites main-

tained that Christ had but a single divine nature, having been on earth more spirit than human being, and was therefore impossible to circumscribe within the limits of a picture. Edessa was predominantly Monophysite in 525, and it is difficult to envisage this faction welcoming the discovery of a relic that seemed to confound their beliefs.

Certainly up until the year 544 the city's major possession, in the eyes of its citizens, was still the reputed letter of Jesus to Abgar, preserved in the civic archives. The letter included (interpolated in the fourth century) a promise by Jesus to protect the city from harm, and the citizens believed in its continuing efficacy. These attitudes were changed by the Persian siege of Edessa of 544, and the deployment of the Mandylion in the manner described by Evagrius. Exactly why is by no means clear, but from the year 544 on, the role of protective device for Edessa tacitly but decisively shifted from the letter to the Mandylion.

The key to the change may well have been the description "not made by hands" given to the Mandylion image by Evagrius. Clearly derived from firsthand viewing of the cloth at the time, it occurs in no earlier account. This description—as already mentioned, a single word, *acheiropoietos*, in Greek—provided those of Orthodox inclination with a ready-made justification for the creation of portraits of Christ. It could be argued that the Mandylion proved Christ was representable because Christ himself had made the image. Conversely the Monophysites could argue that the very fact that Christ had to reproduce his image in such a miraculous manner meant their view was correct, that he was not representable in lifeless colors.

That the Mandylion could protect them was of immense importance to all those living in an age desperately insecure in the wake of the dissolution of the old Roman Empire. This concept, at whose heart lay the Mandylion, created a revolution in images of Christ, magical and otherwise. Within a short space of time Edessa's neighboring towns Melitene and Hierapolis each acquired a copy of the Mandylion. Hierapolis was apparently given the Keramion tile found with the Mandylion. The image on the tile was regarded as having been miraculously created by the Mandylion during its confinement in the niche. In Cappadocia, the town of Camuliana acquired its own rival palladium, an image of Christ "discovered" about the year 554 in a water cistern by a woman who desired to see Christ. It was subsequently carried around Asia Minor by fund-raising priests, who seem to have successfully "sold out" to Constantinople in 574.[6]

About 570 a travelogue attributed to Anthony of Piacenza described a linen cloth with an imprint of Christ, seemingly a copy of the Mandylion, found at Memphis in Upper Egypt.[7]

Many of these copies were themselves regarded as miraculous because of contact with the Mandylion. As Edward Gibbon disdainfully described the situation in his *Decline and Fall of the Roman Empire:*

> Before the end of the sixth century these images made without hands were propagated in the camps and cities of the Eastern empire; they were the objects of worship and the instruments of miracles; and in the hour of danger or tumult their venerable presence could revive the hope, rekindle the courage, or repress the fury of the Roman legions. Of these pictures the far greater part, the transcripts of a human pencil, could only pretend to a secondary likeness and improper title; but there were some of higher descent, who derived their resemblance from an immediate contact with the original. . . . The most ambitious aspired from a filial to a fraternal relation with the image of Edessa.[8]

From our point of view the chief role of the Mandylion at this time was its inspiration of copies of the likeness of Christ in art. Because direct copies of the Mandylion—i.e., copies showing the head of Christ on a cloth background—have not survived from before the cloth's transfer to Constantinople, some scholars have assumed that it was not much copied while it was in Edessa. But it may well be that this was not so. It seems quite possible that during these centuries artists did not copy the full visible area of the cloth, with the gold trellis covering. Instead they copied the "face" area inside the circular halo—and then used this in a limited variety of different formats, each with its own significance.

The purest form, for instance, was that of a disembodied

head in a circle. Two examples of this type have survived—
the first on a seventh-century icon of SS. Sergius and Bac-
chus now in the Kiev City Museum, where it appears on a
medallion between the portraits of the two saints;[9] the second at the center of the huge jeweled cross in the apse of
Sant'Apollinare in Classe, Ravenna, completed shortly before
549.[10] These conform to the way the head, according to our
reconstruction, would have appeared within the nimbus on
the Mandylion.

Of almost equal purity was the second group, differing
from the first only in that a suggestion of shoulders can be
seen, the head otherwise being still disembodied. Two late-
sixth-century pilgrims' flasks (*ampullae*)[11] show this type
clearly, one from the monastery of San Columban, Bobbio,
the other from the Treasury of St. John, Monza, this latter
being one of several such flasks given to Queen Theodolinda
of the Lombards by Pope Gregory the Great (590–604). The
art historian Otto Pacht has shown that these examples were
based on a long-lost mosaic of this same subject once in the
sanctuary of the original Church of the Holy Sepulcher, Jerusalem, at the site of Golgotha, apparently made in the sixth
century.

Of the same type was a "disembodied" head of Christ set
up in mosaic in another of the holiest sites of Christendom,
the apse of the Church of St. John Lateran, Rome, again in
the sixth century.[12] Unfortunately, the work visible in this location today is a late-nineteenth-century restoration, the re-
storers having senselessly destroyed the original. From records of an earlier thirteenth-century restoration it is known
that the haloed face section of the mosaic was originally made
on its own independent bed of Travertine marble, underlining
the special significance of this area.

The fact that this head of Christ in St. John Lateran was
specifically known by tradition as *acheiropoietos*, "not made
by hands," reinforces the belief that it and its related likenesses were copies of the face on the Mandylion. This
seems a much better explanation than that advanced by some
art historians that those of the time believed the head to
have appeared in the apse without human agency.

The same argument applies to another Roman work of the

same period. Otherwise its acheiropoietic appellation would be equally incongruous. This is a strange icon covered almost completely in a hideous silver case made for it in the thirteenth century, and kept in the Sancta Sanctorum Chapel of the Lateran Palace, Rome, the old palace of the popes.[13] It may be ascribed to the third group of likenesses derived from the Mandylion at this period—those of the Christ Enthroned. The Roman work carries the name *Acheropita*, a Latinization of *acheiropoietos*. Yet, as careful cleaning revealed in the early years of this century, it is merely a walnut panel, painted in tempera with the face of Christ set on a full-length figure of the "enthroned" type studied in Chapter XII. Its inscription, now almost entirely effaced, seems to have read "Jesus Christ Emanuel" (God with us).

The inspiration of this sixth-century work, reliably regarded as having been brought to Rome in the last years of that century by Pope Gregory the Great, is relatively easy to determine. Gregory, before he became pope, had been *apocrisarius* or papal legate to the court of Constantinople during the reign of the Byzantine emperor Tiberius II (578–82). Tiberius' rule was a time when interest in acheiropoietic images, in the wake of the discovery of the Mandylion, was at its peak in Constantinople.

In the West there had been few inhibitions about religious images, hence the wealth of pictorial art that Justinian had been able to lavish on Ravenna. But in the East, in deference to the Orthodox/Monophysite conflict, Justinian had exercised restraint, and it was his successor, Justin II, the predecessor of Tiberius II, who opened the door to artistic work in Constantinople. Justin II seems to have authorized the figure of Christ Enthroned as the form in which the face of the Mandylion should be publicly displayed. He thus set up over the imperial throne a majestic image of Christ of this type—regrettably destroyed, but undoubtedly similar in form to that still visible today in the narthex of Hagia Sophia, Istanbul. The emperor prayed and made obeisance before this image at the commencement of each feast day. So important did it become that in just over a century the emperor Justinian II (685–95, 705–11) would display a head and shoulders version of it on the obverse of his coinage, relegating his own standing likeness to the "tail," or reverse side.[14]

To the superstitious Gregory in the sixth century, the effect of this brooding likeness over Tiberius' throne must have been considerable—even more so when he learned that it had been derived from the reputed true likeness of Christ *acheiropoietos* preserved at Edessa. Nor could he have failed to be impressed by the image's reputed protective properties, bearing in mind the ravages his own city of Rome had suffered in that century.

There is, therefore, no difficulty in determining that the icon now in the Sancta Sanctorum Chapel was one specially commissioned by Gregory to take back to Rome. As he would naturally have called this the *acheiropoietos* likeness, it is easy to understand how this gradually became adopted into Latin as *acheropita*. So delighted was he with his acquisition that he seems to have sent a similar likeness with the mission of St. Augustine to the Angles in England—recorded by Bede as carried by Augustine's monks.[15]

As later popes inherited the Acheropita, they, like Gregory, thought the work to have derived protective powers from the miraculous original by which it had been inspired. When Rome was threatened by Lombards during the mid-eighth century, Pope Stephen II personally carried the Acheropita barefoot at the head of a huge procession of people with ashes on their heads, praying for it to deliver their city. Less than a hundred years later, Pope Leo IV (847–51), carried it in a similar procession, this time to remove a huge snake that was causing havoc in the city's center.

Such dramatic faith in the protective powers of the Mandylion obliges one to consider in what manner the cloth was kept in Edessa itself following its rediscovery. The available historical information is relatively plentiful.

In 525, just before the rediscovery, the edifice that had been Edessa's cathedral was destroyed in the flood, and a new Hagia Sophia of Edessa was planned with the purpose of housing the Mandylion specifically in mind.

Superlative descriptions of this cathedral exist. Even Muslims seem to have regarded it as one of the wonders of the world. A particularly detailed description exists in a Syriac hymn of about 569.[16] It paints an evocative picture of a water-circled, stone-built shrine of outstanding beauty, capped with a dome that would seem reminiscent of Hagia Sophia, Constantinople, built at the same period. Wood was banned from the vaulting, and the interior walls were covered with mosaics—significantly, nonpictorial mosaics, undoubtedly because of the prevalence of anti-image feelings in Edessa. Religious messages were instead conveyed by symbolism in the architecture, every feature having a particular significance.

At the eastern end, for instance, the apse was lit by three windows, representing the Trinity. From the floor of the choir there rose nine steps, symbolic, in contemporary thought, of the nine orders of angels, surmounted by a special altar-throne representing the heavenly throne of Christ. It is clear that people at the time thought the cathedral was on a par with the Temple of the Ark of the Covenant. The Syriac hymn states this quite explicitly, and remarks cryptically, "Exalted are the mysteries of this shrine," and elsewhere, ". . . it contains the very essence of God."[17]

The only images permitted, as in the Temple, were cherubim topping the pillars of the sanctuary. The very lack of images can only have added to the awe and mystery surrounding the presence in the cathedral of the greatest of all images, the Mandylion. As the building's greatest treasure, it was kept in a special sanctuary to the right of the apse, guarded by a *higoumenos*, the Orthodox equivalent of an abbot. Twice a week only, the doors of the sanctuary were opened and pilgrims allowed to glimpse the casket containing the cloth, carefully protected by a special grille. And twice a year only, the cloth was removed from its sanctuary and carried within its casket in an elaborate procession accompanied by torches, fans, and spice-filled censers. Each step of the procession represented a stage in the life of Christ, the entry into the church, for instance, symbolizing his entry into the world.

At the culmination of the ceremony, the casket was taken up the nine steps at the back of the apse and laid on the special altar-throne at the top. (At this point, it is worth recalling the importance of the Christ Enthroned style of representation of the Mandylion, discussed earlier in this chapter.) Never in the ceremony within the cathedral were the ordinary faithful allowed even to glimpse the cloth. Only the archbishop, at the end of the service, was allowed to open the casket and glimpse the relic within, lightly sponging it, and then soaking the moisture up again, lightly scattering the drops among the congregation. As summed up by a text of the tenth century:

. . . no one was allowed to draw near or touch the holy likeness with his lips or eyes. The result of this was that divine fear increased their faith, and made the reverence paid to the revered object palpably more fearful and awe-inspiring.[18]

This was evocatively expressed in a Byzantine hymn to the Mandylion:

How can we with mortal eyes contemplate this image
whose celestial splendor
the host of heaven presumes not to behold?
He who dwells in heaven condescends
this day to visit us by his venerable image:
He who is seated on the cherubim
visits us this day by a picture,
which the Father has delineated
with his immaculate hand,
which he has formed in an ineffable manner,
and which we sanctify by adoring
it with fear and love.[19]

In this way the Mandylion was preserved in Edessa for more than four centuries following its discovery, attracting vast numbers of pilgrims to the city, but always kept inaccessible to normal gaze. Some, besides the archbishop, must have seen the cloth. Both Orthodox and Monophysites, despite their religious differences, accepted without dispute the concept that the Mandylion image really was "not made by hands," and they could only have satisfied themselves about this by direct observation.

The air of hallowed mystery ensured that the image of the body would lie unsuspected in the folds to await another era and men of a different city.

CHAPTER XVII

THE CLOTH LEAVES EDESSA

In Constantinople in the early 940s, the Byzantine emperor Romanus Lecapenus celebrated his seventieth birthday and reflected on his reign.[1] Like many others who had sat on the throne, he had achieved his power by usurpation. In 919 he had wrested the Byzantine throne from a mere child—the infant son of Leo the Wise, Constantine Porphyrogenitus ("to the Purple Born").

On the whole he had ruled wisely. The empire was in good order, and after centuries of Moslem inroads into Byzantine frontiers—in which Edessa, not unwillingly, had become part of the Arab Caliphate centuries before—it was now the turn of the Moslems to be on the defensive.

Unlike many of his predecessors and successors, Romanus had thought it unnecessary to murder the emperor he had supplanted. He had brought up the young Constantine Porphyrogenitus in his own court and had married him to his daughter Helena.

Even so, in his old age, Romanus suffered from a troubled conscience and looked to religion as a solace. He thought back to the days of the great image controversy during the eighth and ninth centuries. In those years, he knew the Byzantine and Moslem empires alike had been rent with iconoclasm—fierce destruction of images of all kinds, including the great image of Christ Enthroned above the imperial throne, and the famed acheiropoietic image of Camuliana. Romanus did not have to look far for the signs that the iconoclasts had eventually lost the day—Byzantium now abounded once more with religious art. But, as his priests and soothsayers could not have failed to remind him, there was one thing missing in Constantinople: the famed image which learned defenders of images—St. John of Damascus,[2] Theodore of Studium,[3] and others—had argued throughout the controversy was proof that Jesus had wanted his likeness to be perpetuated, the Mandylion or image of Edessa, so holy, so true, so unmistakably of non-man-made origin that it had remained safe throughout all the destruction around it. In 943 the centenary of image-worshiping Orthodoxy was celebrated in Constantinople. The Mandylion, the greatest of all images, lay hundreds of miles away in Moslem territory. It would be a fitting end to Romanus' reign to move the Mandylion to Constantinople. Recently Constantinople had narrowly escaped devastation by a band of marauding Russians when Romanus' army and navy were operating elsewhere. An uneducated and superstitious sailor, Romanus was bright enough to see that the addition of a new, powerful source of divine protection for Constantinople was bound to be regarded with gratitude by the city's superstitious inhabitants.

Romanus sent his most able general, John Curcuas, on what must surely rank as one of the most bizarre military missions in all history. In a series of brilliant campaigns Curcuas penetrated Moslem territory to cities that, in three hundred years, had never seen a Christian army—Amida, Nisibis, and the neighborhood of Aleppo.

In the spring of 943, Curcuas' army lay outside Edessa's walls, and made known to the city's emir their strange demand, promising that Edessa would be spared, two hundred high-ranking Moslem prisoners released, twelve thousand silver crowns paid, and Edessa guaranteed perpetual immunity from attack by the emperor for just one thing—the Mandylion.

A deal of this kind was quite unprecedented, and not unnaturally the emir did not know what to do. If he accepted, he would face enormous internal opposition from the Christian inhabitants of the city, who enjoyed an extensive trade in pilgrimages from their possession of the fabled relic. If he refused, Edessa would certainly fall, as he could expect no military support from Baghdad.

Anxious that the Mandylion should be preserved, Curcuas occupied himself with minor raids in neighboring territories while the despairing emir sent to his superiors in Baghdad to ask what their orders were.

In H. C. Bowen's *Ali ibn Iza*[4] there is a fascinating account of the deliberations held by the Moslem caliph and his cadis at this point. Had it been "some old icon" under discussion, one can scarcely believe that they would not have immediately told their emir to go ahead and arrange its surrender. Instead, with genuine concern for the relic that had contributed so much to Edessa's prosperity, they deliberated back and forth. But at length it was the Byzantine offer of deliverance of the Moslem captives that won the day.

The emir was instructed to surrender the Mandylion, and the news was imparted to John Curcuas. This was in many ways the easiest stage, for now, early in 944, Curcuas had somehow to wrest the relic from his fellow Christians, and he rightly anticipated duplicity and resistance all the way.

Not the least of his problems was that it was quite unthinkable for a military general to take possession of the Mandylion himself. It would have to be done by a priest, and Abraham, bishop of Samosata, a neighboring town that had recently acknowledged imperial suzerainty, was deputed for the task.

Abraham also appears to have been chosen for another reason. He was one of the few who had some knowledge of the appearance of what he had come to receive. This was a very necessary qualification, as events were to prove. Contemporary sources tell us that when Curcuas' party was admitted, two separate attempts were made by Edessa's clergy to pass off counterfeits instead of the genuine Mandylion.

The attempts may not even have been deliberate. There are reliable documents of the eighth century that claim that a wealthy Edessa Monophysite, Athanasius bar Gumayer, took the Mandylion in pawn at about this time, made a careful copy, and when the Orthodox came to redeem the cloth, deceived them by handing over the copy, arranging for the original to be kept in the Monophysite baptistry.[5] Another copy seems to have been kept by the Nestorians, another rival church in Edessa.

At all events, it was only on their third attempt that Abraham was at last satisfied that he had the true and only

Mandylion in his possession. He also apparently took a copy of the Abgar correspondence at the same time. For Curcuas and Abraham, however, the difficulties were by no means over. The events that ensued form a fascinating illustration of the intense possessiveness that Edessa's Christian population felt toward the Mandylion.

According to Orthodox chroniclers,

. . . the city was in great turmoil as they would not allow their most precious possession to be taken away, which brought them protection against harm. Eventually the Moslem emir managed, by persuading some, using force against others, and terrifying others with threats of death, to get the image handed over. Then there was a sudden outbreak of thunder and lightning with torrential rain, as if by design or arrangement, just as the image and the letter of Christ were about to leave the city of Edessa. Once more those who had clung to these things before were stirred again. They maintained that God was showing by these events that it was not in accordance with Divine Will that these most holy objects should be transferred.[6]

Despite all the emir's efforts to quell the disorder, a running battle seems to have ensued right up to the boat that was to take the Mandylion across the Euphrates. The contemporary chroniclers seem to have regarded it as quite miraculous that the boat managed to depart with the cloth at all.

It was thus, in a scarcely dignified manner, that the Mandylion left Edessa and began what, if it was genuine, would seem to have been its first long journey since the days of the apostles.

In retrospect we may deplore the bullying methods by which the Byzantines had come to acquire it. We may sympathize with the Edessans for what was essentially an act of piracy committed against them by fellow Christians. But events have proven that it was for the best. In little more than two centuries Turkish Moslems took and sacked Edessa in a manner it had never known in all the 1,460 years since its establishment by the Seleucids. Churches that had not al-

ready been devastated during a brief Crusader occupation of
the city were razed. The entire city was thoroughly looted:

> . . . for a whole year they went about the town digging,
> searching secret places, foundations and roofs. They found
> many treasures hidden from the earliest times of the fa-
> thers and elders, and many [treasures] of which the citi-
> zens knew nothing. . . .[7]

If the Mandylion had not been removed earlier by the Byzantines, it would not have survived. Even so, it was as
somewhat tarnished liberators that the Byzantines set off by
boat and by road on the slow journey to Constantinople.

Today, viewing modern Istanbul, it is difficult to visualize
the city they approached—Constantinople, "Queen of Cities."
We have a better mental picture of ancient Athens or Rome.
In the Middle Ages Constantinople lay at the eastern end of
Europe like a remote fairy-tale palace in a wilderness of
hovels. As a center of art, culture, and commerce it was
unrivaled, having preserved intact all the knowledge and experience of the old Roman Empire. Trade poured into it
from all quarters. Its palaces, churches, and shrines were the
envy of the world. Male and female citizens alike wore perfumes and decked themselves with jewelry. Christ himself
was believed to have guided the Emperor Constantine in or-
daining the fourteen-mile circuit of its walls. The emperor
ruled in godlike luxury in an interminable daily round of ceremonial, with visitors prostrating themselves before him.

On August 15, 944, the Mandylion arrived as a new possession of the emperor at the city that was to be its home for
the next two and a half centuries. Even the date was chosen
for its theological significance. The fifteenth of August, the
Feast of the Assumption of the Virgin Mary, was and still is
the most holy feast to the Mother of God in the entire Orthodox calendar. No more appropriate place, therefore, could be
chosen for the Mandylion's first reception in the city than the
Church of the Virgin Mary at Blachernae, close to the northern extremity of Constantinople's western walls, and the most
sacred of all the shrines in the city. The Mandylion tempo-
rarily joined a relic that had up to that time been the "pro-

tector" of the city, the reputed robe of the Virgin, accompanied by an icon placed there in the fifth century during the reign of Leo the Great. In 626, when the Avars were repulsed and their fleet destroyed before Constantinople's walls, the citizens congregated at the Virgin's church at Blachernae to give thanks with the singing of the Akathistos hymn. In 860 the robe of the Virgin was thanked for the repulse of would-be Russian invaders.

Bringing the two god-bearing relics together in the same place was of enormous theological significance. First, symbolically God the Son had come to join his Mother, in the church most sacred to her, on the very anniversary of her most holy Assumption. But more than this, added to the divine protection with which Constantinople was already endowed was that of Christ himself in the form of his own palladian image.

That night the viewing at which the sons of Romanus Lecapenus were present took place. Then the Mandylion was taken by galley along the Golden Horn to the royal palace, where it spent the first of many nights in the imperial chapel of the Pharos. The following day it was prepared for its proper reception by the citizens of Constantinople. From the royal palace it was taken by boat to a point outside the Theodosian walls, and then was carried in its casket around the city in solemn procession, with kings and clergy alike following on foot.

It was borne, in the words of the contemporary chronicler,

like a second ark, or even more precious than that. They walked round the outside of the walls as far as the Golden Gate, and then entered the city with high psalmody, hymns, and spiritual songs and boundless light from torches, and, gathering together a procession of the whole people, they completed their journey through the city center; they thought that because of this the city would receive holiness and greater strength and would thus be kept safe and remain impregnable forever. . . .

It is impossible to describe in words all the weeping for joy and the intercession, prayers, and thanksgivings to God from the whole city as the divine image . . . passed through the midst of the city.[8]

It was appropriate that having been brought from Hagia Sophia, Edessa, the first destination of the procession should be Hagia Sophia, Constantinople, already four centuries old, and ablaze with images sponsored by posticonoclastic emperors. Here, just as in Hagia Sophia, Edessa, the Mandylion was placed on the throne of mercy of the sanctuary and worshiped by the whole assembly.

At the culmination of the proceedings the Mandylion, still in its casket, was taken into the Chrysotriclinium of the royal palace, the great audience chamber of the Byzantine emperors. Here, recalling the Christ Enthroned representation, it was placed on the very throne on which the emperor gave decisions on the most important matters of state. Christ, as present in the Mandylion, had come to Constantinople. Now in the very fullest sense, God and emperor ruled side by side.

One man who watched and took part in these events with intense interest was Constantine Porphyrogenitus, the prince who for more than twenty-five years had waited patiently in the wings as rightful heir to the throne, while his father-in-law, the usurper Romanus Lecapenus, held sway. Constantine was a bookish individual, more interested in ceremonial and the work of artists and craftsmen than in the hard world of imperial politics.

According to palace gossip, he painted and sold his work to supplement the meager allowance granted to him by his father-in-law. It was therefore partly as gratification of his artistic inclinations that he welcomed the Mandylion's coming. But like most Byzantines, he was also too superstitious not to recognize in it a great omen for his own political future.

About the time of its arrival, all sorts of rumors spread about the city. Among them was the story that when the relic had rested at the monastery of Eusebius, on the other side of the Bosporus, a madman had been cured, shouting out, "Constantinople, take the glory and joy, and you, Constantine Porphyrogenitus, your throne!"[9]

Romanus clearly had not long to live. But would Constantine be able to survive the plotting of Romanus' sons Stephen and Constantine? Romanus, aware of his sons' shortcomings, suddenly made Constantine Porphyrogenitus heir to the throne after his death. Stephen and Constantine immediately saw the threat to their own power. On the night of December 20 Romanus' sons staged a coup as their father lay ill in his chamber. Dispatching the old man by boat to a monastery on the island of Prote, they seized power and began to consider how best to dispose of their brother-in-law, but they were forestalled by the citizens of Constantinople. A mob besieged the palace gates demanding the appearance of Constantine Porphyrogenitus, who had to be hauled from his library to show that he was still alive.

For a while Stephen and Constantine were obliged to rule alongside Porphyrogenitus, acknowledging him as senior emperor. But still they plotted, attempting in vain to lure him to a fatal breakfast party. At last, heeding the urgent entreaties of his wife, Helena, Constantine Porphyrogenitus in his turn had the unpopular pair arrested at dinner on January 27, 945. Much to the delight of the Byzantine populace, they were sent into exile.

So within months of the arrival of the Mandylion, Constantine Porphyrogenitus ascended to the throne that was rightfully his. With the superstitions inbred in every Byzantine, he gratefully attributed his success to the Mandylion's arrival, and with astonishing speed acted to demonstrate to all the world this indebtedness. August 16, the date the Mandylion had actually been received by the citizens and made its formal tour of the city, was made the official feast day of the cloth in the Orthodox calendar. He had a special love of the goldsmith's craft and within weeks of his accession he issued a special gold solidus coin, with his head on one side and the Christ Enthroned likeness of Christ on the other, again indicating the link of this likeness with the Mandylion.[10] As a great patron of the arts, he also appears to have inspired another fascinating item from his time, an icon found in the monastery of St. Catherine in the Sinai desert by a team of American art experts.[11] It was originally a triptych with an icon of the Mandylion in the middle, but only the two wings have survived.

One side shows Thaddaeus, the disciple who brought the Mandylion to Edessa. Below him are saints Paul of Thebes and Antonios. The other side shows Abgar, holding the Mandylion. Below him are St. Basil and St. Ephraim the Syrian, the latter Edessa's greatest saint. This is perhaps the earliest surviving depiction we have of the Mandylion showing the cloth itself. But its most interesting touch is that the features of Abgar have been modeled on those of Constantine Porphyrogenitus himself, as is quite clear from other works of art that bear his likeness.

So in the reign of Constantine Porphyrogenitus the Mandylion took on a new location. It found an emperor who set himself and members of his court to try to understand something of the strange character of his new possession. It was Constantine who caused to be written the special feast-day sermon "The Story of the Image of Edessa," which was read in Hagia Sophia, Constantinople, on the first anniversary of the Mandylion's arrival, August 16, 945. This sermon was the document that more than any other has thrown valuable light on the Mandylion's past, up to and including Constantine Porphyrogenitus' reign.

But there was still one item of information it could not reveal, because its author had no knowledge of it at the time—the existence of the full-length figure of Christ that had for nearly a thousand years lain hidden in the Mandylion's folds.

CHAPTER XVIII

THE FULL-LENGTH FIGURE

COMES TO LIGHT

The Pharos Chapel, the shrine in which the Mandylion was kept after its arrival in Constantinople, was part of the imperial mini-city known as the Boucoleon or Great Palace, which stood in the southeastern corner of old Constantinople, flanked by the Sea of Marmara.

Today it is a depressing excursion to walk around the area of Istanbul where the palace once stood. It is cluttered with squalid wooden hovels, the cobbled roadways potholed and littered with refuse. The only real glimpse of the Byzantine

past is afforded by the remains of the sea walls and some mosaic pavements from one of the palace halls viewable within
the so-called Mosaic Museum. Here, a thousand years ago,
graceful buildings stretched as far as the eye could see.
There was a huge hippodrome, a magnificent baths complex,
a senate house, a glittering imperial audience chamber and
accompanying state rooms, exquisitely decorated churches,
an orderly barracks for palace guards, a lighthouse, even a
polo ground.

Somewhere in all this, probably as an annex to the imperial audience chamber, stood the Pharos Chapel, whose
beauty can only be imagined from the awed descriptions of
those who viewed it:

> . . . so rich and noble that there was not a hinge or a
> band nor any other part which is usually made of iron that
> was not all of silver, and there was no column that was not
> of jasper or porphyry or some rich and precious metal.[1]

In this shrine, a veritable Byzantine Fort Knox, the Mandylion had joined the entire collection of relics of Christ's
Passion—among them:

> . . . two pieces of the True Cross as large as the leg of a
> man . . . , the iron of the lance with which Our Lord had
> his side pierced, two of the nails which were driven
> through his hands and his feet, the tunic which he wore
> and which was taken from him when they led him to the
> Mount of Calvary, and . . . the blessed crown with which
> he was crowned, which was made of reeds with thorns as
> sharp as the points of daggers.[2]

The place chosen for the Mandylion's casket was on the
right-hand side, facing the east. Security in the chapel was
impressive, even by today's standards. So closely guarded
was this priceless collection that only those personally invited
by the emperor ever gained access. Such visits were extremely restricted, generally to visiting royalty and select
members of their retinue. The pilgrim of the Middle Ages
had, if anything, an even greater zeal for souvenir-hunting
than his twentieth-century counterparts, and there was a real

practical need for such security precautions. Still, such inaccessibility went far beyond the mere practicalities of ensuring that the relics would not be stolen. As in Edessa, there are no reports of the Mandylion being publicly exhibited at this time.

There are occasional references to it being carried in procession, one being in the year 1036, during the reign of Michael Paphlagos, in which it was accompanied by a second copy of the reputed letter of Christ to Abgar brought to the city four years earlier;[3] another being in the year 1058, when Christian Arab writer Abu Nasr Yahya recorded seeing it in Hagia Sophia.[4]

In none of these instances is there any suggestion of it being removed from its casket for viewing. Expositions to enable monk-artists to make their copies would have been in private. Appropriate to the conditions of faceless anonymity in which these talented individuals worked, these expositions have gone unrecorded.

All this was part of the mystique, the awe that surrounded the emperor and all he stood for. It was characteristic of the Byzantine mentality, which reveled in the mystery of holy things. Brought up on the old classical tales of gods who blinded men who beheld them with unveiled eyes, the Byzantines readily accepted the practice of the most sacred moments of the liturgy being performed out of sight of the congregation, a custom that persists to this day in most Orthodox churches. They were accustomed without question to prostrate themselves before the face of the emperor, making it natural that things pertaining to Christ should be accorded even more reverence. As the inscription read on a twelfth-century Byzantine communion veil now at Halberstadt:

If no Israelite might look directly on the countenance of Moses when he came down from the mountain where he had seen God, how shall I look upon Thy revered Body unveiled, how regard it?[5]

All this makes all the more intriguing the evidence that someone, sometime after the Mandylion's arrival in Constantinople, seems to have undone the gold trelliswork covering the cloth, untwined the fringe from the surrounding nails, carefully unfolded the cloth, and, for the first time since the days of the apostles, set eyes on the concealed full-length figure. Frustratingly, this is another of those moments in the Mandylion's history that has gone unrecorded, yet is crucial to it. It is attested as a real happening from an impressive array of circumstantial evidence.

The first indications, and the most direct, come from western authors. The earliest, datable to sometime before 1130, is an interpolation in an original eighth-century sermon by Pope Stephen III.[6] Referring to the Mandylion, it tells us:

> For the very same mediator between God and man [Christ], that he might in every way satisfy the king [Abgar], stretched his whole body on a cloth, white as snow, on which the glorious image of the Lord's face and the length of his whole body was so divinely transformed that it was sufficient for those who could not see the Lord bodily in the flesh, to see the transfiguration made on the cloth.[7]

Another account, from the prodigious *History of the Church* written by the English monk Ordericus Vitalis about 1130, seemed to derive from the first. According to this version:

> Abgar reigned as toparch of Edessa. To him the Lord Jesus sent . . . a most precious cloth with which he wiped the sweat from his face, and on which shone the Savior's features miraculously reproduced. This displayed to those who gazed on it the likeness and proportions of the body of the Lord.[8]

A Vatican Library codex, also datable to the twelfth century, repeated this tradition in its version of Christ's letter to Abgar:

> If indeed you desire to look bodily upon my face, I send you a cloth on which know that the image not only of my face, but of my whole body had been divinely transformed.[9]

By the thirteenth century, Gervase of Tilbury, a great re-
tailer of the gossip of the time, not only repeated these words
of Christ to Abgar, but added:

> For it is handed down from archives of ancient authority
> that the Lord prostrated himself full length on most white
> linen, and so by divine power the most beautiful likeness
> not only of the face, but also of the whole body of the
> Lord was impressed upon the cloth.[10]

However intriguing these accounts, they are, nevertheless,
unsatisfactory. They carefully avoid discussion of the circumstances in which the image might have been created, it
being, after all, a preposterous idea that Jesus had, in life,
impressed the image of his whole body on cloth. They have
been regarded, understandably, by historians as merely typical examples of the way people of the Middle Ages told tall
stories about religious relics. As evidence, they have little
value except for their seeming relationship to a significant
development at precisely this time in the normally static
world of Byzantine art.

It has already been remarked that there was, in the early
centuries, a considerable reserve about representing Christ
dead. Known examples invariably show Christ's body
wrapped mummy-style, i.e., wound in swathing bands, rather
than in any large shroudlike sheet. Opponents of the
Shroud's authenticity have therefore argued that the Byzantines clearly had no knowledge of the existence of any cloth
answering the Shroud's description at the time (and this is,
of course, perfectly true).

It is significant in the light of the changed Mandylion references that about the beginning of the eleventh century a
dramatic change in representation of Jesus' burial occurred.
Research by Professor Kurt Weitzmann of the Department of
Art and Archaeology at Princeton University, New Jersey,
has shown that in the eleventh century this old mummy-style
entombment scene gave way to a new Lamentation scene, referred to in art history circles as the *Threnos*.[11] The body of
Christ is depicted at the foot of the cross after the crucifixion,
lamented by the holy women, while Joseph of Arimathea and

Nicodemus busy themselves with the funeral arrangements.

Early Lamentation examples include an eleventh-century ivory now in the Rosengarten Museum, Constance, Germany, and a particularly dramatic fresco created about the year 1164 in the tiny Byzantine church of Nerezi, Macedonia. Closely related to these are equally innovative Deposition scenes, one at Nerezi, another forming part of the fresco decoration of the tiny Chapel of the Holy Sepulcher, Winchester Cathedral, England. The common factor to all these is the use of a large, double-length piece of linen, obviously intended to envelop the body over the head, a cloth we would unhesitatingly identify as a shroud.

At precisely this same eleventh- to twelfth-century period, no fewer than three separate but related types of representation of the body of Christ, closely associated with this same development, appeared in Byzantine art.

One group consisted of the Lamentation scene showing Christ's body in a very stiff attitude, with, as a complete innovation in art, the hands crossed over the loins. The Victoria and Albert Museum in London has an ivory of this type dating from the eleventh century.[12] The State Hermitage Museum in Leningrad has a cross reliquary of the eleventh century, formerly in the Count Stroganoff collection, with a scene of this type in enamel carrying the significant inscription "Christ lies in death, manifesting God."[13]

The Pray Manuscript in Budapest, dated reliably to the years 1192–95, has on the reverse of one page a drawing of the same type, unusual for the total nudity of the Christ figure.[14]

On all of these examples, the hands are crossed consistently, the right over the left with an awkward crossing point at the wrists, all forcefully reminiscent of the Shroud.

An intriguing group consists of *epitaphioi*—liturgical cloths still used today in the Eastern Orthodox Church to cover the ceremonial bier of Christ in the elaborate Good Friday procession of the sacred elements.[15] While the earliest surviving examples date from the thirteenth century, their similarity to the independent Lamentation scenes in art suggest their emergence in the twelfth century, their consistent feature

CHIN BAND—virtually universal in Jewish burial procedure. Evidence for the presence of this is seen in the clear gap between the frontal and dorsal images on the shroud. This would have been one of the othonia (bands) of John's Gospel, and not, as some have claimed, the "soudarion."

BINDING OF THE WRISTS—would have been necessary to prevent the arms' returning in rigor mortis to the crucifixion angle. Evidence for the presence of such binding is seen in the gap in the blood flows at precisely this point on the shroud.

BINDING OF THE FEET—the most conjectural of the three. This would appear to have been normal Jewish burial procedure from the account of the raising of Lazarus, who needed to be "unbound" before he could do more than shuffle from the tomb.

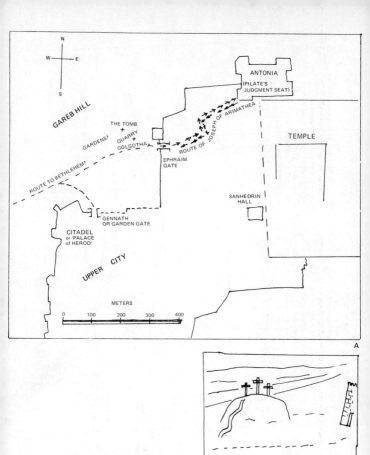

A. Jerusalem at the time of Jesus, showing the route Joseph of Arimathea would have had to take to and from his audience with Pilate. This would have been through streets particularly crowded because of Passover. *(Based on plan of first-century Jerusalem by Dr. Kathleen Kenyon)*

B. According to latest findings, Golgotha was a rocky pinnacle approximately thirty-three feet high, protruding into a quarry which was worked, up to A.D. 70, in a series of working faces rising in terraces. The name Golgotha, meaning "skull," almost certainly suggests that its shape was reminiscent of a human skull. It was close to a road, we know, because passers-by reviled Jesus on the cross.

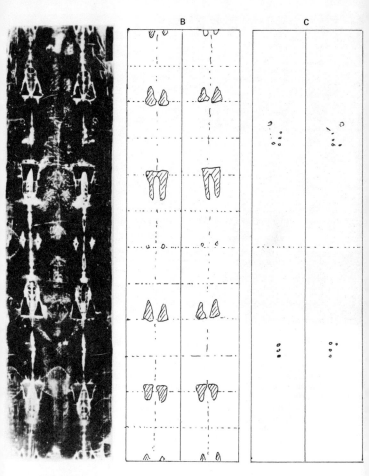

A. The Shroud (in negative) as it is today.
B. The patches added in 1534, after the 1532 fire.
C. The holes from burn damage in an unknown incident preceding 1516.

The weave of the Holy Shroud, seen in close-up. This appears to be a three-to-one twill, broken at intervals by a forty-thread stripe measuring from 10 to 12 cm. in width, making an overall herringbone pattern on the cloth. No similar three-to-one linen samples seem to have survived, but there are examples of silk three-to-one twills from the Roman era—e.g., fragments from a child's coffin ca. A.D. 250, Holborough, Kent, England, and two examples from Palmyra, Syria, ca. A.D. 276. It would seem likely, according to British textile expert Elizabeth Crowfoot, to be of Syrian origin. (*British Society for the Turin Shroud*)

Dr. Max Frei, the Zurich botanist and criminologist, seen in the garden of his Thalwil home examining a specimen of *Amarylis passiflora*, the passion flower. Frei's studies of pollen from the Shroud have thrown remarkable new light on the Shroud's whereabouts during its history. *(Photo by the author)*

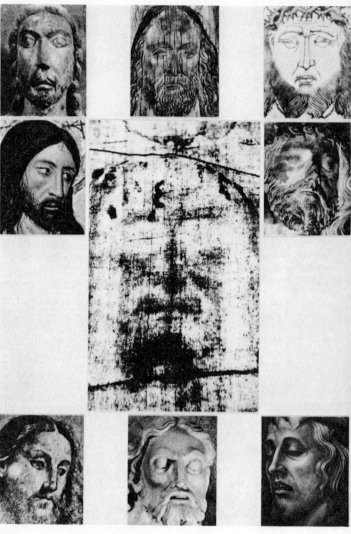

Seen compared to the Shroud face, likenesses of Christ since the thirteenth century, as created by artists of several different nationalities. The same likeness has come down through the centuries. *(Rex Features)*

Christ Pantocrator, from the dome of monastery church of
Daphni, near Athens.

Typical Byzantine Christ portraits displaying Vignon markings on the forehead. (A and B are from the eleventh century; C and D are from the tenth century.)

A. Christ Pantocrator mosaic (detail), dome of church of Daphni.

B. Christ the Merciful (detail), portable icon in mosaic, Ehemals Staatliche Museum, Berlin.

C. Christ Enthroned mosaic (detail), narthex of Hagia Sophia, Constantinople.

D. Christ Enthroned fresco (detail), Church of Sant'Angelo in Formis, Italy.

being, as before, the figure of Christ laid out in death with hands crossed over the loins.

The two most significant epitaphioi, instead of showing the figure of Christ lying horizontally, show him vertically in an apparent standing pose, yet still laid out in death. The first, somewhat clumsily conceived, is preserved in the monastery of the Pantocrator, Mount Athos.[16] The other, executed in gold thread on a dark red ground, is preserved in the Museum of the Serbian Orthodox Church, Belgrade.[17] Although datable to the late thirteenth century, it is most likely to have been based on earlier, now lost, examples. It merits the most careful comparison with the Shroud figure.

The third group, superficially the least apposite, is a series of striking pictorial representations of Christ, showing him not full-length but half-length, bearing the wounds of the Passion, and rising from a coffinlike tomb with his hands in front of him, again in the characteristic crossed-hands pose associated with the Shroud.[18] Of not later than twelfth-century origin, these were known in the East as the *Basileus tes doxes*, the King of Glory; in the West, where they became popular during the fourteenth and fifteenth centuries, as the Christ of Pity.

The western examples are associated with a garbled story, of wide currency during the Middle Ages, in which Pope Gregory the Great, while celebrating Mass in a chapel filled with relics of the Passion, was said to have seen rising from the chalice a powerful vision of Christ covered in wounds, as if rising from the tomb. Christ then administered Mass with his own hands.

There is absolutely no historical evidence for Pope Gregory the Great himself having seen such a vision, the earliest accounts dating many centuries after his time. Instead the story may well be a westernized adaptation of some tangled memory of the incident relating to the Mandylion that we have already reconstructed—that an unknown eastern cleric of the eleventh or twelfth century, in the relic-filled Pharos Chapel saw just such a vision rise from the Mandylion reliquary in the form of the full-length figure on the cloth we now know as the Shroud.

This theory is given credence by the existence of several icons showing the Mandylion and the wound-bearing Christ of Pity figure in the same scene. One of these icons is in the collection of lawyer George R. Hann of Sewickly Heights, Pennsylvania; others are in the U.S.S.R.[19] They suggest an iconographic link between the Mandylion and Christ of Pity that has hitherto gone unnoticed by art historians.

The link is also suggested by the fact that during the late twelfth century the Grail stories emerged in the West, set in the time of the legendary King Arthur, but essentially about a dish or chalice of extreme holiness that forms the goal of a knightly quest. Difficult though they are to untangle,[20] the real core of the Grail stories seems to be not the chalice itself but what it holds—a very special secret vision of Christ, attributed by several authors to inspiration from Constantinople. As in the Pope Gregory story, several have Jesus appearing, covered in wounds at the elevation of the host, and administering Mass with his own hand.[21] In one, the story of King Evalak's shield, the red cross on the shield turns into a bleeding vision of Christ that has powers of protection at a time of extreme danger, just as the Mandylion did.

The most intriguing Grail accounts are of the vision making a few significant changes of form—the wafer of the host first changing into Christ as a child, then Christ as an adult, with, of course, the bleeding wounds. These stories are paralleled by an otherwise incomprehensible passage about the Mandylion from the same text of Pope Stephen quoted earlier in this chapter. This stated that on a Good Friday the Mandylion appeared

. . . at the first hour of the day as a child, at the third hour as a boy, at the sixth hour as an adolescent, and at the ninth hour visible in his full manhood, in which form the Son of God went to his Passion when he bore for our sins the suffering of the Cross.[22]

Difficult though this account is to interpret, it may indicate that when the Byzantines discovered the full-length figure on the Mandylion, they devised a form of super-Mass for special private showings, in which the figure of Christ was made to rise in a series of stages from the casket, each stage being regarded as symbolic of part of Jesus' earthly life. It will be recalled that similar symbolic stages were ascribed to the procession of the Mandylion in Edessa. If this sounds far-fetched, it must be pointed out that the gadgetry required for such a scenario was not only well within the Byzantines' capabilities, but typical of them. For instance, every Friday the Virgin's robe was made to part "miraculously" at Bla-chernae, revealing a precious icon beneath. At imperial audi-ences, emperors such as Constantine Porphyrogenitus de-lighted in startling visiting ambassadors by a mechanism that whirled the throne aloft as if by magic, the emperor then descending in different robes.[23] Once it was discovered that the Mandylion had more to it than merely a face, the fact seems to have had to be kept secret from the general public. The very nature of the Grail stories makes this clear. The secret would be easy to maintain with no public exposi-tions of the Mandylion.

There were, in fact, particularly for the East, very good reasons why it should remain a secret because of the grave clerical embarrassment that any public disclosure would cause. As mentioned earlier, on August 16, 945, the Mandyl-ion was written into the Orthodox calendar with its own feast day on that date and an official history to accompany it. Since the world knew the Mandylion as the facecloth Jesus himself had sent to Abgar, it may well have been unac-ceptable to the Byzantines to attempt to rewrite tradition to account for Abgar having been sent a cloth of the full-length image of Christ, bearing all his wounds. Yet another problem would have been that all the world believed that Jesus had been washed prior to his burial. The very stone on which this service was thought to have been carried out was preserved at Ephesus, and was brought to Constantinople with great ceremony in the twelfth century, the Emperor Manuel I Comnenus reportedly carrying it on his back to the Church of the Pantocrator. When the Mandylion was revealed as the Shroud, it would have seemed impossible to those who had made the discovery that it could have been the cloth used in the tomb—as a body washed before burial could not have left such marks on the cloth. It would have been regarded instead as the cloth used actually to soak up the blood and sweat before the proper preparation and burial—and therefore not a shroud as such.

That such a deduction could be made is evident from the fact that, before the Pia photograph, even some of those who viewed the Shroud as we know it today had similar notions. The seventeenth-century writers Chifflet[24] and Quaresimus[25] both described the Turin Shroud as having been used *ante pollincturam,* before ritual washing, a belief that enabled them to accept other shrouds as authentic as well.

This belief is important as it may well explain the thinking behind the cloth seen in the eleventh- to twelfth-century Lamentation scenes, while still maintaining its compatibility with the Shroud we know today. This same thinking would enable depictions in Byzantine art of mummy-style wrappings for Jesus in the tomb to continue without conflict, as indeed are to be found in icons right up to our own time.

The interesting question is the extent to which this duality of nature of the Mandylion, as the facecloth given to Abgar and as the sweat cloth used at the Lamentation, could be resolved, or remain a conflict in Byzantine minds. All the evidence suggests that the conflict remained. For instance, it is obvious that long after our hypothesized discovery of the full-length figure on the Mandylion, the Byzantines rigidly maintained the old Abgar story, both in art and literature. Extensive scenes of the Mandylion's history are to be found in icons dating as late as the seventeenth century, preserving the old ideas. One may note that chronologically they stop at the tenth century, the Mandylion's arrival in Constantinople, as if an unseen hand had checked the Mandylion's history at that point.

The Byzantines did introduce a new element into the depiction of the Mandylion by placing it, represented as a facecloth, in locations in church decoration symbolic of the sacrifice of the Eucharist.[26] In one fresco it was even depicted on an altar in place of the elements of the host, with Christ himself officiating at the Mass.

In the 1190s they went just a little further. Pope Celestine III at this time was displaying great pride in his copy of the face on the Mandylion, the cloth that history knows as the Veronica. He built a splendid new altarpiece for it within

John VII's chapel in old St. Peter's and showed it to his most distinguished visitors.[27] During negotiations attempting to heal the religious schism between East and West, he seems to have been sent by someone from Byzantium a beautiful *umbella*, or ornamental tapestry canopy to be held over the cloth at such expositions. Although the canopy has since been destroyed, a record of its appearance has been preserved by a seventeenth-century archivist, Jacopo Grimaldi.[28] His careful drawings reveal that there was, as the centerpiece of the umbella, a representation of Christ in exactly the manner of the Shroud. The umbella, the epitaphioi, the Christ of Pity, and the Lamentation scenes add up to a tantalizing clue that the full-length figure on the cloth had now been revealed.

The intriguing gift, the umbella, underlines one puzzling aspect of all the secret new information on the Mandylion—why this should have consistently been recorded in the West rather than in the East? The answer is that it was in the eleventh and twelfth centuries that, in order to find some ally against the growing power of the Moslems, the emperor of Byzantium actively courted visits from magnates of the West. For instance, the patron of Chrétien de Troyes, first known writer of Grail romances, was one of the counts of Champagne, whose connections with Byzantium were not inconsiderable in the period in question. Count Henry II of Champagne had visited Constantinople in 1147, been entertained in every way royally, and even given a Byzantine form of knighthood by the emperor Manuel I Comnenus. Such a man might well have been given a special viewing of the Mandylion. This possibility is admirably illustrated in a description by twelfth-century author William of Tyre of a visit by the Frankish king of Jerusalem, Amaury I, to Manuel I Comnenus in 1171.

He [the emperor] also ordered the interior parts of the palace, the sanctuaries open to none but his servants, the rooms too dedicated to the most secret uses, the basilicas inaccessible to ordinary men, the treasures and ancestral stores of all desirable things, to be shown to them as to his intimate friends. . . . Nothing hidden, nothing sacred, placed in the hidden places of the sacred room from the time of the blessed emperors Constantine, Theodosius, Justinian but was familiarly revealed to them. . . .[29]

This account specifically described the Greeks' astonishment at the emperor's departure from custom. It also lists what the visitors were shown, and here we come to the key question of how the Byzantines handled the problem of the Mandylion's dual nature in the late twelfth century. William of Tyre specifically recorded that the emperor

ordered to be exposed the relics of the saints, the most precious evidence of the Passion of our Lord Jesus Christ, that is the Cross, nails, lance, sponge, reed, crown of thorns, sindon, and sandals. . . .

And in the accompanying French text the sindon was further described as "the cloth which is called the *sisne* in which he was wrapped."[30]

What are we to make of this? Was some hitherto unknown plain shroudlike cloth preserved in the collection? Or was it what we have so far known as the Mandylion, now recognized for its real nature as a burial cloth? To all intents and purposes it seems to have been the latter. This does not mean to say that it was yet regarded as a shroud in the sense of the definitive burial garment, for the word *sindon* would still be consistent with the large cloth of the Lamentation scenes.

But in order that the old Abgar tradition should be maintained, what seems to have happened is that a copy of the original form of the Mandylion was introduced into the collection, a copy that did not occupy the place of the Mandylion on the right-hand side facing the east but was twinned with the Keramion, the pair of relics being kept in two gold caskets hanging in the center of the chapel by heavy silver chains.

This seems to be the only explanation for the mysterious way in which, from the late eleventh century on, burial linens are recorded in the collection of Constantinople, while a Mandylion is also recorded as an independent object. Thus in 1093 suddenly appears the first reference in all history to Constantinople's precious relics of Christ including "the linens which were found in the tomb after his Resurrection."[31]

Then in 1150 an unknown English pilgrim recorded that the collection included "the sudarium which was over his head,"[32] a description exactly corresponding to the way we might suppose the Mandylion/Shroud to have been thought of at the time, except that the same pilgrim refers independently to there being also in the collection "the *mantile* which our Lord held to his face, and on which the image of his face was preserved."[33]

In 1157 an Icelandic abbot, Nicholas Soemundarson, in his list of the relics of Constantinople talks of both "linen bands with the *sveitaduk*"[34] (sweat cloth) and a *"maetull,"* the latter being identified by some scholars as the Mandylion.

The Byzantines recorded in great detail the reception of relics into their city. The obscure way in which the burial linen has thus emerged in the historical accounts suggests a switch in the terminology (due to the discovery) along the lines we have conjectured.

In any case, as none of the aforementioned writers actually saw the relics and had to rely on hearsay, their accounts may well contain confusions quite apart from the imprecisions of the terminology.

The real key to the issue seems to lie in the writings of two authors who both saw the relic collection for themselves, and whose accounts are therefore all the more important.

The first of these was Greek, his name Nicholas Mesarites. He was actual keeper of the relic collection in the Pharos Chapel, and in 1201 had to defend the chapel against a mob during a palace revolution. In an impassioned speech he warned of the sanctity of the shrine in his charge:

In this chapel Christ rises again, and the sindon with the burial linens is the clear proof. . . .

and later

The burial sindon of Christ: this is of linen, of cheap and easily obtainable material, still smelling fragrant of myrrh, defying decay, because it wrapped the mysterious, naked dead body after the Passion. . . .[35]

The phrase "in this chapel Christ rises again" is fascinating. It could be merely symbolic, signifying that the very accumulation of Christ's relics in this one place meant his Real Presence within. Alternatively, in the light of our concept of the figure of Christ rising from the casket of the Mandylion/Shroud it could be a particularly accurate and demonstrative phrase.

The remark that the sindon had "wrapped the mysterious, naked dead body after the Passion" is even more pertinent. It is to be noted that the information is "after the Passion," not "in the tomb," suggesting absolute consistency with our earlier remarks about the cloth having been regarded as not necessarily used for the burial proper. It is to be noted also that the body was described as "naked," surely suggestive that something about the cloth indicated this condition—something that may well have been the presence of the obviously naked figure on the cloth we know today as the Turin Shroud.

The second author was French, his name Robert de Clari, and his description of the Constantinople relic collection has been dated just two years after that of Mesarites, to the years 1203–4. He gives us first an account of the two vessels of gold containing the Keramion and what we have conjectured to be the Mandylion copy.

. . . There were two rich vessels of gold hanging in the midst of the chapel by two heavy silver chains. In one of these vessels was a tile and in the other a cloth. And we shall tell you where these relics came from. There was once a holy man in Constantinople. It happened that this holy man was covering the house of a widow with a tile for the love of God. And as he was covering it, Our Lord appeared to him and said to him (now this good man had a cloth wrapped about him) "Give me that cloth" said Our Lord. And the good man gave it to Him, and Our Lord enveloped his face with it so that his features were imprinted on it. And then he handed it back to him . . . but before he carried it away, after God had given him back

his cloth, the good man took and hid it under a tile until
vespers. At vespers . . . he took the cloth, and as he lifted
up the tile, he saw the image imprinted on the tile just as
it was on the cloth. . . .[36]

It will be noted that although the story concerning the
cloth is just recognizable as that of the Abgar legend, it is a
very watered down and garbled version, without even being
attributed to Edessa. This may indicate that the cloth described was merely a copy, as we have conjectured.

The real interest for de Clari was clearly the fabulous
sydoine he saw for himself, and his account of this deserves
repeating.

. . . there was another of the churches which they called
My Lady St. Mary of Blachernae, where was kept the
sydoine in which Our Lord had been wrapped, which
stood up straight every Friday so that the figure of Our
Lord could be plainly seen there. . . .[37]

In the context of all that we have reconstructed before,
this is a most crucial passage. It has every element. The cloth
is called "the sydoine in which Our Lord had been
wrapped," consistent with the new descriptions of such a
wrapping that we have followed since 1092, but with the
added information, that we have been obliged so far only to
conjecture, that it bore the image of "the figure of Our
Lord." Again intriguingly it follows the concept of the figure
of Christ appearing to rise from the casket, with the information that the sydoine "stood up straight every Friday."

But as much as the passage answers questions, it also
raises them. If what Robert de Clari saw was the cloth the
Byzantines had consistently known as the Mandylion, now
revealed unequivocally as the Shroud, what was it doing out
of the Pharos Chapel, in the church of Blachernae? And why,
for the first time ever, were *public* expositions being held
every Friday?

The location of Blachernae provides the vital clue. As we
have already mentioned, this church, now destroyed, was the
home of the palladian Virgin's robe, which every Friday was
made to appear and miraculously part to reveal an icon of

the Virgin beneath. And as we have also mentioned, this church was always a great rallying place for the citizens of Constantinople in times of distress.

At this point the circumstances in which Robert de Clari saw the sydoine should be made clear. Robert was part of the army gathered together in 1203 for the Fourth Crusade.[38] He and his companions had been transported to Constantinople by a Venetian navy avowedly to restore a deposed Byzantine emperor to his throne prior to the crusade mounting an attack on Moslem strongholds in the Holy Land. They had restored the emperor and had been accepted into the city as by-no-means-welcome guests of Constantinople's citizens.

Rough Frankish soldiers, vulgar in their manners, ill-disciplined and unwashed, suddenly found themselves striding through streets more beautiful than any they had ever seen before, rubbing shoulders with highly cultured eastern Greeks whose perfumes and jewels, worn by men and women alike, struck them as decadent and effeminate.

Neither side liked what they saw of the other, and when the restored emperor found he was unable to raise by taxes the money he had promised to pay the crusaders, the scene was set for an ugly situation. Violent incidents between Franks and Greeks multiplied by the day.

In these circumstances it seems more than likely that the emperor Alexius IV called to mind the fabled protective role that the Shroud/Mandylion had displayed in sixth-century Edessa. It would have been a shrewd psychological move to display the cloth to the superstitious Byzantines for the first time, just as the Virgin's robe was displayed. What a splendid way to convince them that not only the ever-guardian Virgin but Christ himself was with them to protect them from harm. The Blachernae church's rallying-point status made it the natural venue.

This may have been the scene observed by Robert de Clari. It is ironic that this sudden, quite unprecedented round of expositions should have taken place in the very last days that the cloth was to spend in Constantinople.

Relations between Byzantines and Franks worsened, and suddenly the crusaders were no longer merely unwelcome guests; they were besiegers facing besieged, with Constantinople's gates firmly shut against them. All the intentions for a crusade on the Holy Land dissipated in the face of an insatiable greed for the possession of the glittering city in which they had so recently walked.

A determined attack began, all the more vigorous because it was for their own ends. The Byzantines resisted as best they could, but they had long ago lost any interest in war, and their leadership was no match for their opponents' ingenuity. Managing to breach the walls not far from the Blachernae area, the crusaders poured into the city.

All the hatred, all the envy at the glittering Byzantine world that so outshone their own towns and villages was released as the crusaders burst into houses, palaces, and churches and began to claim the spoils of war. Breaking into wine cellars, they quickly became drunk. As Edward Gibbon described it in one of his most memorable passages:

> . . . they trampled under foot the most venerable objects of Christian worship. In the cathedral of S. Sophia the ample veil of the sanctuary was rent asunder for the sake of the golden fringe; and the altar, a monument of art and riches, was broken into pieces and shared among the captors. Their mules and horses were laden with the wrought silver and gilt carvings which they tore down from the doors and pulpit. . . . A prostitute was seated on the throne of the Patriarch, and . . . sung and danced in the church to ridicule the hymns and processions of the Orientals.[39]

It was without doubt one of the most shameful episodes in Western history. Pope Innocent III, when he heard the news, was horrified that a Christian army should have abused fellow Christians in this manner. But by the time the messenger had reached him, the damage had long been done. It took only three days for Constantinople, the queen of cities, to be wrecked in a manner from which she was never fully to recover.

Somewhere in all this confusion the Mandylion/Shroud mysteriously disappeared. Very mysteriously. Robert de Clari's words leave no doubt that this was something that had interested him and he had made specific enquiries. "And no one, either Greek or French, ever knew what became of this sydoine after the city was taken." Yet another stage of the Shroud mystery was about to begin.

CHAPTER XIX

1204 TO THE 1350s—

THE MISSING YEARS

Up to the year 1204, despite all the uncertainties, we have had as a source of strength the fact that there was in existence an undoubted historical object called the Mandylion, and this could have been our Shroud. It is perhaps ironic that this should disappear in the very year that the most positive evidence that Mandylion and Shroud are one and the same emerged for the first time.

From 1204 on, all that was previously tangible seems to dissolve into the mists of history. Ahead yawns a period one may term "the missing years," a historical gap of one hundred and fifty years, from the disappearance of what was unquestionably the Mandylion during the crusaders' sack of Constantinople in 1204, to the mysterious appearance of what is undoubtedly the Turin Shroud in France in the 1350s, in the possession of the knight Geoffrey de Charny.

In many ways a gap of this kind in the historical record was to be expected. In view of the problem that had been faced throughout, the apparent lack of an early history for the Turin Shroud, if the Mandylion/Shroud theory is correct, there *had* to be a period of break for the Mandylion's true identity to be forgotten and for the Shroud to emerge, as it does in the fourteenth century, with total ignorance as to its earlier whereabouts. Had this break not occurred, the mystery that has been so difficult to unravel throughout would have been no mystery at all. Even so, however elusive the Shroud/Mandylion may be from 1204 to the 1350s, it is important to offer at least some theory to throw light on those years. The words of Robert de Clari are worth remembering "No one, either Greek or French, ever knew what became of this sydoine after the city was taken."

One thing was certain. The cloth did not stay in the hands of the Greeks. At the outset it is possible that it was some Byzantine who had access to the Pharos Chapel or the sacristy of the Blachernae church, who perhaps slipped in and secreted it away. If he did, he did not retain it long, perhaps being captured or surrendering it at an early stage for much-needed cash. Certainly it never succeeded in reaching the new Byzantine mini-kingdoms formed by survivors at Trebizond and in the Balkans. No mention occurs in their records of that time. Nor, when in 1261 a Byzantine emperor was able to walk back into Constantinople following crusader withdrawal, did the Mandylion come to light. In the fifteenth-century accounts of the fall of Constantinople to the Turks, the robe of the Virgin played a prominent, though unsuccessful, part in the city's attempt to protect itself. But there was no mention of the Mandylion.

Not that the Greeks forgot the cloth they had nurtured for a little more than two and a half centuries. Far from it. It was written into the Byzantine manual of painting in terms that only underline the eucharistic significance that we stressed in the last chapter: "At the summit of these vaults opening from the dome, draw the Holy Mandylion to the east, and opposite to it the Holy Cup."[1]

While the Byzantine artists were never, in fact, entirely rigid in their following of the exact locations prescribed in the manual, the Mandylion's placing varying slightly, they were punctilious in preserving its memory. It came to be portrayed on countless icons, mosaics, and mural paintings throughout the Balkans and Greece, wherever Byzantine artists had fled after Constantinople was taken from them.

It was frequently depicted in Russian art, the Russians having been converted to Christianity by the Byzantines in the tenth century, subsequently inheriting much of their culture, including the Orthodox tradition in art. Thus, from the thirteenth century it is found depicted in the manuscript of Zakhar's "Prologue," and at about the same date on a superb icon of the school of Rostov-Souzdal. Icons of the fifteenth century, removed by some three centuries from works that had been copied directly from the original, took on certain set types of Mandylion, among them the "Savior of the Wet Beard." From the seventeenth century there are several splendid examples, including an icon in the Icon Museum, Recklinghausen, and a majestic version high up in the dome of the Cathedral of the Assumption, Moscow—the location frequently used for the Christ Enthroned, whose relation to the Mandylion has been traced earlier in this work.

About this same time it appeared on a cross reliquary given to the tsar Peter the Great. It bears the inscription ΘΘΘΘ, an abbreviation of a Greek phrase meaning "miraculous and divine vision of God."

Nor did the apparent failure to protect Constantinople diminish the reputation for powers of protection even of copies of the Mandylion. Battling against the Tartars in Kazan in 1532, Tsar Ivan the Terrible carried a representation of the Mandylion as a protective device on his imperial standard, and was victorious. Such was his gratitude that he dedicated to the Mandylion the first Christian church to be established in the Moslem capital city. Russian nobles had their portraits painted with the Mandylion represented floating protectively over them. Palace doorways were overhung with copies of the cloth.

Perhaps the quaintest detail of all is to be found in photographs of Russian troops entering Thessalonica during the First World War, preserved to this day in London's Imperial War Museum. They carry their regimental colors and these can be clearly seen to be a banner of the Mandylion, virtually identical with that used by Ivan the Terrible, and bearing the inscription "God is with us."

The epitaphios, too, came into its own after the fall of Constantinople, becoming, in the words of one British expert on Byzantine tapestries, "the most important vehicle for embroidery in the Orthodox church, and the one on which embroiderers expended their best efforts."[2]

One is almost tempted to believe that this was a Byzantine attempt to compensate for the fact that, while they possessed the Mandylion, they had failed to reveal its true form to the public. Probably so few knew the full story that the secret died in the sack of Constantinople in 1204, just as the secret of the cloth's whereabouts in first-century Edessa died with the persecution of the Christian population by Ma'nu VI. In Jerusalem and other places of Orthodox worship the priests on a Good Friday and Easter eve still adorn the altar with an epitaphios and scatter among the faithful rose petals with which the cloth has been strewn, as a sign of the coming Resurrection. One cannot avoid the reminiscence of the manner in which water used to gently sponge the Mandylion was similarly scattered among the congregation of the Hagia Sophia cathedral in Edessa.

If the Mandylion/Shroud did not stay in Byzantine hands, where did it go? The surprising fact is that it did not, certainly in any recognizable form, appear in the West. Robert de Clari was quite definite that neither Greek nor Frenchman knew what became of the cloth he saw, suggesting that although he made specific enquiries about it, these were to no avail.

There is a certain degree of confusion about the other cloth he reported seeing, the one said to have been given to a holy man of Constantinople, which, in the last chapter, we suggested may have been a copy. Sir Steven Runciman, in an article written in 1929[3] identified this as *the* Mandylion, and went on to trace its subsequent history as that of a *sanctam toellam* or "holy towel" bearing a picture referred to in a document of 1247 as having been sold by the impoverished Latin emperor Baldwin II to St. Louis, king of France.[4] A major difficulty with Sir Steven's identification is that, whatever the cloth referred to in 1246, it was regarded as one of the most minor of the relics purchased at that time, the major acquisition being the reputed Crown of Thorns. Taken, with the Crown of Thorns, to the Sainte Chapelle, it went on to slumber in virtually total obscurity, never mentioned as one of the major relics of the collection. In 1792 it was destroyed during the French Revolution, thus sealing forever any certainty about its nature.

All other considerations aside, it seems inconceivable that a cloth that had such an illustrious earlier history should, once in the West, have suffered such an obscure fate. The very uncertainty of the matter is made quite clear by the existence of no less than two other claimants to identify with the Mandylion, both having survived to this day. One is an icon carefully preserved under lock and key in the sacristy of the Church of St. Bartholemew of the Armenians in Genoa and known to have been given to a Genoese captain, Leonardo Montaldo, by the Byzantine emperor John V Palaeologus in 1362.[5] This has a Byzantine silver-gilt frame bearing scenes of the Mandylion's history, and a clear Greek inscription: TO ΑΓΙΟΝ ΜΑΝΔΗΛΙΟΝ, "The Holy Mandylion." The other is a somewhat similar looking icon of the face of Christ formerly kept in the church of San Silvestro in Capite in Rome, but transferred in 1870 to the Matilda Chapel of the Vatican. Its frame is baroque, made in 1623 by Sordinora Larutia. Both have been identified by art experts as mere copies of the Mandylion, and of around the fourteenth century.

That rival claimants should have such doubtful pedigrees clearly leaves open the possibility that the present-day Shroud of Turin is one and the same as the Mandylion of Byzantine history. If this is the case, however, the odd aspect is that neither in the Byzantine face-on-cloth form nor in the full-length-figure Shroud form that we know today did this cloth come to light during the next century.

In this context it is important to appreciate that the Pharos Chapel, where the Mandylion should have been kept at the time of the Crusade siege, was spared the looting suffered elsewhere. The priceless relic collection that it housed remained intact, and was carefully catalogued by Garnier de Trainel, Bishop of Troyes (ironically a predecessor of Pierre d'Arcis, the Bishop of Troyes who tried so hard to prove the Shroud a fake a little under two centuries later). De Trainel's list of what he found in the chapel has survived.[6] Other objects that had been in the imperial collection are all there. But there is no record of any image-bearing cloth or shroud.

Speculation is unavoidable. Perhaps it had been kept at Blachernae during the critical period, as Robert de Clari suggested, and was stolen from there by some lone crusader. Possibly. The Blachernae area was certainly among the first to be overrun when the crusaders poured into the city in 1204. Why, when the successful crusader returned home, did he not make public his find? Contrary to what we might expect today, there was, at the time of the crusades, no reason for anyone to keep such a relic hidden because he feared punishment for having stolen it. Immediately after Constantinople's sack a weak and tardy ban on the looting of relics was imposed by Count Baldwin of Flanders as part of his attempt to check the abuses and use some of the spoils to pay the Venetians. But too much looting had already gone on for the order to be treated with much respect, and there are numerous accounts of knights and churchmen who returned to the West with stolen relics, to be greeted with adulation, not recrimination. The Bishop of Soissons brought back to a grateful see dozens of relics, including a reputed arm of John the Baptist and the finger which doubting Thomas thrust into Christ's side. The highly respectable monastic establishment at Cluny delightedly received the head of St. Clement, stolen from Constantinople's Church of St. Theodosia. Relics brought trade through pilgrimages to wherever they came to rest. Enormous sums of money were paid for them, the Crown of Thorns alone changing hands for the princely sum of ten thousand marks. There was every incentive to publicize their whereabouts. But no one brought to light the Mandylion/Shroud.

If, therefore, the cloth survived—and de Clari does not suggest that it was destroyed—there would seem to have been devious circumstances in which it "went underground" in a way that has never previously been identified.

For the reasons just mentioned, this was unusual and helps in developing a picture of the unknown keeper or keepers.

The period of "going underground" extends through more than a century and implies a certain continuity of ownership. One must expect a group of owners rather than an individual.

Furthermore, if they were not actually among the crusaders who took Constantinople in 1204, the group must have been closely connected with them. They must have possessed considerable wealth; otherwise surely there would have been too great a temptation to sell the relic, either openly or on the black market. It was, after all, worth a prince's ransom.

They must have had the wherewithal to ensure its concealment and security—no mean feat over five generations. They must have possessed some very strong motive for acting in such a curiously secretive manner. Only Christians would have been interested in keeping the cloth to themselves. Who, therefore, had such a high opinion of themselves that they considered Christ's most precious relic their exclusive right?

Finally, and not least, they must, if the Shroud/Mandylion identification is valid, have had some historical link with Geoffrey de Charny, the French knight who was the Shroud's first authenticated owner. None of this might appear to provide any real substance with which to identify the Shroud's possible guardians between 1204 and the 1350s, but as it happens there is one historical group of suspects who fit these requirements with uncanny precision.

Some eighty years before the capture of Constantinople two French knights, Hugh of Payens and Geoffrey of Saint-Omer, with seven companions had founded the Crusader Order of Knights Templars or "Poor Knights of Christ of the Temple of Solomon,"[7] so called because they were given land close to the site of the ruined Temple in Jerusalem. By 1204 they had become both wealthy and powerful, attracting to their ranks men of the noblest blood, distinguishing themselves as fearless crusaders, and building across Europe and the Near East a series of virtually impregnable fortresses.

In a precarious age these fortresses were of no small importance, and became recognized as useful storehouses for national treasures and valuables of all kinds. Kings and popes alike came to bank with the Templars, giving the "poor knights" the reputation, if not the reality, of possessing enormous wealth. Because of this role the Templars were one of the principal sources of finance for the Fourth Crusade, although they themselves took little part in it. They were also in a position to act as guardians, traders, and pawnbrokers for the flourishing trade in relics, genuine and false alike, that ensued from the Fourth Crusade. Thus the means of acquiring the Mandylion/Shroud were there. Also, the Templars' heavily guarded monastery-fortresses provided the means of keeping the cloth's whereabouts secret for a considerable period. The question that therefore arises is whether there is any valid reason for believing that this might have taken place.

The answer is surprisingly affirmative. The Templars' daytime business dealings with the money entrusted to them were impeccable. But at night dark mysteries surrounded their internal doings. Chapter meetings were held at midnight behind locked doors. Initiates were sworn under pain of death never to reveal the details of the ceremony by which they were admitted to the order. Most significant of all, at the beginning of the fourteenth century all Europe buzzed with gossip and rumors of a strange object they were said to be hiding—a mysterious "head" that they were believed to worship idolatrously at secret ceremonies, prostrating themselves before it to the Saracen war cry "Yallah."

According to one account, ". . . it was a certain bearded head, which they adored, kissed and called their Savior."[8] Another described it as an idol, which

> they venerate as God, as their Savior. Some of them, or most of those who attend the chapters, say that this head can save them, that it has given them all the wealth of the order, that it makes the trees flourish and the earth fruitful. Also they bind or touch this idol with the cords with which they gird themselves.[9]

The mystery cult was no mere rumor. It was of great importance to the Templars, and one of the key factors in the order's downfall. For with the tinge of heresy it raised, it provided the excuse needed by Philip the Fair, king of France, for his long-cherished plan to confiscate the Templars' now legendary wealth by accusing the order of corruption.

In view of the Templars' military strength, Philip could only achieve his plan by surprise. He succeeded brilliantly. At daybreak on Friday, October 13, 1307, acting on orders they had been allowed to open only the day before, seneschals throughout France seized and imprisoned without warning every Templar they could lay their hands on, from the lowliest servant to Jacques de Molay, grand master of the order, along with his private bodyguard of sixty knights. In the hands of Philip's Inquisition, the Templars were subjected to merciless torture and forced to confess to a series of most perverted religious practices, the truth of which has long been argued by historians. Tangled with the knights' "confessions" of their lurid sexual aberrations are found the other confessions of great importance to us, the Templars' own descriptions of the mysterious "idol" or "head."

It is important to consider the possibility that, if indeed the Templars had acquired the Shroud, then they, like the Byzantines, might have displayed it as the "disembodied" head reconstructed in earlier chapters, though no longer with the Parthian trellis cover. Likewise, they may well have had special "holy" copies made, kept in jeweled cases similar to those we know to have been used for the Veronica, for the Sancta Sanctorum Acheropita, etc. It is then significant to discover that, while there is a wide variation in accounts of the "head," for reasons to be considered shortly, the consistent picture is that it was ". . . about the natural size of a man's head, with a very fierce-looking face and beard."[10]

Philip the Fair appears to have known this much before he laid hands on a single Templar. He had informers, but he may even have gathered something of it firsthand, having taken refuge in the Paris Temple during a city riot in 1307. He knew, for instance, that viewing of the head was the privilege only of a special inner circle of the order, as is clear of his instructions to his seneschals that the "ydole" was in the form of

a man's head with a large beard, which head they kiss and worship at all their provincial chapters; but this not all the brothers know, save only the Grand Master and the old ones.[11]

But why should there have been such a fuss about some representation of a man's head? Why should it not have been clear who the man was? Why should only select brethren have been allowed to see it? And why should it have been regarded with fear?

Seasoned knights as they were, those knights who spoke of it—and many refused point-blank—described themselves as having been quite literally terrified. One used this as his ex-

cuse for not being able to describe it, saying that it had filled
him with such terror he hardly knew where he was.[12] Another, Brother Raoul de Gizy, had this to say:

INQUISITOR: Now tell us about the head.
BROTHER RAOUL: Well, the head. I've seen it at seven chap-
    ters held by Brother Hugh de Peraud and others.
INQUISITOR: What did one do to worship it?
BROTHER RAOUL: Well, it was like this. It was presented,
    and everyone threw himself on the ground, pushed
    back his cowl, and worshiped it.
INQUISITOR: What was its face like?
BROTHER RAOUL: Terrible. It seemed to me that it was the
    face of a demon, of a *maufé* [evil spirit]. Every time
    I saw it I was filled with such terror I could scarcely
    look at it, trembling in all my members.[13]

Puzzling as the testimony may seem, the "terror" appears to
have been no act for the benefit of the Inquisition, to throw
them off the scent of finding the head. Its genuineness is readily confirmed for us by a Minorite friar's most graphic description of an incident which took place at a Templar preceptory in England some while before the persecution
began:

He was guest of the Templars at the preceptory of Weth-
erby in Yorkshire, and when evening came he heard that
the preceptor was not coming to supper, as he was arranging some relics he had brought with him from the Holy
Land. And afterwards, at midnight, he heard a confused
noise in the chapel, and getting up he looked through the
keyhole, and saw a great light therein, either from a fire or
from candles, and on the morrow he asked one of the
brethren the name of the Saint in whose honor they had
celebrated so great a festival during the night, and that
brother, aghast and turning pale, thinking he had seen
what had been done among them, said to him, "Go thy
way, and if you love me, or have any regard for your own
life, never speak of this matter."[14]

The crucial question is the head's identity. It is of considerable significance that it is precisely the most holy images of

Christ that caused real fear at this time. Pope Alexander III in the twelfth century had ordered Gregory the Great's Acheropita image in the Sancta Sanctorum chapel to be veiled because it caused a trembling dangerous to life. In the Grail legend it was the image of Christ that similarly made the knight Galahad tremble. So what was the Templar head?

One American author has suggested that it was some Gnostic or Moslem demon that the Templars had taken to worshiping as a result of their long sojourn in the East.[15] But damning though the Templar's confessions appear, there is little convincing evidence for the order's adherence to any non-Christian or satanic cult. For instance, suggestions that the idol was Mahomet are quite absurd because, far more than the Christians, the Moslems shunned any form of portraiture, human or divine.[16]

Moreover, had the Templars become involved in any serious heresy, there would surely have been some martyrs for its cause among such a brave order of knights. Yet there is not a single instance of this in the evidence that has been preserved. They either died under torture, refusing to confess that they held any heresy, or, to put an end to unbearable torment, they "confessed" to the sins of which they were accused, then promptly and unreservedly asked forgiveness. All this was not lost on one of the leading Dominican theologians of the day, Pierre de la Palu, who, although belonging to an order which had no love for the Templars, nevertheless appeared before the Inquisition at great personal risk to state that having heard the trial evidence he found the Templar denials far more worthy of confidence than their apparent confessions.[17]

The possibility must be considered that, rather than heretical or satanic, the Templar head was the divine likeness in a form mortal men were not normally privileged to view; in other words something not only Christian but with the very mystique we have already seen the Byzantines attach to the Mandylion.

In this connection there are several significant clues. For instance, in one of the post-1204 Grail romances, the Templars actually figure as the guardians of the Grail.[18] Like the Grail the Templar "idol" was regarded as having fertility properties; one account specifically states it was "the Savior" who "makes the trees blossom and ripens the harvest."[19] The identity of the head as Christ is hinted at by several sources, some accounts talking of the head being displayed at a ceremony taking place just after the Feast of SS. Peter and Paul. SS. Peter and Paul is celebrated then, as now, on the twenty-ninth of June. The next feast in order in medieval times would have been that dedicated to the Holy Face, celebrated just two days later on July 1.

Insufficient attention has been given to a remark made by the abbot of Lagny in evidence against the Templars to the effect that at their chapters the priest had nothing to do but repeat Psalm 67. Alongside other depositions that the words of consecration were omitted at the special Templar Mass, it can at least be conjectured that the Templars deliberately omitted them (as we are told they were omitted in the Grail legends) because of the believed presence of Christ himself, in a far more positive form than in the normal Mass, via his image. This seems to find ready support from the mention of Psalm 67, this being not only a most beautiful Christian chant but also highly suggestive of the object of Templar adoration:

> God be merciful to us and bless us
> And *cause his face to shine upon us*
> Selah
> that thy way may be known upon earth
> Thy saving health among all nations
> Let all the people praise thee. . . .
>
> Selah
> Let the people praise thee
> O God,
> Let all the people praise thee,
> then shall the earth yield her
> increase
> And God, even our own God, shall
> bless us.
> God shall bless us, and all the
> ends of the earth shall fear him.

As has been noted by the great Inquisition historian Sir Charles Lea, it is certainly strange to find such a chant coming from the lips of men alleged to be idolaters.[20] But more than this, its very content seems to explain certain curious "sins" with which the Templars were charged. For instance, could not the cry "Selah," occurring twice in the psalm, when repeated in unison, have sounded uncannily like the Saracen war cry "Yallah" that the Templars were accused of addressing to their idol? May not the psalm's call for God to make "the earth yield her increase" seem the most likely origin of claims that the Templars held their idol to "make the land produce and the trees blossom?"

Above all, does it not seem plain that the object to which Psalm 67 would have been addressed could scarcely have been some hideous demon—but instead was much more likely a Christian, but terrifying, holy representation of God—in his human likeness as Christ, the Savior of the World?

This is hinted at in the case of a now lost example recorded in Jerusalem in 1277. The Templars' stronghold in Jerusalem, the site of their foundation, was finally overrun by the Moslems in 1244. Thirty-three years later the victorious sultan, Baibars, inspected their castle and is recorded to have discovered inside the tower "a great idol, in whose protection the castle had been placed: according to the Franks who had given it its name [this is an unreadable word, made in diacritic letters]. He ordered this to be destroyed and a *mihrab* constructed in its place."[21]

The French archivist Riant, commenting on the passage, directly suggested, "Could this have been the 'idol' of the Templars, or the image of Christ?"[22] What were for Riant two alternative possibilities, may really have been one. Recalling the Mandylion's renowned palladian properties, the information is surely significant that the castle had been placed in the protection of the "idol."

But by far the most direct piece of evidence for the source of the Templar "idolatry" took the form of a still extant copy that has hitherto gone unrecognized as such. During a severe gale in Somerset, England, in 1951, the ceiling plaster collapsed in the outhouse of a cottage belonging to Mrs. A. Topp in the village of Templecombe. It revealed in the roof, covered with coal dust, a curious panel painting. The presence of a keyhole and hinge marks indicated that at one time it had been used as a door to the cottage coal house. But it clearly had an earlier and more illustrious origin.

For the Templars had in 1185 acquired property in Templecombe and built there a preceptory used for recruiting and training new members of the order before sending them off for active service in the East. From its distinct medieval style there seems little doubt that the painting was once the property of the order in Templecombe. Above all, from its nature as a bearded male head, with a reddish beard, lifesize, disembodied, and, above all, lacking in any identification mark, it corresponds precisely to descriptions of the Templar "idol," of which it may well be the only surviving copy.

Today the restored painting hangs in the tiny Church of St. Mary, Templecombe. It is important because it dispels any idea that the Templar "idol" might have been some form of bust. It conforms, too, to some of the most rational Templar descriptions: "a painting on a plaque,"[23] "a bearded male head," "lifesize,"[24] "with a grizzled beard like a Templar's." (The Templars cultivated their beards in the style of Christ). Its likeness to the Byzantine copies of the Mandylion, although painted in a different (late medieval) style, is, to say the least, remarkable. Perhaps most significantly of all, although appearing to be Christ, it bears no halo, which could well be the explanation for all the mystery about whom the image represented—the statement of some Templars that they thought it was their Savior, the speculation of others, obviously uninitiated, that it might have been Hugh of Payens, the founder of the order. It explains, too, why copies of the Templar head were never found—without identification marks they were not recognized for what they were. But it indicates something more. With the extremes of veneration the Templars paid to their "bearded head," it can scarcely be supposed that their artists ignored a thousand-year-old tradition and omitted the halo out of irreverence. Rather, it would have been because of the desire to reproduce directly a special characteristic of the "original" object from which the copy was made.

The reader can now have little doubt where all this is

leading—to a working hypothesis that the lost Mandylion/Shroud, with its virtually unique, nonhaloed, "true likeness" of God's assumed form, was the original Templar "idol" from which the Templecombe panel and other similar versions in Templar hands were copies. That there were such copies is not only indicated by the variety of descriptions of the idol—some in jeweled cases, others plain—but also by information that in England alone there were four—according to a Minorite friar, one in the sacristy of the Temple in London, another at "Bristleham," a third at Temple Bruern in Lincolnshire, and the fourth at a place beyond the Humber. The manner in which the image was painted in the Templecombe version suggests that, if indeed the original of the Templar idols was the Mandylion/Shroud, it had retained the stretched-out, face-only form.

Comparatively few definitive studies have been published on the Templars, and according to one as yet unpublished source, a manuscript made available by Miss V. Godfrey-White, the knights' relationship with the image of Christ went far deeper.[25] According to Miss Godfrey-White, enormous influence was exerted on the order by St. Bernard of Clairvaux (1091–1153),[26] who made repeated reference in his writings to a "newness of life" with the ultimate purpose that we may be "admitted to contemplate the glory of the unveiled countenance of the Lord Jesus,"[27] "included in the number of those to whom the prophet David alluded when he said 'They shall walk, O Lord, in the light of thy countenance, and in thy name they shall rejoice.'"[28]

As Miss Godfrey-White goes on to show, St. Bernard may have intended the Templars as an elite, privileged to enjoy a fleeting foretaste of the "newness of life" upon earth[29]—in return for the unflinching heroism expected of them in protecting and reclaiming the holy places of Christendom, and for a particularly severe vow of chastity:

> . . . if any of the Brethren do not keep chastity, he cannot come to perpetual rest nor can he see God, as witness the Apostle who says "Search after peace with all, and keep chastity, without which nobody can see God."[30]

St. Bernard almost certainly knew nothing of the Mandylion, and the experience he referred to was most likely, in its early form, psychological only. But wittingly or unwittingly he laid the ground for a cult of the relic, in its Shroud form. Each Templar was given on initiation the exclusive right to wear a white mantle, later superimposed with a red cross, the latter directly symbolic of the crucified body of Christ. The initiation ceremony, over which great secrecy prevailed, took place almost invariably in a copy of the rotunda of the Church of the Holy Sepulcher in Jerusalem. Many Templar churches and chapels were built round with this in mind, and in their center, as at the Templar Vera Cruz Church of Segovia in Spain, there was often an actual model of the tomb of Christ, in the form of a two-storied structure with steps leading up.[31] At some stage the special ceremony was devised for initiated members of the order whereby they were given a momentary glimpse of the supreme vision of God attainable on earth, before which they prostrated themselves in adoration.

The crux of the Templar saga lies in the nature of this ceremony. If they had acquired the Mandylion, the only object that could give them the original likeness of God as he had appeared on earth in human form, still this could not be in all places at once. Just as the Byzantines had created special "acheiropoetic" copies of the Mandylion in the sixth century, generally by placing ordinary painted versions in contact with something that had in turn been in contact with the original, the Templars adopted the same theory for their purposes. In the Inquisition evidence there are several references to members of the order receiving on initiation a little cord that had been in contact with the "head."[32] The panel copies would no doubt have been "treated" the same way.

The parallels with the Byzantines go even deeper. By an ironic twist of history, just as the plethora of images in early Byzantium brought about charges of idolatry, leading to the backlash of iconoclasm, so the Templars ran into exactly the same doctrinal difficulty, despite their attempts to avoid it by secrecy. The Templars appear to have used the same method of worship of their "idols" as that practiced before the holiest images in Byzantium—total prostration, or "proskinesis" as practiced also before the face of the emperor.

It is easy to see how, to uninitiated western eyes this would have appeared not as the ultimate in mortal religious experience, as was intended, but as the grossest idolatry, for which men went to the stake as heretics. Churches contained images, but as objects of instruction, not of direct worship. And for this to be accorded to a human likeness bearing no markings to distinguish it from the earthly order . . . small wonder Templar initiates were sworn never to reveal the details of their ultimate in ceremonies. Small wonder these took place during the night, behind locked doors, with sentinels posted. And small wonder that, in ignorance of the original "idol's" true nature, and accelerated by Philip the Fair's cupidity, the end result was the Templars' cataclysmic downfall. They vainly defended themselves against what were chiefly trumped-up charges of heresy, but concocted with just enough substance to stick.

The question remains of the Shroud's subsequent whereabouts if indeed it was ever in Templar hands. We can only guess at the answer, but we do know the main treasure of the Templars was kept until 1291 at Acre, in their great castle jutting out into the sea. When Acre fell, the treasure was whisked by sea to Cyprus. The knights failed to settle on Cyprus, and the treasure is shortly after described as being taken by sea to Marseilles, then traveling north to Paris in a huge, heavily guarded baggage train. Its home in Paris was to be the new Templar headquarters set up at the Villeneuve du Temple, a huge fortress opposite the king's palace, the Louvre. And it would seem that here, about the beginning of the fourteenth century the original idol, although shown only secretly, attracted the attention that was to become a major factor in the order's downfall.

The servitor Stephen of Troyes told the Inquisition of the mysterious object he saw at one of the Templars' Paris ceremonies. It was

. . . brought in by the priest in a procession of the brethren with lights; it was laid on the altar; it was a human head without any silver or gold, very pale and discolored, with a grizzled beard like a Templar's.[33]

Other descriptions, clearly referring to copies, included mention of gold and silver cases, wooden panels, and the like. But the Paris head is different. One gets the distinct impression that this was the holy of holies, accorded ceremonial strikingly reminiscent of that used by the Byzantines. The paleness and discoloration referred to are clearly characteristic of the Shroud, as of course is the mention of the beard. Even more intriguing is a description from the *Chronicles of St. Denis* in which we are told it seemed to be ". . . an old piece of skin, as though all embalmed and like polished cloth."[34]

To anyone who has seen the Shroud, this is not an altogether impossible description. Even today the cloth is characterized by a surprising surface sheen.

When Philip's men made their surprise swoop on the Paris Temple on the fateful Friday the thirteenth, they met fierce resistance and only afterwards were able to begin searching, in vain, for the Templars' "idol." In England, where Philip later encouraged similar action against the Templars, orders were given for a meticulous inventory to be made of all Templar goods seized.[35] Again nothing was found. One can only speculate on what happened in the short term to the Templars' most precious possession. Certainly the Templars had some awareness that trouble was brewing for them. The order's grand master, Jacques de Molay, had come back to Paris specifically to ask for matters held against them to be cleared up by a papal enquiry. He may have arranged for the "idol" to be safeguarded by the family of one of the local masters of the order. Or, as would seem more likely, it may have been possible for someone to slip away to such a family the relic, cut away from any frame or casket, merely folded inside a jerkin, while the remaining knights fought valiantly against Philip's men.

While pondering such speculation, we come across the most challenging clue of all to the possibility that it was the Templars who had the Shroud, and that it was in the family of one of the masters of the order that it found its new home.

Philip the Fair behaved with abominable cruelty to the Templars, killing most of the knights for heresy, torturing others to death,[36] and holding the leaders in prison for seven years pending sentence to be passed by a papal commission, the only legal body entitled to determine their fate. Pope Clement and his cardinals, embarrassed by Philip's high-handed manner, dallied until March 19, 1314. Then, on a public scaffold in front of Notre Dame, the four principal masters of the order were brought out and asked to repeat their "confessions" before Clement's commissioners, with the promise that if they did so, although they would remain in prison, they would be spared execution.

No one supposed the matter would be anything but a mere formality. Two of the masters accepted the "deal" and were led off to spend the rest of their days in the king's gloomy dungeons. But to the surprise of most present, the remaining two acted differently, and with a courage that rings down the centuries. Pale from considerable suffering and long captivity, the grand master, Jacques de Molay, together with the order's master of Normandy stepped forward with quite unscripted confessions. They had been guilty, they said, not of the crimes imputed to them, but to their shame, of uttering falsehoods about their order under the duress of unbearable torture and the threat of execution. Instead of the scandalous sins and iniquities of which it had been accused, the Templar Order was pure and holy, and had nobly served the cause of Christianity.

This is, of course, entirely consistent with our theory that the Templars were innocent of the Inquisition's charges, and that the object of their worship, although secret, was utterly Christian. But for the papal cardinals the episode was both embarrassing and unexpected. Stunned, they retired to deliberate. They were forestalled by the swift action of Philip the Fair. The Templars had to be silenced before they could do further damage to his reputation. On his own initiative he ordered the immediate execution of the pair as relapsed heretics.

The site chosen was a small island in the Seine, the Ile des Juifs, today incorporated into the Ile de la Cité. As the sun dipped below the Paris housetops, Jacques de Molay and his companion, facing at their own request the Cathedral of Notre Dame, slowly burned to death, refusing all offers of pardon for retraction, and bearing their torment with a composure that won for them among the spectators the reputation of martyrs.

De Molay, it was said, called on the Almighty to bring justice down on Philip the Fair and the pope, and, by one of those strange quirks of fate, both had died painful deaths within a year.

There is one more twist to the story, of considerable relevance to our attempt to reconstruct the history of the Shroud —the name of de Molay's companion at the stake, the aforementioned master of Normandy. It was Geoffrey de Charnay.

CHAPTER XX

FOUND ONCE MORE—AS THE SHROUD

Geoffrey de Charnay, the Templar, was burnt at the stake in 1314. Geoffrey de Charny, first recorded owner of the Shroud in the West, began appearing prominently in French military records from 1337 and lived until 1356. Is it possible that there was a family connection between the two and that by this link the Shroud passed unrecorded from the ruined Order of Knights Templars into the de Charny family of Lirey?

One may discount any problem over the difference in spelling of the two names. Like English spelling up to the time of Dr. Johnson, there was little standardization in medieval French. For clarity we will adopt the most frequent modern usages of the two names, but when one turns to the original documents, Geoffrey the Templar is referred to as "Gaufrido de Charnaio" and "Gaufridus de Charneio" in the *Procès des Templiers;* Geoffrey de Charny of Lirey is referred to as "Joffrois de Chargni," "Geffroy de Chargny," and "Geffroy de Charny" in Froissart, "Gaufridus de Charniaco" in the *Continuation de la chronique de Richard Lescot,* and

"Gyeffroy de Charni" in the *Livre Messire Geoffroy de Charni.*

The real difficulty in trying to trace a relationship is the paucity of information. A genealogical search is being made of the origins or family of Geoffrey the Templar via the Centre d'Entr'aide Généalogique, Paris, so far without success.[1] The most that can be gleaned of his personal history is that he was from Anjou, a province just the other side of Paris from Champagne. He was admitted into the Templar order around the year 1266, at the age of eighteen, and spent some of his time in Cyprus. As we have seen, he rose to become master of Normandy, one of the "grandes dignitaires" of the order, and is unlikely to have married or produced any children because of the strictly imposed vow of chastity. Any lands he might have possessed would have been confiscated by the king during the suppression.

As for the Shroud-owning Geoffrey de Charny, although he was one of France's bravest and most brilliant generals during the reigns of Philip VI and John the Good, there is mystery about his origins. He is referred to as only *probablement* the son of a Burgundian Jean de Charny, who lived about 1314.[2] In the earliest records he is described merely as "messire Geoffrey de Chargny." The impression created by the known details of his life is overwhelmingly of a self-made man—or a man struggling to regain some lost family honor.

In the absence of genealogical proof, one can only speculate that the two Geoffreys were related, perhaps great-uncle and great-nephew. The name de Charny is sufficiently rare to make this moderately likely. The intriguing fact is that the more one learns of the life of the younger de Charny, the more his possession of the Shroud as a secret Templar inheritance makes sense.

One of the points stressed about him back in Chapter X was his virtually unquestionable integrity. His exploits in battle won him many honors, and the English chronicler Froissart described him on the field of Poitiers as the bravest and most *prud'homme* of all combatants.

Yet a pall of mystery seems to hang over how Geoffrey acquired the Shroud. His military adventures took him throughout Europe and the Near East, hence there was every

The Vignon markings—how Byzantine artists created a living likeness from the Shroud image. (1) Transverse streak across forehead, (2) three-sided "square" between brows, (3) V shape at bridge of nose, (4) second V within marking 2, (5) raised right eyebrow, (6) accentuated left cheek, (7) accentuated right cheek, (8) enlarged left nostril, (9) accentuated line between nose and upper lip, (10) heavy line under lower lip, (11) hairless area between lower lip and beard, (12) forked beard, (13) transverse line across throat, (14) heavily accentuated owlish eyes, (15) two strands of hair.

Vignon markings on the eleventh-century Christ Pantocrator at Daphni. All of the listed markings appear except numbers 6 and 7.

	Enthroned Portraits					
MARKING	S. Apollinare Nuovo (6th C)	S. Pontianus (8th C)	Hagia Sophia Narthex (10th C)	S. Angelo in Formis (10th C)	Daphini Pantocrator (11th C)	Cefalù (12th C)
1 Transverse streak across forehead		√	√	√	†	√
2 3-sided square between brows		√	√	†	†	†
3 V shape at bridge of nose		√	√	√	√	√
4 Second V within marking 2					√	√
5 Raised right eyebrow		√		√	√	√
6 Accentuated left cheek	√	√	√	√		√
7 Accentuated right cheek	√	√		√		√
8 Enlarged left nostril	√		√	√	√	√
9 Accentuated line between nose & upper lip	√	√	√	√	√	√
10 Heavy line under lower lip	√	?	√	√	√	√
11 Hairless area between lower lip & beard	√	?	√	√	√	√
12 Fork-beard				√	√	√
13 Transverse line across throat				√	√	√
14 Heavily accentuated owlish eyes	√	√		√	√	√
15 2 strands of hair	√		√	√	√	√

† v. stylised
? painting obliterated at these points

Incidence of the Vignon markings on portraits of Christ Enthroned in Byzantine art.

Nonsuffering version of the Veronica, fifteenth-century French panel painting, artist unknown.

Above: Seventeenth-century icon of the Mandylion in the collection of H.M. the Queen, Buckingham Palace. *(Collection of the Queen's Pictures, Buckingham Palace; by courtesy of H.M. Queen Elizabeth)*

Right: The Shroud (detail). The cloth Byzantines called the "Mandylion" disappeared in the thirteenth century. The cloth we call the "Shroud" appeared mysteriously in France in the fourteenth century. Could they have been one and the same thing?

Mandylion (detail) from fresco
of Spas Nereditsa (now destroyed).

Vignon markings on 1199 copy of Mandylion at Spas Nereditsa:
(1) transverse streak across forehead, (2) three-sided square between brows (very stylized), (3) V shape at bridge of nose, (4)
second V within marking 2, (9) accentuated line between nose
and upper lip, (10) heavy line under lower lip, (11) hairless area
between lower lip and beard, (12) forked beard, (14) heavily
accentuated owlish eyes.

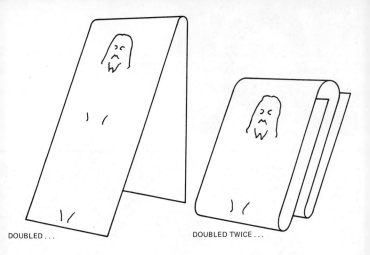

DOUBLED . . .

DOUBLED TWICE . . .

Reconstruction of the Shroud "doubled in four." The burn marks would not, of course, have been present before 1532.

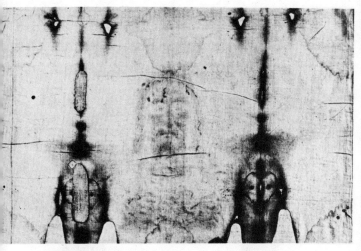

DOUBLED IN FOUR:

How the Shroud may have looked in the tenth century.
A. Mandylion copy, Spas Nereditsa

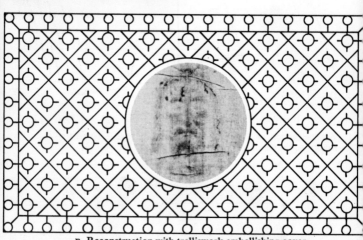

B. Reconstruction with trelliswork embellishing cover

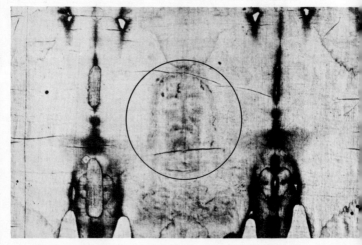

c. The Shroud today. The disfiguring burn marks were not made until 1532.

opportunity for him to "discover" it abroad. But not a single contemporary document suggests this. A late text implies that he may have been given it by "the king." But again, no document of the time records this, despite the survival of excellent archival sources. In fact, despite Geoffrey's valor, it would have been quite out of keeping for any French monarch to make such a gift to a commoner, even supposing there were evidence that the French monarchy once possessed the Shroud, which there is not.

The real core of the mystery, already hinted at in Chapter X, seems to concern the curiously neglected fact that no actual record of Geoffrey's possession of the Shroud seems to occur in his lifetime. It is important that we review some of the known details.

In June 1353 Geoffrey is known to have obtained from King John the Good a "rent" with which to found the collegiate church of Lirey. The canons of this church are known to have eventually housed the Shroud there. Although many authors impute the donation of the Shroud to the year 1353, the fact is that in the deeds of the church's foundation, normally full of details of donated relics, etc., there is absolutely no mention of the Shroud.[3]

The significance of this omission is reinforced when, on May 28, 1356, the completed church was accorded a eulogistic address by the diocesan bishop, Henry of Poitiers. Again no mention of the Shroud is made. As noted in Chapter X, Henry of Poitiers is the very bishop who, according to his successor Pierre d'Arcis, was responsible for all the fuss that the Shroud was a forgery. It seems inconceivable that, had the forgery episode already occurred, he would be found praising the canons and their founder as liberally as he did on this occasion. Yet if the forgery episode had not taken place, there was scant time left for it to do so, as within four months Geoffrey was lying dead on the field of Poitiers.

From 1357 has survived a complete list of the relics in the Lirey collegiate church, derived from a letter signed by twelve bishops granting indulgences to those who came to venerate them.[4] Geoffrey was now dead, but still the Shroud is not mentioned. Similarly it is not referred to in the special

Mass which, as required by their foundation, the Lirey canons were obliged to say for Geoffrey's soul.

Did Geoffrey publicly reveal his possession of the Shroud at any stage of his lifetime? It seems that he did not. Then why did Bishop d'Arcis, writing forty years later, associate him with the expositions suppressed by Bishop Henry of Poitiers? The clue to what really happened at Lirey seems to lie in a damaged, but still distinct, pilgrim's medallion preserved in the Musée de Cluny, Paris. This was discovered during the nineteenth century by a Frenchman, A. Forgeais, who specialized in retrieving old historical amulets from the Seine, the one in question being found by the Pont au Change.[5] The medallion represents a shroud being held up by two clerics wearing copes, and Forgeais mistakenly supposed it to be the so-called Shroud of Besançon. But the French archivist M. Perret[6] has recently shown Forgeais to be wrong. First, the shroud itself has the frontal and dorsal images so characteristic of the Shroud of Turin, whereas the Besançon shroud is always depicted as a frontal image only. The most conclusive evidence, however, lies in the coats of arms on either side of a quaint representation of the Holy Sepulcher. The left-hand coat of arms is unquestionably that of Geoffrey de Charny, corresponding precisely to Froissart's description: ". . . gules, three inescutcheons argent"—i.e., three small shields on a red ground. The right-hand coat of arms is that of Geoffrey's second wife, Jeanne de Vergy.

The very existence of this medallion supports d'Arcis's otherwise unconfirmed information that there was a popular cult of the Shroud at this early period—it is in fact the earliest known full-length representation of the Shroud. But the real point of interest is the inclusion of the arms of Jeanne de Vergy. They raise the possibility that, instead of the expositions having taken place in Geoffrey's lifetime, they were conducted on the instructions of his widow after his death—i.e., sometime between 1357 and the death of Bishop Henry of Poitiers in 1370.

This opens up an entirely new field of thought, and one much neglected by previous researchers. In particular it raises what from the evidence seems not at all an unlikely possibility, that Geoffrey had some particularly strong reason for not wishing to state how the Shroud had come into his possession;[7] also that, although he seemed to be making plans to announce the Shroud's existence, he was not able to do so before his death.

Why should this have been the case? After all, we know that Geoffrey was a deeply religious man, as is quite clear from his composition of somewhat turgid religious verse and his foundation of the collegiate church. It cannot have been that the Shroud was of no interest to him. Also, he certainly enjoyed friendly relations with Bishop Henry of Troyes, at least up to May 28, 1356, as is quite clear from the latter's enthusiastic presence at the completion of the Lirey church. So why could he not take the latter into his confidence about the Shroud? It is clear that he did not, for the bitter accusations of fraud described by Pierre d'Arcis need otherwise never have taken place.

The whole issue revolves around the deep mystery of how Geoffrey came to acquire the Shroud, and it is important to establish the right guidelines. If he had obtained it legally, there is not the slightest reason why he should have been secretive over its existence. Yet everything seen so far suggests he was secretive.

Similarly, when d'Arcis accused the family of fraud thirty or so years later, this was surely the time for them to quash the clamor by giving a clear explanation of how the cloth came into their possession. Yet it is apparent that they did not do so.

Had Geoffrey obtained the cloth illegally? If the answer is yes, the immediate question is how. It is quite inconsistent with what we know of his character for him to have stolen the cloth, there being in any case no one at that time on record as possessing the relic or reporting its loss. The reader will by now be realizing the trend of the evidence—that Geoffrey had inherited the Shroud from the Templars. His reticence in these circumstances would therefore be readily understandable. The memory of their savage downfall was too recent for something so closely involved with it to be revealed without careful preparation.

When the hard evidence for this is considered, some of the references made by Bishop d'Arcis more than thirty years after Geoffrey's death take on a hitherto unsuspected meaning. D'Arcis, the bishop whose memorandum to Pope Clement VII provides the strongest part of the case for the Shroud being a fourteenth-century forgery, was, it may be recalled, a legal expert of no small standing. He could be expected to choose his words carefully, and in this context his closing remarks to the pope bear more careful scrutiny than they have hitherto been accorded:

> . . . if health had allowed I should have presented myself personally to your Holiness to state my complaint to the best of my ability, for I am convinced that I cannot fully or sufficiently express in writing the grievous nature of the scandal, the contempt brought upon the Church . . . and the danger to souls.[8]

Now d'Arcis scarcely showed restraint in his denunciation of the Shroud's exhibitors, accusing them of fraud, avarice, and downright misrepresentation. What scandal was it, therefore, that he could not mention in writing? What recent historical event might the Shroud have been associated with that could, if resurrected, have brought a hornet's nest down around the Church's ears?

Though it has hitherto been unsuspected, careful examination of what is known from the writings and activities of Geoffrey's last years strongly suggests that at the back of his mind he was planning a revival of the Templar order in a new and different form.

On New Year's Eve, December 31, 1349, Geoffrey was captured by the English during a secret night attack on Calais. He spent some eighteen months languishing in prison in England, in which time he had ample opportunity to ponder the future role of the grim relic we suspect lay hidden in his strongbox back in France. As the story runs, the idea came to him that, should he be released, he would build a church in honor of the Virgin Mary. No sooner had this thought passed through his mind than two angels appeared, opened the doors of his prison, and he was set free.

History offers a slightly less fanciful version. What secured Geoffrey's release was not angels but hard cash—payment by his king, John the Good, of a substantial ransom of twelve thousand gold écus, which enabled him to return to France sometime around July 1351. But it was not unusual in medieval times for those in mortal peril, such as sickness or captivity, to make vows to go on a pilgrimage or perform some pious task, should they be spared. A century earlier St. Louis had made and fulfilled a similar vow when stricken by a serious illness. Geoffrey may well, therefore, have seen the payment of the ransom as the miraculous answer to his prayers, and this is what determined him after his release to carry out his private pledge to build the Lirey church.

This is borne out by the five years between his release and his death in 1356, a period which reveals a markedly stronger religious outlook than had hitherto been apparent. Despite almost nonstop military activity due to the ever-present dangers from the English, he found time to set in motion the Lirey foundation. And to this period may be ascribed Geoffrey's composition of his streams of verse and prose on chivalry, none of it of great literary merit, but highly illuminating as to his frame of mind.

Chivalry, the pursuit of the knightly ideal, was very much in vogue, crossing all national frontiers, even if it tended to be applied exclusively to those of noble class. But with Geoffrey it went deeper, taking on a strange melancholy piety. What is most striking about his writings is the strong religious connotations with which they are charged, often almost indistinguishable from those of the defunct Templars. This is clearly seen in the mode of reception he proposed for the initiate knight:

. . . when one wishes to make a new knight, first it is fitting that he should confess and repent. Then, the day before reception, he should be immersed in a bath, minded that his body should be cleansed of all sin. Then he should go to lie on a freshly made bed with white sheets, which signifies the repose of conscience.

After this the knights should come to dress him in clean linen, symbolizing that from this time on he should be thought pure and free from sin. Then should be added a crimson garment, which represents that he is prepared to shed his blood to defend the faith of Our Lord. And then he should put on black leggings, as a reminder that it is from the earth that he had come, and to the earth he will return. He should also be girded with a completely white belt, signifying that he should live in chastity. . . . Then he should be conducted with great joy to the church, and there solemnly await daybreak, praying to Our Lord that he would pardon the evil days and nights of times past. And on the coming of the next day they should go to Mass.[9]

The baptism, the white garments, the night vigil, the white belt, the emphasis on chastity, the daybreak Mass—all find ready parallels in what we are able to deduce of the Templars' reception ceremony. And Geoffrey stressed chivalry's close compatibility with the role of a priest—again recalling the warrior-monk life of the Templars.[10]

But there is more. On January 6, 1352, scarcely six months after his release from captivity, Geoffrey became one of the founder knights of an exclusive new religious-military order, the Order of the Star,[11] pledged, like the Templars, never to flee in battle. Directly recalling the Grail romances, the order was set up "on the style of the Round Table," and the cofounder with Geoffrey was his similarly religiously minded king, John the Good.

Was Geoffrey trying to revive the Templars under a different name? Did he intend the Shroud to again become the object of worship for a select order of rigorously initiated knights? The Order of the Star was too short-lived to make this clear. According to one account it was broken up in the very year of its foundation. According to another it survived only three or four years longer, as the Order of Our Lady of the Noble House.[12] Certainly, like Geoffrey himself, it did not survive the Battle of Poitiers.

If one might point to one day on which, more than any other, the mystery of the Shroud's origins was sealed, that day must be September 19, 1356, the day of the Battle of Poitiers.

Five miles from the main town, amid a landscape little changed to this day, Geoffrey and his king rode out to meet the English army of the Black Prince. Geoffrey's role was a particularly proud one, for little more than a year earlier, in recognition of his valor, he had been appointed *porte-oriflamme,* bearer of the sacred banner of St. Denis, the royal battle standard of France. It was this banner, of red silk split into points like a flame and borne on a gilt staff, which Geoffrey carried as they surveyed, from a high ridge, the English army drawn up behind a hedge.

Ostensibly, the French should have won. They outnumbered the English three to one; they were better placed; and, in deciding to make their attack on foot, they thought they had learned the lessons from their disastrous defeat at Crécy ten years earlier. As it happens, they vastly underestimated the brilliant strategy of Edward the Black Prince combined with the immensely superior firepower of the English long bow.

Froissart, perhaps the father of all war correspondents, has left to posterity a more than usually detailed and vivid account of the fighting, culminating in the episode in which the recklessly chivalrous King John the Good stuck steadfastly to his vow never to flee in battle. When all was clearly lost, he stayed on foot, ax in hand, in a last desperate bid to save his throne. Froissart specifically notes that Geoffrey de Charny was by his side, "the whole of the hunt upon him" because of the clearly visible banner, bearing himself with unfaltering courage in hopeless circumstances. It was Geoffrey's ax that felled an Englishman about to strike John down. It was with his own body, the banner of France still in his hands, that he stopped the final lance-thrust before the king despairingly surrendered and was taken into captivity.

So the English made their first, and as it happens, decisive mark on the Shroud's history. In taking Geoffrey's life, and with him most of his fellow members of the Order of the Star, who also vainly stood their ground on the battlefield, they effectively severed for all time the vital information about the Shroud's past that Geoffrey might, at some future stage, have been intending to reveal. Geoffrey's intentions with their Templar overtones must remain in the realm of speculation.

But if it was not Geoffrey who brought about the expositions of the Shroud that so incensed Bishop Henry of Poitiers, who was the real offender? From Geoffrey one must turn to those left behind, in particular to his widow, Jeanne de Vergy. What is known about her? She was still a comparatively young woman, left with a son of tender years (another Geoffrey de Charny, whom to avoid confusion we will call Geoffrey II), together with responsibility for a very new church composed of a dean and five canons, whose foundation had been something very close to her husband's heart.

It is important to consider her predicament, particularly her financial circumstances. Although Geoffrey was very highly regarded by his king, there is no evidence to suggest that he was a rich man. His only lands of any consequence were minor seigneuries that, due to the devastations of the Hundred Years' War, would have yielded little income. Both the kings under whom he served had financial difficulties, and in 1349 Geoffrey's annual grant of one thousand livres was actually cut to five hundred livres, to be paid in rents from the seneschalties of Toulouse, Beaucaire, and Carcasonne.[13] Although in compensation this was made a hereditary right, the choice of these seneschalties could scarcely have been to Geoffrey's advantage, for they were far to the south, and suffered badly from the English invasion. Nor would his prolonged absences from his estates have helped the collection of these dues, which was always notoriously inefficient.

This situation is made even clearer by the fact that while other French noble families paid their own ransom money when captured, Geoffrey's ransom of 1352 was paid by the king, after a delay of eighteen months.[14] History specifically records that this gesture by John the Good was in lieu of other payment for Geoffrey's services.[15]

As for the foundation of the Lirey chapel, this was not the work of a rich man. It was a modest structure of wood,[16] which fell into considerable disrepair in less than a century.[17] The upkeep of its dean and canons was paid by an annual rent of 140 livres made out by the king in Geoffrey's favor in June 1353,[18] specifically for this purpose, a grant which, without doubt, was seriously jeopardized by the king's capture and imprisonment in England immediately following Geoffrey's death in September 1356.

That Jeanne de Vergy was indeed in very real financial

difficulties after Geoffrey's death is confirmed by the fact that within two months of the Battle of Poitiers she begged the regent of France for letters officially passing over donations previously granted to her husband for the benefit of their son.[19] No time was lost in preparing the letters; they were signed on November 21, 1356. It is unlikely that they were of much help to her. Following the battle all France was in a dreadful state. Even before the battle, prices were rising alarmingly. Politically the country was in an unprecedented situation, with the throne technically vacant, even though the king was still alive, in prison in England. The Dauphin was a minor, inviting several plots to oust the Valois line from the French throne. The countryside was being ravaged by marauding bands of English and Navarrese troops. And from England came the demand for a ransom of three million écus for John the Good's release.

For a family that relied so heavily on the king's patronage, such times must have been very hard. And in the circumstances, with no husband to support her, Jeanne could scarcely regard Geoffrey's beloved foundation as anything but an expensive luxury that would have to be disbanded. Undoubtedly this would have been the inevitable outcome but for a piece of inspiration that came perhaps from Jeanne, perhaps from the Lirey clergy. If money was not to be had from estates or from the king, what about the Shroud? Couldn't the bloodstained relic from Geoffrey's strongbox be used as a sure source of income? Wouldn't this indeed be the fitting way of saving the church so dear to Geoffrey's heart?

The modern reader might question how this would be possible, but to the medieval mind it would have been obvious. The power of relics to attract crowds of pilgrims had not diminished; rather it had reached an all-time peak only six years earlier. The year 1350 had been declared a Papal Jubilee Year, and many thousands had flocked to Rome for the special expositions of the Holy Veronica that were now a regular feature of these events. All who made such journeys brought offerings of money to expedite the relic's powers of salvation, and, of course, like modern tourists, they bought pious souvenirs such as the de Charny medallion already referred to. Above all, there was a vogue at precisely this time for dwelling in morbid detail on the more horrendous aspects of Christ's Passion. This trend had come with the teachings of St. Francis of Assisi a century earlier, and Francis's assumption of the stigmata following a special vision of Christ. Artists now showed copious bleeding in their renderings of the crucifixion where previously depiction of Christ's blood was restrained or absent altogether. Mystics such as the English Richard Rolle of Hampole (ca. 1300–49) and St. Bridget of Sweden (1303–73), contemporary with Jeanne de Vergy, attracted much attention by their lurid and graphic visions of how Christ died, a popular preoccupation intensified by the fact that at this time the Black Death was sweeping Europe. The climate was therefore exactly right for the appearance of such a macabrely detailed relic of the Passion as the Shroud.

What Jeanne de Vergy could not anticipate was the severe shock its revelation would cause, and the sheer disbelief that would be aroused by its introduction from such an inexplicably humble quarter. For, as already noted, Jeanne was still comparatively young, and the Lirey clergy were new and inexperienced. They seem to have failed to appreciate that the very momentousness of what they had brought to light was bound to cause enormous consternation. Had it been a reputed nail of the crucifixion, an arm of John the Baptist, or a finger of St. Thomas, few questions would have been asked. Relics such as these were part of everyday life. Their very anonymity made them plausible and acceptable. But the Shroud was something different. A fourteen-foot length of linen, stained with the blood of Christ, and bearing the image of the back and front of his crucified body—why, it was incredible! Was there anything in the Gospels to suggest that such a stupendous relic was preserved? Where had it been before this time? And how had it come into the hands of this relatively modest French family? The memorandum of Pierre d'Arcis is clear testimony that precisely these questions were asked.

It is also clear from the complete absence of any reference to him in the available documents that Geoffrey I was not around to offer an explanation when the matter came up; the reasonable inference from this being that he was already dead. As for Jeanne and the Lirey clergy, they appear to have been tongue-tied by all the controversy, and either unable or unwilling to throw any light on how they had come by the cloth, apart from the implication that it had belonged to Geoffrey.

The Bishop of Troyes's enquiry could scarcely fail, in these circumstances, to cast serious doubts on the honesty of the Shroud's exhibitors. The de Charny family's strained financial resources offered an obvious solution—the cloth was the work of an artist who had cunningly painted it, the motives of the dean and his canons "only of gain," a point that d'Arcis repeatedly emphasizes.

All that was needed was an artist prepared to attest that the Shroud was "a work of human skill, and not miraculously wrought or bestowed." This, one may judge, was the unfortunate manner in which the Shroud made its first public appearance on the western historical scene. It was quickly over. From the absence of any known formal action taken against them, Jeanne and the canons appear to have been too frightened to uphold their right to the expositions, and hurriedly secreted the cloth away again to await a less hostile era.

Immediate events made it easier for them to do so. The financial burden was given a welcome lift in 1358, when Geoffrey II was granted estates confiscated from Josserand de Macon, which had been long due to Geoffrey I for his valor at the siege of Breteuil in July 1356, three months before his death. Jeanne herself remarried a little while later, becoming the wife of Aymon of Geneva, a wealthy and influential nobleman who was uncle of the future Clement VII, an Avignon pope who was to play a major part in the drama to follow. After the furor the Shroud was stored safely away from possible controversy, probably at the de Charny castle at Montfort.

In 1370 Jeanne de Vergy and her now grown son, Geoffrey II de Charny, watched proudly as, at long last, in the Eglise des Célestins, Paris, the remains of Geoffrey I de Charny were solemnly transferred to a hero's tomb, paid for by the king.

Another nineteen years went by before expositions were renewed. The fact that Geoffrey's son and successor renewed the expositions is important. That it was done at all is remarkable, bearing in mind the earlier hostility. But the most intriguing aspect is the manner in which Geoffrey II went about it. This reveals clearly that, as an honorable and now seasoned knight like his father, he was aware of the possible recurrence of trouble over the issue of the Shroud's origins, yet determined despite this that the relic should be made known and established.

Ironically, most of the evidence on which the events may be reconstructed derive, of necessity, from the formidable d'Arcis memorandum. Although hostile, it has a fund of reliable information. For instance d'Arcis makes it clear that, unlike his father, Geoffrey II openly involved himself in the struggle to establish the Shroud as an object of pilgrimage. D'Arcis describes him as holding out the Shroud in his own hands to display it to pilgrims on important feast days, and when attempts were made to stop the expositions, he himself made approaches to the necessary authorities on the Lirey canons' behalf.

It is important, therefore, that we know something of the manner of man Geoffrey II was. His integrity seems to have been every bit as strong as that of his father. Six years after the latter's death he took up a military career, participating in the recapture of French territories lost to the English, first under the Count of Tancarville, and later under the Duke of Burgundy. The able and methodical King Charles V of France had succeeded John the Good, and for him Geoffrey carried out confidential diplomatic work. By 1371 most of the ground won by the Black Prince had been regained by the French, and in 1375 Geoffrey was rewarded for his part by being appointed to the post of *bailli* for Caux.

Few Shroud scholars have stopped to ask what this post was, merely translating it, with little further thought, as "bailiff." In fact, the post involved considerably more. The *bailli*, the northern equivalent of *seneschal*, was responsible directly to the king for a region of which generally he was not a native. His functions were something of the order of mayor, chief of police, judge, tax collector, and army mobilization officer all in one. In terms of influence Geoffrey was well placed, with the kind of post in which there was little likelihood of finding himself in financial difficulties. The year

1388 saw him transferred to the larger region of Mantes, a town which must have stirred family memories, having been the scene of a treaty between John the Good and Charles the Bad of Navarre back in 1354 at which Geoffrey I had been one of the chief negotiators.

By 1389 he was a highly respected and well-rewarded individual, with few apparent leanings to involve himself in a religious feud. What therefore impelled him to renew the Shroud expositions, and why did he choose this time? First, it is apparent that the Shroud expositions were no mere whim but the result of careful thought and preparation.

On the political scene King Charles VI of France, a boy of twelve at the death of his father, had been on the throne for more than ten years, and a year earlier had more or less fully taken over the role of kingship from his four regent uncles. Geoffrey, therefore, chose a rare settled period, fortuitously as it happened. Three years later the king lost his reason and spent most of the next thirty years in an enfeebled state of mind, to the general disruption of the realm.

As for the motives that impelled Geoffrey to act at this time, perhaps one may be forgiven for suggesting, with little positive evidence to go on, the influence of Jeanne de Vergy, now of advanced years. The date of her birth is not known, but she can have been little short of sixty at this time, no mean age for this period. Only a year earlier she had lost her second husband, Aymon of Geneva, uncle of the reigning Avignon pope, Clement VII. She may well now have pressed her son to revive the veneration of Geoffrey I's beloved Shroud and extinguish the old controversy, both before her own death and, more particularly, before her strong family link with the pope could grow cold.

In this connection it seems to be more than just a twist of fate that her son, Geoffrey de Charny II, should have married Marguerite de Poitiers, niece of the very Henry of Poitiers, Bishop of Troyes, who during the 1350s had condemned the Shroud as a mere painting. In an age when marriages were frequently "arranged" for social and political advantage, it is not unreasonable to suppose that Jeanne thought such a matrimonial alliance would both seal old wounds and provide her son with useful connections to what was a highly episcopal family.

But her prime target appears to have been Pope Clement VII, her nephew through her recently deceased husband. Clement, although the first of the "antipopes" of the Great Western Schism, was recognized as head of the church throughout France. There are strong indications that he was party to at least some of the true facts behind the Shroud's origin before any complaint arose, and thereby partial to the de Charny cause. This is implicit in the careful arrangement that went into renewing the expositions of the Shroud, in which a substantial degree of family influence can be detected.

It is significant that Geoffrey II, a layman, made no attempt to refer to Pierre d'Arcis, Bishop of the Troyes diocese in which the Lirey church was situated, and the obvious man to approach. Instead he went higher, and obtained the necessary permission with suspicious ease from Cardinal de Thury, Clement's legate and nuncio. It was under this cover that the Shroud was exposed to the veneration of many thousands of visitors on feasts and holidays.

Difficult though it is to be sure of procedural matters during this time, it seems scarcely orthodox that de Thury should have made no attempt to consult d'Arcis in the matter or even formally to notify him that he had given such permission. D'Arcis positively states that he was ". . . neither cited nor heard,"[20] and goes on to point out that in Lirey the letters of the cardinal were regarded as approval by the pope himself, which one suspects they may well have been.

The most indicative feature of some prior collusion is, however, that as a cautious measure to avoid the previous controversy, Geoffrey and Clement appear to have thought out and agreed in advance to a careful formula for describing the cloth that admitted any direct claim for it as the true Shroud.

This feature has embarrassed previous Shroud authors, who have tried to gloss over it one way or the other. It has also been used as a trump card by those who have opposed the Shroud's authenticity. For the fact is that in the various contemporary documents we possess Geoffrey II referred to

the cloth only as an image or likeness. This is the way it was
described in de Thury's authorization, which Geoffrey presented as his permission to conduct the expositions, and
which was presumably to his liking. But as d'Arcis was quick
to realize:

. . . although it is not publicly stated to be the true shroud
of Christ, nevertheless this is given out and noised abroad
in private, and so it is believed by many, the more so because, as stated above, it was on the previous occasion [i.e. in 1356/57] declared to be the true shroud
of Christ. . . .[21]

This passage is extremely important, for it really gives in a
nutshell what Geoffrey was trying to do, and why the Shroud
came to be regarded, up to our own time, as a fourteenth-
century forgery.

Geoffrey, the cautious king's official, trained in patient di-
plomacy by the court of Charles V, was probably using his
family connections to establish a foothold of respectability for
the Shroud, circumspectly introducing it as an image or likeness (for it was this, too) in the hope that by reputation in
the course of years its true nature as Christ's relic would be
recognized and its future assured. The need for uncontested
acceptance was the whole point of omitting to describe it
openly as the true Shroud. It was also the reason for referring directly to papal authority, in order to minimize inter-
ference and maximize the chances of success.

If there is any lingering suspicion that Geoffrey may have
genuinely thought the Shroud was only a copy or representation, this may be totally dispelled not only by the lengths to
which he went in defending the expositions but more particularly by the exceptional manner in which he exhibited it.
While the Shroud appellation might be omitted for purposes
of expediency, the ceremonial that Geoffrey insisted should be
attached to its exposition clearly revealed what he believed
in his heart:

. . . the cloth was openly exhibited and shown to the
people in the church aforesaid on great holidays, and fre-

quently on feasts and at other times, with the utmost solemnity, even more than when the Body of Christ our Lord
is exposed: to wit, by two priests vested in albs with stoles
and maniples and using the greatest possible reverence,
with lighted torches and upon a lofty platform constructed
for this special purpose. . . .[22]

With little doubt it was this ceremonial, sheer idolatry if
the cloth was only a painted copy, that more than anything
else incensed Bishop d'Arcis.

This is the heart of the complex issues brought to light by
the d'Arcis memorandum, and through these apparently con-
tradictory circumstances there are very strong reasons for
Geoffrey and Clement to act the way they did, particularly in
order that the Shroud's origin should not be revealed.

It was not simply a case of Geoffrey wanting to suppress
his family's association with the fallen order. The issue went
considerably deeper, threatening the entire shaky founda-
tions of the Avignon papacy. It had been an Avignon pope,
Clement V, who had played a prominent part in the suppression of the Templars, goaded on by the French king Philip
the Fair. Now in 1389, with another Clement at Avignon,
there was strong pressure for the papacy to be returned to
Rome, where there was already a holder recognized outside
France, in the person of Benedict IX. It only needed French
passions about the reputed innocence of the Templars to be
stirred again, brought about by revelations that their "idol"
had been no Moslem demon but the Shroud of Christ, and
Clement's authority, along with his splendid Avignon palace,
would be worth nothing.

All this, of course, could not have been known to Pierre
d'Arcis. And one can fully understand this highly intelligent
and responsible prelate's reaction to what must to him have
appeared outrageously fraudulent and idolatrous conduct.
Abuses relating to relics were notorious at this time—evident,
among many other sources, from any schoolboy's reading of
the Pardoner in Chaucer's *Canterbury Tales*.

Here was a knight with a piece of cloth that more than
thirty years ago had been claimed as the Shroud and invoked
such a searching enquiry about where it had come from that

it had been guiltily withdrawn without any explanation offered. This was a clear enough indication that it had been made fraudulently. The knight was now not openly saying what it was, yet was attracting thousands of pilgrims—and their offerings—by rumor that it was the Shroud. And he was using backdoor methods, approaching the papal representative to authorize the expositions rather than his local bishop, who would, after all, know more about the matter. All this could scarcely have seemed more clear-cut evidence for fraud and misrepresentation, and Bishop d'Arcis was not afraid to say so.

What he did not know was that Clement already knew of the Shroud, knew equally clearly that its origin must not come to light, and was determined that his relations' right to the expositions should be upheld.

This undoubtedly lay behind the otherwise inexplicable manner in which Clement acted. Presented with such a formidable complaint from a loyal and well-established bishop of one of the major sees in Christendom, any self-respecting pope would surely have seen clear need for the circumstances to be investigated. Yet Clement's first reaction was to try to stifle the issue, upholding the de Thury letters of authority and, without any enquiry into the circumstances, sentencing d'Arcis to "perpetual silence."

His difficulty was that he was dealing with a bishop of some mettle. D'Arcis had great pride in his reputation as a jurist and was not to be silenced, even by a pope, when injustice was being allowed to go unchecked only eleven miles from his doorstep. This is what brought into being the powerful memorandum, in which d'Arcis made no bones about his astonishment at Clement's attitude.

> . . . it is a wonder to all who know the facts of the case that the opposition which hampers me in these proceedings comes from the Church, from which quarter I should have looked for vigorous support, nay, rather have expected punishment if I had shown myself slothful or remiss. . . .[23]

What is surprising is not Clement's subsequent limitations on the Lirey expositions, which the Shroud opponents have made so much of, but the extent to which he was prepared to go to uphold Geoffrey de Charny. Even though challenged this far, he still refused an enquiry. As a concession to d'Arcis he asked for a modification of the number of candles used and the richness of vestments worn, and he reaffirmed that the Shroud should be called only a "likeness or representation."

But to Geoffrey he did not even mention the latter requirement, as if it was understood already. Above all, he refused to order the expositions to be stopped, despite d'Arcis's strong demands, and reimposed on his recalcitrant bishop the demand for perpetual silence about the matter.

Seen in this light, the whole otherwise baffling episode becomes highly understandable. The trend of previous research by Shroud authors has been to try, quite unsuccessfully, to disprove or discredit what d'Arcis was saying. This was all the more difficult to do as the bishop had held the see of Troyes for twelve years and had a high reputation for integrity.

The truth is that virtually all d'Arcis's facts were correct, but the issue hinged on how they were interpreted. D'Arcis wrongly saw in the apparently guilty way that the Shroud was displayed a clear case for believing the relic to be a fraud.

He saw the lack of any information about its origin as strong support for this same view. He did not realize that by shouting so loudly about the seemingly underhanded methods of the Shroud expositions he was hindering a pious attempt to introduce a genuine relic for public veneration.

So was born the whole deep stain on the Shroud's authenticity, a stain that even d'Arcis could not have foreseen would last to our own time. But however much damage had been done to the Shroud's reputation, and it was considerable, by far the most important outcome of the affair was that expositions were not stopped but allowed to continue. This was the vital foothold the de Charnys needed, and Clement had gone as far as he dared to ensure it.

CHAPTER XXI

YEARS OF GRADUAL ACCEPTANCE

The rest of the Shroud's history is not in dispute. Geoffrey II de Charny survived the Pierre d'Arcis controversy by only a few years. He died on May 22, 1398, shortly after a crusade to Hungary, and was buried in the church of the Cistercian abbey of Froidmont, near Beauvais. His tombstone, with an elaborately carved effigy of him as a knight in armor, survived until the First World War, when the whole abbey was reduced to ruin.

On Geoffrey's death, responsibility for the Shroud fell to his daughter, Margaret de Charny, a pious and strong-willed woman who was to play a remarkable part in determining the future course of the Shroud's history.

She would have been little more than a girl at her father's death, and because her mother swiftly remarried, it was she who inherited the paternal seigneuries of Lirey, Montfort, and Savoisy.

Within two years she married Jean de Baufremont, a union which appears to have been marked by tragedy. First, it was childless, which in the light of subsequent events would seem to have been due to infertility on Margaret's part. Second, in 1415 Jean suffered the same fate as Margaret's grandfather Geoffrey, death at the hands of the English, this time at the Battle of Agincourt.

Following her mother's example, Margaret de Charny lost little time in remarrying. Her new husband was Humbert of Villersexel, a nobleman of the Franche-Comté who had the titles of Count de la Roche and Lord of St. Hippolyte sur Doubs. He was wealthy, and for Margaret this was opportune.

Up to this time the Lirey canons had maintained custody of the Shroud, keeping it in the church built by Geoffrey I. But after Agincourt the countryside was ravaged by marauding bands, and both Humbert and Margaret feared for the relic's safety. With the consent of the Lirey canons it was taken for safekeeping to the de Charny castle of Montfort near Montbard, and on July 6, 1418, Humbert issued this receipt:

> During this period of war, and mindful of ill-disposed persons, we have received from our kind chaplains, the dean and chapter of Our Lady of Lirey, the jewels and relics of the aforesaid church, namely the things which follow: first a cloth, on which is the figure or representation of the Shroud of our Lord Jesus Christ, which is in a casket emblazoned with the de Charny crest. . . . The aforesaid jewels and relics we have taken and received into our care from the said dean and chapter to be well and securely guarded in our castle of Montfort.[1]

The receipt ended with a promise that when France's troubles were over, all would be returned to the Lirey canons, including the Shroud. Most likely at the time this was the intention, probably because Margaret had seen little of the strange cloth that was part of her inheritance.

But Margaret's mind appears to have been changed. The Shroud was soon moved from Montfort to Humbert's domain at St. Hippolyte sur Doubs, and stored in the Chapel des Buessarts, which to this day preserves souvenirs of its stay.[2] Expositions came to be held each year on the banks of the Doubs in a meadow known as the Pré du Seigneur, and a minicult of the Shroud appears to have grown up, with many copies made, among them a cloth that subsequently achieved wide renown as the "Besançon Shroud," a work destroyed during the French Revolution.[3]

Elaborate entombment sculptures of Christ became fashionable at this time, seemingly under the Shroud's influence. The trend spread well beyond eastern France.[4]

But one fact appears to have sorely troubled Margaret—the cruel hand of fate which had left her childless. Through twenty years of marriage to Humbert she remained barren, and when in 1438 Humbert died, she must have been conscious that she was now going to die without direct heirs. This raised the problem of who should inherit the Shroud, and one can detect from subsequent events the extent to which this occupied her thoughts during her remaining years. She appears to have been determined that, despite Humbert's promise, the Shroud should no longer be kept by the canons of Lirey. There was sound reason for this. The church founded by Geoffrey I had been a modest enough wooden structure, and after ninety-odd years it was in a deplorable state of repair. Margaret appears to have regarded it as an inadequate home for a relic that she now clearly cared for deeply.

She also appears not to have been prepared to trust her own relatives, again with good reason. The nearest relation, Francis de la Palud, her nephew by marriage, was a most colorful character who had lost his nose at the Battle of Anthon and wore a false one of silver. His exploits had been the cause of no little international friction, and although he inherited all Margaret's husband's estates, she seems to have regarded him as quite unsuitable as an heir to the Shroud. But neither did she choose to bequeath the relic to her half brother Charles de Noyers, whom she at least trusted to negotiate on her behalf on several occasions. Nor did she give it to her cousin Antoine-Guerry des Essars, to whom, at her death, she left the lands of Lirey.

This was all the more strange from the point of view that she was under considerable pressure, from shortly after her husband's death, to return the Shroud to the dean and canons of Lirey.[5] In May 1443 she was summoned before the parlement of Dôle, and agreed to hand over all the jewels and reliquaries taken into safekeeping by Humbert—except the Shroud. In return for various payments toward the upkeep of the Lirey church she was allowed to keep the Shroud for three more years. At the end of this period she showed no signs of being prepared to surrender the Shroud, and was summoned this time before the court of Besançon. She was allowed to keep the Shroud for another two years, on payment of the Lirey canons' legal costs and more church upkeep. Two years later this agreement was renewed for a further three years, this latter extension being negotiated on Margaret's behalf by Charles de Noyers. One senses in these negotiations a tacit recognition that this intrepid woman was unlikely to hand over her beloved Shroud in her lifetime, both parties seeming to believe that the problem would be solved by Margaret's death, which, as she would by now have been in her sixties, could not be far off.

But the canons reckoned without Margaret's determination and farsightedness. Although of advanced years, Margaret now seems to have set out on a deliberate hunt for suitable heirs.

Perhaps in a move to check out the promising house of Hapsburg, in 1449 she traveled north to Belgium. A contemporary chronicler, Cornelius Zantiflet, a Benedictine, recorded her in this year at Chimay in Hainault, exhibiting the Shroud before a great crowd of people. Just like the bishops of Troyes, the Belgian clergy were suspicious of the cloth's credentials, and the Bishop of Liège asked Margaret to produce some certification. All she could offer were the bulls of Clement VII describing the cloth as only a "figure or representation" of the Holy Shroud. Although Zantiflet noted that the cloth's image must have been produced by an "astonishing art," Margaret failed to find among the Belgians the interest she was seeking and returned to the south. An exposition held at the castle of Germolles, near Mâcon, in 1452 seems to have been similarly abortive.

A year later the tide turned. On March 22, 1453, Margaret was in Geneva, and a curious transaction appears to have taken place on that date between her and Duke Louis of Savoy. According to a still extant document drawn up between the two parties,[6] Louis ceded to Margaret the castle of Varambon and the revenues of the estate of Miribel, near Lyon, in return for "valuable services." Margaret was now in her seventies, and one can scarcely suppose that at this stage in her life she should have been particularly interested in acquiring real estate. As is clear from subsequent documentation, the gift of the Shroud was the "valuable service" referred to, and Margaret had clearly chosen Louis and his successors to take over the relic from her.

Her choice of the House of Savoy, and the fact that she handed over the Shroud in this manner while fighting legal battles with the canons of Lirey, provides ample evidence of her high ideals for the cloth's future. Certainly there had been considerable amity between the de Charnys and the

House of Savoy. Margaret's father, Geoffrey II de Charny, and her second husband, Humbert de Villersexel, had been created knights of the Order of the Collar of Savoy by earlier dukes.

But her real motive appears to have centered on the very considerable piety of the Savoy family at this period. Duke Louis was a direct descendant of Saint Louis (1214–70), the king of France who had acquired the reputed Crown of Thorns for the Sainte Chapelle, Paris. Duke Amadeus VIII, Louis of Savoy's father, had become late in life Pope Felix V. And Louis himself cultivated a constant retinue of Franciscan friars whom he used as confessors.[7]

In addition Louis had an equally pious wife, the radiantly beautiful Anne de Lusignan, a princess of the ruling house of Cyprus. In the crusader period the Lusignans had been kings of Jerusalem and continued at their coronations to claim this as an empty title.

Anne and Louis, as rulers of Savoy, represented to Margaret a rising dynasty, wealthy and powerful enough to give the Shroud the security it so desperately needed in a troubled age, and influential enough to bring it to the full attention of the highest dignitaries of western Christendom.

These factors alone would have been sufficient. But it is tempting to speculate that there may have been something more about the Savoy family that persuaded Margaret to pass it on to them, something, perhaps in the eagerness of Anne de Lusignan which indicated that there was more than met the eye. On coming into the possession of the Savoy family, the Shroud took on a new but not unfamiliar role. While it had been with the de Charnys, there was never the slightest suggestion that the relic possessed palladian or protective powers. When not being described, for formality's sake as an image or likeness of the Shroud, it was merely the image of Christ upon the Shroud, and that was that.

But for the House of Savoy it swiftly became the family palladium, the divine protective device to be invoked by the ducal family in times of difficulty—just like the Mandylion. In its earliest days with the family it was carried about with them on their travels like a holy charm, to safeguard them against the dangers of a journey.

St. Francis de Sales (1567–1622), who took a great interest in it, used precisely the word "palladium" to describe it. The genealogist Guichenon (1778) described it as a "preservative against all kinds of accidents."[8] Seventeenth-century engravings show it as a standard fluttering above Duke Victor Amadeus and his wife, inscribed with the words "In this sign, conquer," the very words that inspired Constantine the Great to win the Battle of the Milvian Bridge. Subsequently in engravings it became associated with the preservation of the whole city of Turin.

How should this have come about when there is not precedent for such an association while it was preserved with the de Charnys? It may, of course, have been merely a natural reaction that might have been the same if they had come to possess any other relic. But it is tempting to relate Anne de Lusignan's eagerness to possess the Shroud to her background. Until her marriage Anne had lived in Cyprus, which had been her family's home for three centuries. Every year on August 16 those of the Orthodox faith on the island celebrated the coming of the Mandylion to Constantinople, the feast day that had been instituted by Constantine Porphyrogenitus in 945 and was still maintained despite the loss of the cloth in 1204. The focal point of these celebrations was the church of the Acheiropoietos at Lapithos, a church dedicated to the Mandylion and founded by a man reputed to have been the very "bishop" who discovered the Mandylion in Edessa in the sixth century. Anne, being a Catholic, would not have taken part in these celebrations, but it is unlikely that she would have been unaware of them, Lapithos being no great distance from the Lusignans' palace. It seems, therefore, at least possible that she may have recognized Margaret de Charny's Shroud, if not as the Mandylion, as something akin to it, and regarded it as a heaven-sent gift for the protection of the status-seeking family that she now headed.

While Margaret was wheeling and dealing in high places, there was, however, one group of men who waited with ever-growing impatience—the canons of Lirey. Legally, right was on their side. Not only had Margaret's grandfather founded their church to house the Shroud; they possessed in addition the all-important receipt from Humbert de Villersexel, promising the relic's return to them. On May 29, 1457, seemingly ignorant of the transfer of the Shroud to the House of Savoy, they petitioned Margaret again for its return, this time excommunicating her when, yet again, she failed to comply.

Two years later it appears that Margaret was approaching her end. Charles de Noyers, her half brother, seems to have persuaded the Lirey canons to recognize that they would now never recover the Shroud, and it was best to negotiate for compensation. For their part the canons would appear to have conceded to this grudgingly. A sixteenth-century manuscript in the Bibliothèque Nationale's collection for Champagne seems to sum up their feelings about Margaret. "The said Shroud of the Lord the perfidious woman handed over, and, it is said, sold it to Duke Louis of Savoy."[9]

The excommunication was somewhat reluctantly lifted, and on October 7, 1460, Margaret de Charny, the last of her line, went to her rest content that her duty to the Shroud had been done.

She had indeed done well. Remarkably, even in her lifetime documents had begun to stop referring to the cloth as merely a "figure or representation" of the Shroud, the clumsy but necessary formula adopted by her father. After her death, seen in the glittering circles that surrounded Louis and Anne of Savoy, the cloth grew in reputation. As has already been noted, the Savoys cultivated in their train a retinue of Franciscan friars minor. In 1464 the order elected as Minorite General no less a personality than the theologian Francesco della Rovere, at that time engaged in a theological controversy concerning the blood of Christ. Rovere, if he was not actually a member of Duke Louis's retinue at one stage, certainly seems to have seen the cloth at this time for he alluded to it in these words:

. . . the Shroud in which the body of Christ was wrapped when he was taken down from the cross. This is now preserved with great devotion by the Dukes of Savoy, and it is colored with the blood of Christ.[10]

The clause "when he was taken down from the cross" indicates the view, already discussed, that the cloth tended to be regarded more as a preburial wrapping. But the words "colored with the blood of Christ" demonstrated for the first time real confidence that the Shroud could now be regarded as a major relic of the Passion.

The passage, in a work specifically entitled *The Blood of Christ*, was written by Rovere in 1464, the year he became Minorite General. His subsequent ecclesiastical career was meteoric. Within three years he was a cardinal, in another two he became Pope Sixtus IV. His work on *The Blood of Christ* was actually published in the second year of his pontificate, giving the Shroud for the first time proper recognition from the Holy See.

Nor was this the limit of his support. In 1471 Duke Amadeus IX, the sixteen-year-old son of the now deceased Duke Louis, began the enlargement and embellishment of the ducal church at Chambéry, in order to make it a worthy home for the Shroud, and Sixtus granted numerous privileges to the clergy of this church.

When in 1502 the work on the edifice had been brought to a satisfactory completion by a succeeding duke, on June 11, in an elaborate procession of all the clergy of Chambéry, with cross and lights, the Shroud was carried by the richly vestmented Bishop of Grenoble into its new home. For the benefit of the enormous crowds who followed, it was exhibited on the high altar, then carefully deposited in a special cavity in the wall behind the altar, closed by iron doors and locked by four keys.

Four years later Pope Julius II, a nephew of Francesco della Rovere, issued, at the petition of Bishop Louis de Gorrevod, approval for this chapel to be called the Sainte Chapelle of the Holy Shroud, a title giving it the status of the already celebrated shrine of the same name erected by St. Louis in Paris for the Crown of Thorns. At the instigation of Bishop Gorrevod, a bull was also issued, pertaining to Chambéry, for the institution of a Feast of the Holy Shroud, with its own proper Mass and Office, assigned to May 4, the day after the feast assigned to the finding of the True Cross. Within half a century of the death of Margaret de Charny the cloth, whose authenticity had hitherto seemed so difficult to believe, had achieved respectability, a respectability made even more apparent when in 1511 the future King Francis I of France, accompanied by Queen Anne of Brittany, made a pilgrimage to visit it, a pilgrimage repeated four years later by the same Francis, now king, after his victory at the Battle of Marignac.

The Dukes of Savoy must have been delighted with their acquisition. Gifts flooded to the Sainte Chapelle—stained glass, Flemish sculpture, rich draperies, ornamentation from Cyprus, jewel-studded reliquaries.

As history demonstrates, however, this was a heyday, swiftly brought to an end by a succession of troubles. The first, and the most pertinent to the Shroud itself, took place on the night of December 4, 1532, when the fateful fire broke out in the Sainte Chapelle's sacristy, causing the extensive burn marks that disfigure the cloth to this day. The event caused many to claim that the cloth had not survived at all but had been replaced by a copy. So strong was this rumor that Duke Charles III was obliged to request from the pope a special commission of a cardinal and three bishops to come to Chambéry to investigate and officially deny it. Suspicions were not, in fact, satisfied until two years later, in 1534, when the repair work by the Poor Clare nuns enabled the now scarred Shroud to be shown in public once more.

Within three years there were dangers of a different sort— French troops on the move, in a tide of invasions. For safety the cloth was taken to Vercelli, then to Nice, at that time within Savoy territory. Returned to Vercelli in 1549, four years later, on November 18, 1553, it was hidden in the house of canon Antoine Claude Costa while French troops sacked the city.

In fact this period of threat to the cloth's survival passed as swiftly as it had come. The Peace of Cateau Cambrésis in 1559 enabled the forceful Duke Emmanuel Philibert to gain some control over his dominions, and on June 4, 1561, in an elaborate procession accompanied by trumpeters and torches, he had the Shroud returned to the Chambéry Sainte Chapelle, now restored to at least some of its former splendor. On August 15, for the first time in a quarter of a century, the Shroud was again exhibited on the chapel's high altar.

The days of the Shroud's stay in Chambéry were, however, now numbered. Following the treaty, Chambéry was unsatisfactorily situated as a capital for the dukes of Savoy, and Emmanuel Philibert was too astute a prince not to realize it. He saw Turin as the logical center of his dominions but needed the right sort of excuse to bring the Shroud there.

In 1578 that excuse came. Charles Borromeo, the saintly Archbishop of Milan, made it known that he was intending to make a pilgrimage on foot to revere the Shroud because of a vow he had made during a severe plague that had afflicted Milan. Emmanuel Philibert volunteered to have the Shroud brought to Turin to save the pilgrim the rigors of the mountainous journey necessary to reach Chambéry. The cloth never returned to Chambéry.

The scene of the archbishop's arrival in Turin was one of immense emotion, carefully recorded by contemporary painters and chroniclers. Borromeo, who made the entire journey from Milan on foot in four days, was received into the city to the roar of a gun salute and salvoes from the arquebuses of Emmanuel Philibert's infantry. His feet were bleeding badly, but steadfastly he made his way first to the cathedral and then to the duke's own chapel, where he spent forty hours in private adoration of the Shroud. The following Sunday in the square in front of Turin's Palazzo Madama, the castle of the dukes, a platform was set up on which were assembled a colorful array of dignitaries, the papal nuncio, the Venetian ambassador, various princes, knights of the Order of St. Maurice, seemingly hundreds of ecclesiastics, all surrounded by a vast crowd of spectators.

As Borromeo was escorted to the chair reserved for him, he was asked to say a prayer for the assembled gathering. He found himself tongue-tied by emotion. When the Shroud was brought out, in a manner which was to set the scene for many Turin expositions to follow, he broke down and wept. Three times Turinese bishops held up the cloth to the crowd. Then it was taken into the cathedral for further veneration.[11]

Expositions of the Shroud in front of the Palazzo Madama became a regular feature of Turin life each May 4. Each vied with the last for magnificence. The duke's family and visiting dignitaries would assemble in the shade of a richly embroidered panoply, with the Piazza del Castello in front of the palace crammed with spectators. Three bishops, robed in their finest vestments, would hold up the Shroud before the people. At the 1615 exposition one of these bishops was another future saint. This was Francis de Sales, who, like St. Charles Borromeo, found himself overcome by emotion at the experience. It was a hot day and perspiration from his brow accidentally fell onto the Shroud. Standing next to St. Francis was Turin's cardinal, Prince Maurice, who chided him for his carelessness. St. Francis said nothing, but recorded afterwards how he had been minded to say that Jesus himself had not been so delicate not to shed blood and sweat for these to be mixed with ours to give eternal life. Pictures of the Shroud were subsequently to be among his most cherished possessions. His protégé, Saint Jeanne Françoise de Chantal, founder of the Order of the Visitation, was present at yet another exposition in 1639.

It would seem from all this that the Shroud's authenticity was now beyond question, but not quite. In 1670 the Congregation of Indulgences in Rome granted a plenary indulgence to Shroud pilgrims "not for venerating the cloth as the true Shroud of Christ, but rather for meditating on his Passion, especially his death and burial," a tacit cognizance that even now the Shroud's credentials were not wholly sound.

Even so, the enthusiasm of the dukes of Savoy for the relic they cherished could not be diminished. The Turin chapel built to house the cloth in the 1580s was by the last decade of the seventeenth century regarded as inadequate, and a magnificent replacement in the Piedmontese Baroque style was commissioned from the architect Guarino Guarini, carefully planned to link cathedral and palace, being accessible from the latter without the need for the ducal family to descend among the people. While the finishing touches were being made to the new chapel, a Turin worthy, the blessed Sebastian Valfré, assisted by Duke Victor Amadeus II and his wife Anna of Orléans, carefully made small repairs to the Shroud where some of the patches sewn on by the Poor Clares showed signs of wear. On June 1, 1694, accompanied by yet more ceremony, the Shroud was solemnly carried into the chapel that has been its home to the present day, and locked away behind the grille above the high altar.

During the eighteenth century, the frequency of expositions declined, seemingly through genuine concern that the relic's condition should not suffer from such constant handling. In 1750 Duke Victor Amadeus III had the Shroud displayed for his wedding to Maria Ferdinanda of Spain. This set a precedent whereby expositions tended to be reserved for such special occasions rather than held as an annual event.

Thus in the nineteenth century there were only five expositions—one in 1805 for the benefit of a visit by Pope Pius VII, one in 1815 for the same pope's safe return to Italy after being held captive by Napoleon, one in 1842, one in 1868 when Princess Clotilde of Savoy, working on her knees, made a few small repairs to the cloth, and the final 1898 exposition for the benefit of the Italian kingdom's fiftieth anniversary, in which the revelatory Pia photograph was taken.

It was, of course, this photograph that brought the Shroud into the twentieth century in a way that no one hitherto could have envisaged. As we have seen earlier, in the very years that Catholic historians were busy updating the image of the Church by writing off relics such as the Shroud as unfortunate products of a gullible past, science was finding it could not be dismissed so easily.

In 1973, in the wake of Pope John XXIII's *aggiornamento*, Pope Paul VI found he could neither conceal his personal views that the Shroud was authentic nor, in the light of the as-yet-inconclusive scientific testing, wholly give the case for the Shroud's authenticity the full weight of papal authority.

He made his feelings clear in his television address:

. . . I personally still remember the vivid impression it made on me when, in May 1931, I had the good fortune to be present on the occasion of a special celebration in honor of the Holy Shroud. Its projection on a large, luminous screen and the face of Christ represented thereon appeared to me so true, so profound, so human and so divine, such as I have been unable to admire and venerate in any other image. It was for me a moment of extraordinary delight.

Whatever may be the historical and scientific judgment that learned scholars will express about this surprising and mysterious relic, I cannot but wish that it will lead visitors not only to deep sensitive observation of the exterior and mortal features of the marvellous figure of the Savior, but also introduce them to a more penetrating vision of his inmost and fascinating mystery.[12]

He had no way of knowing that within four years science would have a yet more positive say in favor of the Shroud's authenticity.

Statue of Parthian King Uthal of Hatra (second century A.D.),
showing style of trelliswork that may have been used to em-
bellish the Shroud and transform it into the Mandylion. (*Direc-
torate General of Antiquities, Bagdad*)

A. Mandylion on Ivan the Terrible's battle standard, Museum of Arms, Moscow.

B. Russian troops of the First World War, carrying the Mandylion as their battle standard. (*Imperial War Museum, London, Ref. No. Q32210*)

Pilgrim's medallion of the Shroud exhibited at Lirey, ca. 1357. The first known representation of the Shroud entirely full length—i.e., with both frontal and dorsal images visible. The shields are the arms of Geoffrey de Charny on the left (according to Froissart, "gules, three inescutcheons argent"—i.e., three small silver shields on a red ground) and the arms of Jeanne de Vergy, Geoffrey's second wife and subsequent widow, on the right. The roundel in the center represents the Empty Tomb. From a damaged amulet found in the Seine by the Pont au Change and now in the Musée de Cluny, Paris. (*Ref. 75 CN 5261, Service de documentation photographique de la Réunion des musées nationaux*)

I Luero Ritratto del Santiss. Sudario, dedicato alle Altezze Sereniss: di Maria Adelaide, Maria Anna e Maria Lodouica Princi. pesse della Real Casa di Sauoia, in questa prima Impressione. dall'Vmiliss, e ossequiiss. Seruitore Pietro Antonio Boglino in Torino

Exposition of the Holy Shroud in the seventeenth century, in the presence of Princesses Maria Adelaide, Maria Anna, and Maria Louise of the House of Savoy. Engraving on silk in the collection of Sherborne Castle, Dorset, England. *(Photograph by H. Tilzey, Yeovil, by kind permission of Simon Wingfield Digby, Sherborne Castle)*

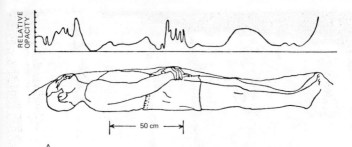

A

Above: Graph produced by Doctors Jackson and Jumper showing scan of image intensity of the Shroud at each point along
ridge line, compared with the lay of the cloth on model. The
intensity of the image can be seen to increase in a direct ratio
to the distance of each body feature from the cloth.

Below: The ridge line along which the scan was made. *(By
courtesy of Drs. John Jackson and Eric Jumper, Colorado
Springs)*

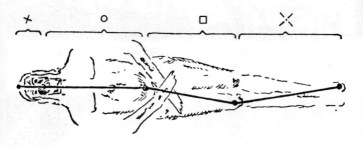

B

Relief image of the entire Shroud (frontal and dorsal images seen side by side) as produced by the VP-8 Image Analyzer. *(Drs. Jackson and Jumper)*

Relief image of the Shroud face produced by Mottern's VP-8 Image Analyzer. *(Drs. Jackson and Jumper)*

The precise shape of a hand-valve wheel seen imprinted as a permanent "shadow" on the side of a gas tank following the searing light of the Hiroshima atom bomb. (*USAF photo*)

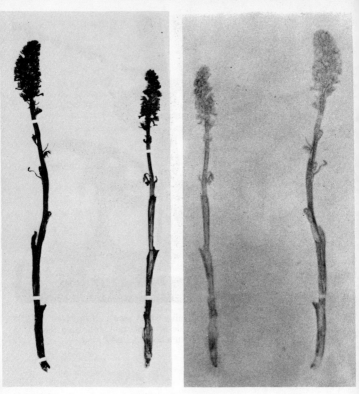

Herbals seen in positive and negative (*Photos by R. Conway*)

Part V
THE SHROUD—A PARANORMAL PHENOMENON?

CHAPTER XXII

THE CONTINUING RESEARCH

In the sunshine of New Mexico, forty oddly assorted individuals gathered on the morning of March 23, 1977, for the first United States Conference of Research on the Turin Shroud. The venue, set against the picturesque Sandia Mountains, was the Ramada Inn, Albuquerque.

While it was to be expected that some among the gathering would be churchmen, the novelty was their denominational diversity. Hosts Fathers Rinaldi and Otterbein of the U. S. Holy Shroud Guild accepted with gratitude the interest from Rome and Turin signified by the presence of special Vatican representative Monsignor Giulio Ricci. They delighted in the new Anglican interest marked by the attendance of fearlessly independent-minded British theologian Dr. John Robinson, of Trinity College, Cambridge, and American Episcopalian priest Fr. David Sox. And they welcomed the colorful and keenly questioning presence of four members of the Christian Brotherhood Commune from Santa Fe.

But where the real significance of the conference lay was in the serious-minded men who represented its core—more than twenty active and highly qualified scientists.

There were a few, principally pathologist Dr. Robert Bucklin and medical school professor Joseph Gambescia, who had studied the Shroud for more years than they cared to remember. For the rest the subject was new and, because of its very diversity from their normal work, intensely interesting. There were image-enhancement specialists such as Donald Janney of the U. S. Atomic Energy Commission's Los Alamos Scientific Laboratory, Jean Lorre and Don Lynn of the Pasadena Jet Propulsion Laboratory, and Bill Mottern of Albuquerque Sandia Laboratory. There were physicists and physical chemists such as Ray Rogers and Bob Dinegar of the Los Alamos Laboratory. Even spectroscopy was represented in the person of Roger Morris of Los Alamos.

These men were for the next two days to carry on animated discussions using a terminology that seemed light years removed from a possible first-century grave cloth—terms such as "emissivity," "X-ray fluorescence," and "neutron activation." Dr. John Robinson spoke for all laymen present in remarking afterwards how much of the scientific language was far outside his field of knowledge. But the aspect that impressed him deeply was the caliber of the men involved and the seriousness with which they considered the possibility of the Shroud's authenticity: "There is no one in this thing who is being either gullible or just dismissive."

How had it all come about? The space-age scientific tone had undoubtedly been set by two youthful Air Force Academy assistant professors whose research and initiative had brought the meeting into being.

Physicist Dr. John Jackson, a USAF captain, first became intrigued by the Shroud negative image as early as 1968. The aspect that particularly fascinated him was one first commented on by Paul Vignon, that the image appeared at least to have been created at a distance—i.e., by some form of emanation from the body rather than by direct contact. This seemed to him the logical inference from the finely graded tones of the body image revealed by the photographic negative. The point that Jackson felt needed research was the actual measurement of the distances involved in the image formation, and the evaluation from this of any data that might suggest how the image had been produced. At Albuquerque, Jackson decided to set up a modest research project along these lines[1] and enlisted the help of his long-standing friend, aerodynamicist Dr. Eric Jumper, also a USAF captain.

High on their priorities for preparation work was the making up of a "dummy" Shroud from a piece of muslin cut to the exact dimensions of the original. Onto this Jackson projected a transparency of the Shroud while Jumper carefully transcribed all the main features—the burns and patches, the shadings relating to eyes, nose, hair, fingers, arms, the stains of apparent blood—every observable marking.

Next they decided to try to find a model matching as

closely as possible the height and main physical characteristics of the man of the Shroud. Because of the interest of their friends and associates, they had no difficulty in recruiting some eleven volunteers for "matching" purposes. Each was checked with the Shroud figure transcribed on the muslin and one, an Air Force officer, fitted almost exactly. Interestingly, his height, 5 feet 10½ inches, and weight, 175 pounds, corresponded closely to the physical characteristics of the man of the Shroud deduced by medical men, as described in Chapter III.

Asked to lie on a table, the officer model was then covered with the muslin "shroud." By ensuring that each feature of the transcribed image was positioned over the corresponding part of his body it was possible to reconstruct exactly the original disposition of the man of the Shroud. Jackson subsequently observed "there was but one way to cover the body correctly."

The officer was then photographed from the side, first with the "shroud" in position and then with it removed. By correlation of the two photographs it was possible to measure off along the respective ridge lines of "shroud" and "body" the perpendicular distance of cloth from body at every point.

Following this, Jackson and Jumper ran the image of the Shroud under a micro-densitometer, a machine for measuring image intensity, following exactly the ridge line from which the data of cloth-body distance had been obtained. The resulting graph revealed clearly a varying intensity of the image at each landmark, giving in itself a distorted outline of the Shroud "body."

The real satisfaction for Jackson and Jumper came from their next graph, a mathematical correlation of the relationship between image intensity and cloth-to-body distance. This revealed what they had scarcely dared hope for—a perfect curve, demonstrating beyond question that there was a positive and precise relationship between image intensity and the degree to which the cloth was separated from the body at any given point. The very homogeneity of this data spoke volumes for some strange but scientifically measurable process of image formation, and in particular a process that had acted over a distance rather than by direct contact.

This discovery was significant, but what was to follow was even more so. Early in 1976, while still at Albuquerque, Jackson, following another line of enquiry, was advised to consult Bill Mottern, image-enhancement specialist at the Sandia Laboratories. The meeting, which took place on February 19, was one Jackson will never forget. Mottern had not even heard of the Shroud before, but as Jackson talked about it, he asked whether a specific laboratory machine might be of help. This was an Interpretation Systems VP-8 Image Analyzer, a device which plots shades of image brightness as adjustable levels of vertical relief.

Jackson handed over an ordinary three-by-five-inch transparency of the Shroud, obtained from the Holy Shroud Guild, and Mottern set this up in the machine and casually flipped the switches.

The next moment he and Jackson gaped astonishedly at the result. On the television screen to which the image analyzer was linked was the Shroud figure, seen for the first time ever from the side, in perfect three-dimensional relief. Using a facility built into the machine, Mottern rotated the image to view the other side. The effect was the same. Details such as the hypothetical "pigtail" discussed in Chapter IV now showed up clearly with a depth that confirmed the feature as thick, tightly compressed hair gathered at the back of the neck in the fashion of the early Jews. A separate photograph of the face also showed up with the same high-relief effect.

For Jackson it was an unforgettable experience, emotionally as much of a surprise as Pia's 1898 discovery of the Shroud negative, and scientifically one of enormous satisfaction, being instant verification of all the careful work with the officer model.

To one who is not a scientist the significance may not seem obvious until one understands the unusualness of such a perfect result. An ordinary photograph, being two-dimensional, simply does not contain sufficient information relating to distance and proportions to be immediately translatable into a meaningful three-dimensional image, however good the equipment used. Jumper and Jackson verified this for themselves using positive and negative photographs of Pope Pius

XI. These showed up with immediate distortions, the nose flattened, the mouth contorted, the eyes far too deeply set. As he subsequently observed:

> Only when the degree of illumination received from an object depends in some way upon its distance (as for example in a stellar photograph) would three-dimensional analysis and reconstruction be possible. Otherwise no less than two photographs separated by a known distance are required to build a true relief image.[2]

The evening of the meeting with Mottern, Jackson could scarcely contain his excitement. He phoned Jumper, described the discovery, and then spoke of an additional observation from the three-dimensional pictures. There was something strange about the eyes, he said. Each had a curious unnatural bulge to it viewed in three-dimensional form—as if something had been laid on it.

Jumper, whose wife was out, was obliged to stay at home that evening to mind the children. But Jackson could not rest. He began searching his library, hunting out references to ancient Jewish burial practices. In an article in the 1898 *Jewish Quarterly Review* he found the information he was looking for. It was a custom, the article said, among Jews and certain other nationalities to lay coins or pieces of potsherd over the eyes when laying out a corpse for burial, the intention being to keep the deceased from seeing the way by which he was carried to his last home.[3] A small coin laid over each eye, Jackson realized, would match the configuration of the "bulges" exactly.

Within months of the discovery, both Jackson and Jumper were moved by the Air Force to take up their present assistant professorships at Colorado Springs. Although preoccupied with their new responsibilities, they realized that in the Shroud they had found a quest that had to be followed through. Familiar from their work with the complex scientific hardware developed for the U.S. space program, they sought every means to apply it to Shroud research.

Away to the southwest in Pasadena, California, two highly skilled image-enhancement specialists of the Jet Propulsion

Laboratory were working on photographs being received of the Viking Mission to Mars when Jackson called on them for their help. One was technician Jean Lorre, the other supervisor Donald Lynn. Although Catholic, Lynn knew virtually nothing about the Shroud until contacted by Tom Dolle of the Santa Fe Christian Brotherhood. It was through Dolle that Jackson's visit was arranged, and fortunately the Laboratory authorities gave their consent for the use of the image-enhancement equipment for Shroud research.

In their spare time during Sundays in the summer of 1976, Lorre and Lynn worked on the negatives and slides of the Shroud provided for them by Jackson. The first step was to scan the material in order for it to be translated into numerical light values—an extension of the same micro-densitometer work undertaken earlier by Jackson and Jumper in Albuquerque. The information was fed into the image-processing laboratory's IBM computer, after which Lorre and Lynn were ready for application of their specialized techniques.

A lot of the early work was concentrated on the image of the face, involving mathematical removal of the visibility of the cloth weave and the distracting crease lines. Jackson and Jumper were particularly eager that computer enhancement might reveal more information on the apparent coins over the eyes, such as an identifiable image or inscription.

In this hope they remained disappointed. It was possible to make out shadows, slightly irregular in shape, in the area of the "bulges" that could be the outline of small coins. It was even possible to say that in size and uneven roundness they were consistent with the lepton, the "widow's mite" of the New Testament. That was all. Any further information on the coins intrinsic in the Shroud was certainly not available via the three-by-five-inch negatives that the scientists had to work with.

But this was by no means all that Lorre and Lynn's work brought to light. Using a process not unlike that of Mottern's VP-8 Analyzer, they produced a directional or gradient image of the Shroud, on which detail of a directional character was enhanced, thereby giving an effect of relief to the two-dimensional image. This had a particularly striking effect on the scourge marks on the dorsal image. Viewed from a forty-five-degree angle in one direction, those seeming to have been delivered by a flagrum wielded from the left stood out most markedly. Viewed from the opposite angle, the same characteristic could be noted of the marks that appeared to have been delivered by a flagrum wielded from the right.

The significance of this was that it was the only aspect of the Shroud image that showed any directionality—and one to be expected of strokes already suggested as going one way and then the other. For the rest of the Shroud image there was *no* directionality, and this argued powerfully for the image not having been made by an artist. In their work on the enhancement of the image of the face, Lorre and Lynn produced one scan which showed information they had mathematically taken out of the image, an apparently meaningless set of vertical and horizontal lines. To the scientists this was not meaningless. It was visual confirmation that whatever created the image was some nondirectional process, something virtually impossible for an artist to simulate.

It was in a mood of some excitement, therefore, that the conference was held at Albuquerque. Never before had the Shroud been so seriously considered by men of such diverse academic backgrounds.

Jackson and Jumper consulted many other scientists on the image-enhancement work, such as Donald Janney at the Los Alamos Laboratory and Don Devan of Information Science, Inc., of Santa Barbara, California. Fired by their enthusiasm, others of related disciplines became involved, among them archaeologist and physical chemist Ray Rogers of the Los Alamos Laboratory, and thermography and X-ray fluorescence specialist Captain Joseph Accetta of the USAF weapons laboratory, Albuquerque.

Then, quite independently of Jackson and Jumper, onto the scene came Dr. Walter McCrone, a microanalyst from Chicago. McCrone has a laboratory equipped with some two million dollars' worth of microscopes and microprobes that make it perhaps the best in the world for extracting the maximum possible information from the most minute sample.

McCrone was featured in the London *Sunday Times* in January 1974 as having shortly before brilliantly debunked the authenticity of Yale University's Vinland Map, allegedly a map of the New World predating Columbus. From samples quite invisible to the unaided eye he had discovered that while the parchment was genuinely of medieval date, the ink used to draw the map contained traces of a synthesized pigment, anatase, not developed until about 1920. Questioned by the author about the viability of using his methods on the Shroud, McCrone expressed an already latent interest in the relic, and was confident that his laboratory was fitted for the task. He was put in touch with the U. S. Holy Shroud Guild.

For eighteen months the Guild and McCrone waited for news of the Turin commission's findings before submitting a formal application to take samples. When the commission's report was released and it became apparent that there were sizable samples of the Shroud with Professor Raes in Belgium, McCrone flew to Ghent to negotiate their analysis by his laboratory. Here he met disbelief from Raes's colleague, Professor Apers, at what could be done in America, and his hopes of being able there and then to return to his laboratory with the samples were dashed. As if to settle the matter, Turin almost immediately demanded the samples be returned to them.

At the Albuquerque conference McCrone spelled out in detail the sort of results he could achieve if only he could be allowed the most minute samples. Most dramatic, he explained, were the recent improvements in radiocarbon dating. A few years ago the Libby method, the only one understood by the Italians, would have required the destruction of 20 to 25 grams of sample, an understandably unacceptable quantity. Since 1970 steady improvements in apparatus and techniques, particularly the introduction of highly specialized mass spectrometers, had reduced the amount of sample required to, at the time of the conference, some 60 milligrams or 1.6 by 1.6 cm. of material—less than the samples cut away for Professor Raes's purposes in 1973. No longer applicable were the old reservations about the fire of 1532 and the drenching with water invalidating any radiocarbon reading. The very samples taken for Professor Raes could be used, and would not even be totally destroyed.

Given a three-month period for the counting of beta

tracks, and with due allowance for the recalibration of carbon 14 that has followed cross-checking with dendrochronology, a dating accurate to plus or minus one hundred years was possible, enabling the settling once and for all, of the question of whether or not the Shroud is a fourteenth-century forgery.

Nor was this the only possible application of McCrone's microanalytical techniques to the Shroud. Using an ion microprobe, vastly more sensitive than the electron microscopes used by the Italian commission, and the very instrument with which he had revealed the Vinland Map's fraudulence, McCrone claimed his laboratory could identify the nature of the Shroud image, and very possibly the method of image formation. The uniqueness of the ion microprobe lies in its ability to distinguish and identify which of the 104 chemical elements are present in any given sample. It can identify, he explained,

> on one tiny spot of one of my scalp hairs, for example, more than thirty trace elements attesting to the fact that such a hair can only have come from my head, that my calcium level ensures good membrane equilibria, the iron level that I am not anaemic, the potassium level that my hyperactivity is under good control, the zinc that I need not fear schizophrenia, and the lithium is protection against manic depressive behavior. Finally the vanadium and chromium levels announce that I am sixty, plus or minus two to three years.[4]

All this from a portion ten times smaller than the human eye can see. As McCrone concluded in respect to the Shroud:

> If we could get a fiber on which it has been observed that on one side there is an indication of an image we would definitely be able to tell an elemental composition difference between the portion of the fiber that has the stain or the image and the portion that does not have such an image.[5]

To the men at Albuquerque in March 1977 that possibility seemed a pipe dream. They had no idea that its realization could be a mere eighteen months away.

CHAPTER XXIII

THE 1978 EXPOSITION

On August 1, 1977, Italy's *Osservatore Romano* broke the news that having reached the age of seventy-five Cardinal Pellegrino of Turin had retired from archdiocesan duties. The man to be appointed in his place was the former archbishop of Bari, Anastasio Ballestrero.

Ostensibly the announcement simply meant that a younger man was taking over the spiritual responsibility for Turin's considerable domestic troubles, among them a huge unwanted immigration into the city of Italians from the South, a Communist civic administration, and terrorism from the Red Brigade.

But for the Shroud the appointment meant far more. For it was to be Ballestrero who within a year of coming into office was to mount the first full-scale exposition of the Shroud in forty-five years.

Nineteen seventy-eight was the four hundredth anniversary of the Shroud's arrival in Turin, too major an event to be celebrated by a mere television exposition, as adopted by Cardinal Pellegrino in 1973.

Although the prospect of literally millions of pilgrims descending on Turin had daunted Pellegrino, Ballestrero had no such qualms.

A man with a Pope John XXIII air about him, he has a bluff, peasant way of getting things done, and his handling of the long-overdue exposition and testing of the Shroud was to be no exception.

Considerable planning and expense were needed within a short time.

For full-scale exposition of the Shroud Turin needed to be made ready for visitors, streets and public buildings cleaned, signposting erected, and special crowd control barriers prepared. On the cathedral steps special gantries needed to be built, and inside the cathedral a special posse of security men needed to be on guard day and night to avoid the Shroud becoming yet another Red Brigade object of ransom.

Ballestrero sought help for these requirements from the unlikeliest source, Turin's Communist administration. He succeeded to a greater degree than anyone could have believed, the Communist mayor agreeing to give Turin a total face-lift for the exposition, embracing Ballestrero's requirements, and costing in the region of a million pounds.

Not included in this were certain items which Ballestrero may well have thought more seemly to be provided by the Church than by the State.

In particular the Shroud itself needed a bulletproof glass exhibition case, special lighting, plus some scientific means of protecting the cloth from the effects of continuous illumination.

Valuable technical advice for this requirement was forthcoming from the University of Turin, but there was nevertheless an unavoidable $20,000 which needed to be found to cover basic costs.

Ballestrero, insisting that even for this purpose there was nothing available from his funds, turned to Father Rinaldi as spokesman for the American scientists.

If the Americans were so enthusiastic for the exhibition and testing, surely they could find the money for the Shroud's frame?

After a hasty interim loan from British financier Lord Craigmyle the money was found.

A further need was at an ordinary human level for helpers outside and inside the cathedral to guide visitors, hand out leaflets, control queues, and above all, in the most unobtrusive manner possible, keep those actually viewing the Shroud moving on.

Ballestrero appealed for local volunteers to work long hours for six weeks. More than a thousand came forward to give their time free.

As if he had not already asked for more than anyone else would have dared, Ballestrero insisted on one further requirement. During the time of the exposition no form of commercialism related to the Shroud was to be operated within a wide radius of the cathedral.

Just as the Shroud itself would be shown without charge, so also any ancillary exhibition, film, or concert should be mounted free. This would ensure that no visitor could go back to his native country claiming that the Shroud exposition was just another commercial gimmick.

The test of all Ballestrero's thinking was to come on August 26, 1978, preview day for a subsequent forty-two consecutive days of expositions. At 11 P.M. pressmen from around the world, now in far greater numbers than those who had attended in 1973, were given their first introduction to the form of display of the Shroud within the cathedral.

The effect was breathtaking. There were no candles, none of the ornamental bric-a-brac of former days. Against the darkness of the rest of the cathedral the Shroud appeared suspended in space, and illuminated as if from within. Although there had been a return to the traditional horizontal manner of displaying the cloth, the simplicity was even more striking than in 1973.

The money for the frame had been well used. The lighting was ideal for photography which was now freely permitted, and behind the scenes a complicated apparatus maintained the Shroud in an inert atmosphere, with temperature and humidity at constant levels.

During the next forty-two days some 3,333,000 people were to file within ten feet of the Shroud, each given a free six-language information sheet, each gently kept moving by the volunteers.

It was an extraordinary time, marked in part by being synchronous with, and indeed outrunning, the sadly brief pontificate of Pope John Paul I. This "Pope who smiled" was elected in the very hour of the first Mass of the expositions, 6 P.M. Saturday, August 26. He died before the expositions were over.

However, quite apart from the events in Rome, the expositions had their own unique atmosphere.

As the crowds daily grew larger the already generous opening times, 7 A.M. to 10 P.M., became more and more stretched. It was an eerie experience to stroll into the cathedral square at 6:15 in the morning, while it was still dark, to find literally thousands of people already scurrying to join queues.

The last Mass of the expositions, on the evening of Sunday October 8, was one vast sea of people, Anglican, Episcopalians, and even Greek Orthodox among them, some so moved that, like Anglican bishop John Robinson, they felt it entirely natural to receive Roman Catholic Communion.

There can be no doubt, therefore, that in his handling of the expositions Ballestrero scored a powerful spiritual coup.

Even so there was one further related hurdle which had been waiting for him from when he took office. What would *his* reaction be to the pleas for American testing of the Shroud, which Father Rinaldi had vainly made known to Cardinal Pellegrino for so many years?

After the Albuquerque conference a similar meeting on the Shroud had been held in London in September 1977 to launch the British Society for the Turin Shroud.

Drs. Jackson and Jumper, with a few colleagues, had attended this, then, with Father Rinaldi as interpreter, had flown on to Turin to put directly their new proposals for scientific work on the Shroud.

They could hardly have chosen a more auspicious time. Ballestrero had been appointed a mere six weeks, but it was already evident that there was a new mood, receptive to testing, in the air.

Italian scientists who had stepped into the shoes of the 1973 Commission received the Americans cordially, and while they were detectably anxious not to be upstaged, it was also clear that there was sufficient general agreement for the Americans to be able to return to put their plans in motion, with a target date of access to the Shroud at the end of the 1978 exposition, during the week commencing October 9.

Back in the States there were to follow months of the most intense discussion and planning, including the design and construction of a huge frame with soft magnets on which the Shroud could be mounted for photographic purposes.

There were many difficulties.

There was no ready source of finance for the project. Those who wanted the opportunity to test the Shroud had to beg or borrow any equipment they needed, and find the money themselves for their air fares and hotel bills.

There were uncertainties about the amount of time that would be allowed for scientific work—early on it was feared that this would be only twenty-four hours, but this subsequently became extended to five days.

Shortly before flying out to Turin a special "dry run" on a dummy shroud was held in Connecticut to work out the "choreography" of the test program, and to ensure that every last detail, including electrical outlets and current, had been foreseen.

Although this went well, it could not rehearse the Americans for one setback they encountered immediately on arriving in Turin, the bureaucratic obstructiveness of Italian customs officials when confronted with the vast array of special equipment flown into Turin from the United States.

To the chagrin of the scientists the apparatus was impounded, causing days of frustration and uncertainty, and it was eventually only the archbishop's own countersignature on the customs bond that secured its release.

This over, before access to the Shroud could take place, there had to be one final "curtain raiser" in the form of a two-day International Congress on the Shroud, held at Turin's St. Paul Banker's Institute on October 7 and 8.

Mounted by Italian academics and clergy chiefly to demonstrate that Italy's scientific technology was not far behind the Americans, with few exceptions it was not remarkable for bringing to light new information.

Drs. Jackson and Jumper attended it, and politely listened to the papers, including one by Turin's Professor Giovanni Tamburelli, demonstrating how he too could produce a 3D image like theirs.

At last, late in the evening of Sunday October 8, the goal of all their sleepless nights and months of planning came to be realized.

As Jackson and Jumper, along with their colleagues and a contingent of European scientists, hovered expectantly in the adjoining Royal Palace, in the cathedral the last of the Shroud's over 3 million visitors were escorted out, and the frame lighting switched off. In strict privacy the cathedral's

Palatine clergy began the delicate task of removing the Shroud from the frame.

The room in which Jackson and Jumper waited was one which they had grown accustomed to in the last few days. An ornately frescoed chamber once used for visiting princes, now thanks to the work of them and their colleagues, it had been transformed into something more resembling an operating room.

Amid cables strung across the floor stood the specially constructed frame on which the work on the Shroud was to be carried out. It was while the scientists were making last-minute modifications to this (they had spotted minute rust marks) that suddenly, with scant ceremony, a group of young men brought the Shroud into the room.

The cloth was carefully laid out, and the red silk protective covering removed. Those present, most of whom had not previously had the opportunity to examine the Shroud at close range, crowded round intrigued.

As many subsequently commented, this viewing alone was sufficient to convince them that they were not dealing with a simple forgery.

But there was a job of work to be done, and for the first night the Shroud was the responsibility of the Europeans, although some Americans stayed on as observers. It had been agreed that Max Frei should take further dust samples, and it was a revelation for those present to see him at work on this.

As he dabbed pieces of sticky tape on to the linen, then peeled these off with an alarming, though harmless tearing noise, it was realized that the Shroud linen really was still in remarkably good condition, and could stand up to more handling than might be expected.

When it came to the Americans' turn, Drs. Jackson and Jumper were to supervise alternately day and night for the next five days as step by step their twenty-five-man team managed to carry out every item of the experimental work they had so carefully planned.

By direct permission of Ballestrero, and supervised by Turin physicist Professor Gonella (general co-ordinator of the combined American and European research work), minute samples from image-bearing areas of the Shroud were taken for the ion microprobe analysis that had been proposed by Dr. McCrone.[1]

Where necessary, the Americans were assisted by Poor Clare nuns, direct successors of their long-dead sisters who more than four hundred years previously had repaired the Shroud after the 1532 fire.

Also high on the agenda was X-ray fluorescence work, particularly important for identifying the nature of the image by spectroscopic means, all elements having characteristic emission aspectra when excited by X rays.

Into the same category came X-ray transmission work and infrared thermography.

Another quite separate branch of the American work was an enormously complex and far-reaching photographic exercise, carried out under the supervision of the two highly experienced specialists from the jet propulsion laboratory, Don Lynn and Jean Lorre.

This included conventional black-and-white photographs and color photographs, microphotos, infrared and ultraviolet pictures, many taken of the Shroud section by section following a grid system planned back in the United States.

Thanks to the same farsightedness, it was even possible for the first time to photograph the back of the Shroud without removing the holland cloth backing.

This was made possible by the unstitching of one edge of the Shroud, carried out by the Poor Clare nuns, and deployment of special fibreoptic equipment able to "see" the underside.

The volume of data created by all this work is enormous, and there is a code among the scientists that until all the information has been carefully assembled, assimilated, crosschecked, and evaluated none of it will be released.

This process may take until 1980 or even 1981.

However frustrating this may be in the interim, what we can be assured of is that at last Turin has made the Shroud freely available to the most intense scrutiny of science. No special conditions have been imposed on the American scientists regarding publication of results.

Whatever the outcome, there is to be no censorship, no

fudging of evidence, and the credit for this new and unprecedented step forward in Shroud studies must undoubtedly go to the wisdom and farsightedness of Archbishop Ballestrero. All he has asked for is to be kept informed.

Sadly, by way of a postscript, it should be noted that over the carrying out of just one test only there remains some uncertainty, albeit rapidly diminishing.

The test in question is the already mentioned carbon 14 process, the only available scientific means of dating the Shroud linen.

The man most vocal in asking for this test, although not the one who would carry it out, was, as already noted, the Chicago microanalyst Dr. Walter McCrone.

McCrone is a most charming and undemanding individual, but unfortunately he seems to have become the largely innocent victim of a particularly sensitive piece of Italian power politics.

On September 19, 1977, with Jackson and Jumper, McCrone was received cordially in Turin, and his information on the latest C-14 methods, new to the Italians, greeted with considerable interest. Had he continued to remain wedded to the Jackson-Jumper test proposals, all might have been well. But sometime during the visit McCrone was approached on his own, in confidence, by Monsignor Ricci and his English-speaking assistant, Mary Elizabeth Patrizzi.

Ricci and Patrizzi explained that they were good friends of ex-king Umberto (theoretically still the Shroud's owner), and they could probably arrange a very quick way of McCrone obtaining Shroud samples, by a direct approach to Umberto, who happened to be nearby in Geneva.

Two days later McCrone found himself face to face with Italy's former king. Umberto agreed that McCrone should have his permission to take samples of the Shroud. As a preliminary it was arranged that McCrone should take back with him and test samples of another cloth relic in which Monsignor Ricci had a special interest, the Sagrado Rostro of Oviedo.[2]

The Oviedo samples were obtained, and shortly after McCrone introduced Ricci and Patrizzi to various laboratories in the United States then innocently sent out a general memorandum about what he had done. His mistake was to misjudge the extent to which his independent and hitherto clandestine action would offend the delicate negotiator on the Americans' behalf, Father Peter Rinaldi.

For what McCrone did not appreciate was that Ricci and Patrizzi's friendship with King Umberto was not a mere social nicety. They were prominent members of Italy's royalist party, and by an alliance with them he had cut off the very support which he might otherwise have expected to receive in Turin.

While Cardinal Pellegrino, when in office, had continued to pay a certain lip service to Umberto, times had dramatically changed under Ballestrero.

It was not for his spiritual qualities, deep though these are, that Ballestrero had obtained his million pounds' support from Turin's Communist mayor. With a peasant air, and very much a man of the people, Ballestrero is not the sort to meddle with those wishing to return to the days of the monarchy.

As events were to prove, during the exposition he was personally to reject permits of access to the Shroud granted in writing by the king. Effectively, by his mission to Geneva, McCrone had committed diplomatic suicide.

For the future the radiocarbon dating test will most likely still be carried out on the Shroud, despite this gaffe.

During 1978 a new breakthrough in radiocarbon dating, using very minute samples, was achieved by a laboratory at the University of Rochester, Rochester, New York, under the direction of nuclear physicist Dr. Harry Gove.[3] Rochester is able to date the Shroud using a sample as small as 5 milligrams weight—an eminently practical proposition, as Professor Raes was given bigger samples for mere weave analysis in 1973.

At the Turin Congress Dr. Gove explained to the Italian scientists and clergy the advantages of the new method. It was publicly agreed that Gove could be allowed portions of the Raes samples, providing an independent laboratory was available to cross-check Gove's work using separate portions of similar size.

At the very end of 1978 the Brookhaven laboratory in the United States, a highly respected institution often used by the

Smithsonian, announced that it too was now capable of dating micro-samples of the Shroud type.

Accordingly, at the time of this book going to press diplomatic moves are in hand to make the samples[4] available to the two laboratories, and in the light of Archbishop Ballestrero's known receptiveness, Father Rinaldi is optimistic about the outcome. Further minute fibers of the Shroud, although too small for carbon dating, are currently under detailed analysis by Dr. Ray Rogers, archaeologist and thermal chemist of New Mexico's Los Alamos Scientific Laboratory. It is even probable that despite the Umberto episode, Dr. McCrone will be invited to assist with his special expertise in ion microprobe analysis and ultrasonic cleaning.

It is to be hoped that if the radiocarbon test is carried out within the next year the results will be available in time to be married with those of the other elements of the U.S. research program. Although while they sift and check their data the U.S. scientists remain prudently reticent about discussing their findings, from their general air of optimism there seems little doubt that we are on the very brink of the Shroud's fullest possible scientific authentication.

CHAPTER XXIV

THE LAST MIRACLE

It is now more than eighty years since Secondo Pia revealed for the first time that there is literally more to the Shroud than meets the eye. In those years the cloth has emerged slowly but inexorably from being a subject of crankish speculation to one of intense scientific, historical, and theological interest. To what extent the future may provide "proof" that the Shroud is the one which wrapped Jesus remains to be seen. All that can be said is that at the time of writing an enormous quantity of new data on the Shroud has been obtained, and while we wait for this we must be content with the still significant interim conclusions available from the findings discussed in this book.

For instance, from the careful analysis of the Shroud's textile fibers by Professor Raes the linen can be said to offer no inconsistency with known weaves of the first century A.D. It also beyond doubt bears traces of cotton that confirm it has come from the Middle East.

The chemico-microanalytical work by the 1973 Italian commission scientists, while inconclusive, suggests that of whatever substance the Shroud image is composed it is not of any readily identifiable pigment that would have been used by a medieval artist.

The work of Drs. Jackson and Jumper corroborates this by indicating, from the manner in which the image was formed, that no human agency was involved.

The palynological research of Dr. Max Frei provides the strongest possible evidence that at some stage before its known post-fourteenth-century peregrinations in France and Italy the Shroud was in Palestine and Turkey including the Anatolian steppe region of Turkey in which Urfa/Edessa stands.

Frei's evidence thereby strongly corroborates the author's theory that the Shroud and the Mandylion are one and the same. Although this theory cannot be considered conclusively proven, it certainly invalidates any argument that the Shroud cannot be genuine because there is no documentary record of it before the fourteenth century.

Medical opinion is as firmly emphatic today as in the time of Vignon and Delage that, whatever the substance of the image, it is genuinely the imprint of a human corpse which has suffered the agonies of crucifixion.

Lastly but by no means least, comparison of gospel evidence with the imprint of that corpse strongly suggests that if it is to be identified with anyone in history, that identity must be none other than Jesus Christ.

All these conclusions, provisional though they are, seem sufficient to rule out the old claim that the Shroud is merely a painting by a fourteenth-century artist.

Paradoxically, however, they do not provide the slightest grounds for acceptance of the obvious alternative—that the image is the simple product of the blood and sweat with which Jesus' body was soaked at the time of the burial. More than seventy years ago careful experiment convinced Vignon[1] and Delage that straightforward contact could not be the explanation for the Shroud's image, all attempts at reconstruction producing grotesquely distorted results both in positive and negative. More recent research by Professor Judica-Cordiglia[2] and others has indicated the same, and this was also the author's verdict on viewing the Shroud at close range in November 1973.

From the sequence of the Passion anyone would expect the blood flows to have transferred onto the cloth with proportionately different degrees of completeness according to the time of day at which the original wounds were inflicted. One would also expect most, in the course of rolling and unrolling over the last two thousand years, to have scaled off. Instead, it is quite evident that all flows have transferred onto the Shroud in appearance at least in their entirety, and that, quite unnaturally, they have remained intact. The information from the Italian commission that the "blood" has not penetrated the fibers and was not positively identifiable as blood seems only to confirm that there probably is no actual blood on the Shroud. If there was blood in the first place, either all hematic substances were rendered unidentifiable by the heat of the fire of 1532, or they were transformed and "fixed" by the image-creating process itself.

Either way, the deduction must be that, if the Shroud image was formed neither by human artifice nor by ordinary natural means, it must have been by some unknown image-forming process. It is in attempting to define something of the nature of this third alternative that we arrive at the Shroud's paramount mystery.

A first, essential condition for what is visible on the Shroud has to be that the position of the cloth was relatively flat over the body. This may well have been made possible by the packing of blocks of aromatic spices around the body in the tomb, suggested in Chapter IV. This does not have to have been done with great precision. There are one or two anomalies on the Shroud, such as the apparent disproportionate length of the lower right arm. The Albuquerque conference's youngest speaker, Cadet McCown, considered a maximum deviation of sixteen degrees quite reasonable.

With regard to the image-forming process itself, one suggestion has been that what happened on the Shroud was something akin to images made by certain preserved plants. For centuries it has been normal in the collecting of botany specimens to sandwich these between thick sheets of paper. After a long period of time there tends in some cases to "develop" on the paper, both above and below the plant, strikingly precise images in a sepia color closely akin to that of the Shroud. Examples are found in almost any herbarium or botanical collection,[3] being particularly prevalent in the case of specimens of the genus *Petasites* and similar fleshy plants. Unfortunately the images take some seventy or more years to develop properly, in marked contrast to the thirty-six hours maximum allowed "exposure time" for the Shroud. Since, apart from a minor study by Dr. Jean Volckringer,[4] all too little is known of how these images are formed their relevance must remain for the present an open question.

A far more promising suggestion has been that the image is some form of scorch, the color being the sepia of the first stage of the oxidation process preliminary to actual burning. In 1966 British author Geoffrey Ashe,[5] without having seen the Shroud, demonstrated the possible relevance of this. By the simple expedient of exposing linen to the radiance from a heated brass ornament Ashe was able to produce a cloth image of a character not unlike that of the Shroud, something all those experimenting with vapors and blood-coated corpses had failed to do.

This idea gained credibility with the author and with Dr. Willis and others at the 1973 exposition. On close study of the Shroud color there seemed a great similarity between the character of the scorches from the 1532 fire and the tones of the body image. Just over three years later the validity of this subjective impression was demonstrated scientifically at Albuquerque.

Spectroscopic analysis operates on the principle that every chemical element has its own characteristic wavelength. Scientists are able to determine, by careful measurement of the wavelengths of emitted light, the chemical composition of, among other things, the atmosphere of distant planets. The application of this relatively simple and totally nondestructive method to the Shroud was rejected in 1973 by Professor Delorenzi of the Turin commission, largely, it would seem, through ignorance.

At Albuquerque spectroscopy's relevance was brilliantly demonstrated by Dr. John Jackson. He took an ordinary color photograph of the Shroud supplied to him by Father Otterbein and had this color-scanned in Don Lynn's laboratory to isolate the simple proportions of blue, red, and green present in the different physical features of the image. He gave all these features—the burn marks, the body images, the blood, the hair, etc., different symbols and plotted on a graph their different color intensities compared with their neutral densities as shown up by micro-densitometer scanning. The result was remarkable. Spectroscopically "body," "blood," and burn-mark features all recorded the same intensity. Although Jackson was the first to acknowledge that the data he was dealing with were far from ideal, the implication for future research was self-evident—the Shroud image had pronounced similarities to a scorch.

The obvious question is how a genuine dead body, cold in the tomb, could produce some kind of burning or radiance sufficient to scorch cloth, acting in so controlled a manner that it dissolved and fused blood flows onto the cloth, yet created at the same time the perfect impression of a human body? The concept is mind-boggling. Yet, if the evidence already presented for the Shroud's authenticity is to be believed, *something* along these lines appears to be the only explanation.

Not far from anyone's minds at the Albuquerque conference was the idea that it might have been some kind of thermonuclear flash—a singularly appropriate speculation, considering that they were sitting not two hours' drive from the site of the first atomic-bomb test at Alamogordo in 1945. Adding some weight to this speculation were some unexpected photographic properties of the first atomic bomb dropped on Hiroshima, as attested by *Hiroshima* author John Hersey:

The scientists noticed that the flash of the bomb had discolored concrete to a light reddish tint, had scaled off the surface of granite, and had scorched certain other types of building materials, and that consequently the bomb had, in some places, *left prints of the shadows that had been cast by its light.* The experts found for instance, a permanent shadow thrown on the roof of the Chamber of Commerce Building (220 yards from the rough center) by the structure's rectangular tower; several others in the look-out post on top of the Hypothec Bank (2,050 yards); another in the tower of the Chugoku Electric Supply Building (800 yards); another projected by the handle of a gas pump (2,630 yards). . . .

A few vague human silhouettes were found, and these gave rise to stories that eventually included fancy and precise details. One story told how a painter on a ladder was monumentalized in a kind of bas-relief on the stone façade of a bank building on which he was at work, in the act of dipping his brush into his paint can; another how a man and his cart on the bridge near the Museum of Science and Industry, almost under the center of the explosion, were cast down in an embossed shadow which made it clear that the man was about to whip his horse. . . .[6]

The correspondence of these radiation images with the phenomenon on the Shroud itself is, of course, by no means total. The Shroud was, after all, seemingly scorched from within rather than from without, and by a process of necessity far more controlled than the blast from an atomic bomb.

Nevertheless the impression is inescapable that, rather than a substance, some kind of force seems to have been responsible for the image. This is suggested by the information in the 1973 commission's report that the image affected only the topmost surface of the fibers, and whatever created it had neither seeped nor penetrated the fibers and was insoluble and resistant to acids. Whatever formed the image was powerful enough to project it onto the linen from a distance of up to four centimeters (according to Jumper and Jackson), yet gentle enough not to cause distortion in areas where there would have been direct contact. This factor is particularly obvious on the dorsal image, where the cloth would have received the full weight of the body.

The concept of a force is implicit from the manner in which the image seems to have been created with a marked upward/downward directionality, without any diffusion, and leaving no imprint of the sides of the body or the top of the head. Also the image-forming process seems to have shown no discrimination between registering the body surface, the hair, the blood, and even inanimate objects—i.e., the two coins discovered by Jackson and Jumper. All would seem to have been imprinted on the cloth with the same even intensity, and with only the most minor color variation in the case of the blood.

The idea then, of some thermonuclear flash being the force in question is obviously more than idle speculation. Dr. Jumper certainly treated the hypothesis seriously, arguing that as a diffusion process would have to involve penetration of the fibers and saturation, a thermal discoloration or light scorch could explain many of the characteristics of the Shroud image. Further, as any remotely lingering energy source, such as a laser, would have caused images penetrating the entire cloth, or even destruction of the cloth, if the image is a scorch it must have been by some high-intensity, short-duration burst, acting evenly upward and downward.

Thermal chemist Ray Rogers of the Los Alamos Scientific Laboratory, very active at the recent testing, said very much the same thing, using the words "flash photolysis," and speaking of a mere millisecond of time.

While we await definitive analysis of the Shroud stains, this concept may be as near as we can get to whatever created the Shroud image. It is certainly awesome enough, but there are additional factors to be borne in mind that are unique to this one cloth in Turin.

Other shrouds have survived, some from Egyptian tombs dating from many centuries before the time of Christ. A few, including those of known martyrs, bear imprints—but nothing approaching the perfect photographic likeness of the Shroud of Turin. If a similar imprint had appeared on the shroud of an Egyptian pharaoh or a Chinese emperor, it would be considered just some freak of nature, and dismissed with little further thought. But it occurred, from all that one can determine, only on the shroud of Jesus of Nazareth, a man reputed to have worked miracles and to have risen from the grave.

The Gospels are quite explicit that Jesus was a man with a power, a power he is specifically recorded to have felt drawn from him, as in the case of our now-familiar woman with the issue of blood who touched the hem of his robe.

It was perhaps manifestation of this power which took place at the Transfiguration—the extraordinary incident described by three gospel writers when, on a high mountain, the aspect of Jesus' face changed and he appeared in brilliant light, his clothing "dazzlingly white" and "as lightning" (Mt. 17:1–8, Mk. 9:2–8, Lk. 9:28–36).

It may be that this power has some affinity with the mysterious "energy body," sensitive to human moods and emotions and displaying curious characteristics in the case of psychics, which Russian scientists have been able to study by their discovery of Kirlian photography.[7]

Even from the limited available information, a hypothetical glimpse of the power operating at the moment of creation of the Shroud's image may be ventured. In the darkness of the Jerusalem tomb the dead body of Jesus lay, unwashed, covered in blood, on a stone slab. Suddenly, there is a burst of mysterious power from it. In that instant the blood dematerializes, dissolved perhaps by the flash, while its image and that of the body becomes indelibly fused onto the cloth, preserving for posterity a literal "snapshot" of the Resurrection.

However the image was formed, we may well be entranced by the fourteen-foot length of linen in Turin. For if the author's reconstruction is correct, the Shroud has survived first-century persecution of Christians, repeated Edessan floods, an Edessan earthquake, Byzantine iconoclasm, Moslem invasion, crusader looting, the destruction of the Knights Templars, not to mention the burning incident that caused the triple holes, the 1532 fire, and a serious arson attempt made in 1972. It is ironic that every edifice in which the Shroud was supposedly housed before the fifteenth century has long since vanished through the hazards of time, yet this frail piece of linen has come through almost unscathed.

Frustratingly, the Shroud has not yet fully proven itself to us—not uncharacteristic of the gospel Jesus, who at certain times seems almost deliberately to have made his presence obscure, as in his post-Resurrection appearance to Mary Magdalen when she mistook him for a gardener, and in his walking, shortly after, as an unrecognized stranger with the two disciples on the road to Emmaus.

But one cannot help feeling that it has its role to play, and that its hour is imminent.

APPENDIX A

RECONSTRUCTED CHRONOLOGY OF

THE TURIN SHROUD

(Based on the theory that the Shroud is the same
as the "Mandylion" or "Image of Edessa" lost from
Constantinople in 1204)

Circa 30 A.D.   Crucifixion of Christ. (Disciple Addai or Thaddaeus, "one of the seventy" (see Lk. 10:1) travels to Edessa,
bringing with him a mysterious "portrait" (*Doctrine of Addai*). Abgar V, toparch of Edessa, is cured of a disease and
converted to Christianity (see Eusebius of Caesarea, *History
of the Church*, bk. i, chap. 13).
   *To disguise its nature as "unclean" burial linen, "Shroud"
   is made up as a "portrait," folded so that only the face
   is visible. It is taken to Edessa (now Urfa, in eastern
   Turkey).*

Circa 57   Ma'nu VI, second son of Abgar V, succeeds to the
throne of Edessa. Ma'nu reverts to paganism and cruelly
persecutes Edessa's Christians. (The "portrait" disappears.)
   For safety it is hidden in a niche above Edessa's west gate.

Circa 177   Renewed toleration of Christians at Edessa under
Abgar VIII (177–212). For a period Abgar's tiara on coins
actually seems to feature the Christian cross (British Museum Edessa, cat. 13). But "portrait's" whereabouts remain
unknown. The memory of it grows dim, and legends con-
centrate on an apocryphal correspondence between Christ
and Abgar V.
Parthian rule in Edessa ceases, and is eventually replaced
by that of the Byzantines. City suffers severe floods roughly
once each century.
   *For centuries the Shroud's existence remains completely
   unknown while it rests in hermetically sealed conditions.*

525   Severe flood at Edessa, causing loss of 30,000 lives and destruction of virtually all major public buildings. During work on rebuilding the walls a cloth is discovered hidden in a niche above the west gate. It is found to be impressed with an image of Christ *acheiropoietos*—"not made by human hands" (Evagrius, "Ecclesiastical History" Migne, *PG*, LXXX, vi, 2, 2748–49). Without the slightest dispute the cloth is identified as the original portrait brought to Abgar. The Emperor Justinian from Constantinople lavishes money for flood prevention scheme at Edessa, and the building of a beautiful shrine for the cloth, the Cathedral of Hagia Sophia, Edessa.

From this time on a new, definitive, front-facing likeness of Christ appears in art.

The Shroud is rediscovered, but no one realizes its true nature.

544   The cloth, subsequently to be referred to as the "Mandylion," is described by sixth-century writer Evagrius as miraculously preserving Edessa from an attack by a Persian army.

It is regarded as so holy that access to the cloth is very rare. But an authoritative likeness of Christ is formulated from the visible image.

639   Moslems gain control of Edessa from the Byzantines. Christian population of Edessa is tolerated and the Cathedral of Hagia Sophia, housing the Mandylion, is admired and preserved.

Circa 700   Faced with crippling taxes, Orthodox Christians of Edessa surrender Mandylion in pawn to rich Monophysite Athanasius bar Gumayer. Athanasius is said to have substituted a clever copy for the original. If this story is correct, the latter comes to be stored in the Jacobite church of the Mother of God, Edessa.

A strange swap occurs.

723–842   Both Byzantine and Moslem empires suffer outbursts of "iconoclasm" in which countless icons and manmade images are destroyed. But the Mandylion survives unscathed.

Spring 943   Byzantine imperial army under General John Curcuas besieges Edessa. Following instructions from Constantinople, Curcuas promises emir of Edessa that he will spare the city, release 200 Moslem prisoners, grant Edessa perpetual immunity from attack, and pay 12,000 pieces of silver if the Mandylion is handed over to him.

Summer/Autumn 943   Caliph and cadis of Baghdad debate whether or not the Mandylion should be handed over, and show great reluctance to let such a prized relic pass from their hands. Eventually ex-vizier Ali ibn Iza convinces them that the liberation of Moslem prisoners outweighs all other considerations.

Early summer 944   Abraham, bishop of Samosata, is deputed to receive the Mandylion in the name of the Emperor. Abraham appears to recognize the Orthodox copy as spurious, and is only satisfied when he has the Monophysite and Nestorian copies of the Mandylion also handed over to him. Moslems and Edessan Christians demonstrate against the handover of the cloth. Abraham and the Bishop of Edessa, carrying the Mandylion, are followed by rabble to the banks of the Euphrates. Here they cross by boat to safety.

Mandylion stays for a short while at Samosata, then continues journey by road to Constantinople.

It is met by Paracoemomene Theophanes at the mouth of the river Sagaris. Shortly before its arrival in Constantinople it stays in the sacristy of the monastery of St. Eusebius, in the Optimatan theme.

The cloth leaves Edessa.

August 15, 944   Mandylion reaches Constantinople. At the Church of St. Mary of Blachernae, privately, in the sacristy, it is taken out of its casket and venerated by the future emperor Constantine Porphyrogenitus, together with Stephen and Constantine Lecapenus, sons of the reigning emperor. The Lecapeni find it "extremely blurred." Later the same night the Mandylion is taken by galley to the Palace of the Boucoleon, and placed in the Chapel of the Pharos.

A contemporary account, the "De imagine edessena" describes the image as a "moist secretion without coloring or artificial stain," and that it did "not consist of earthly colors."

August 16 The Mandylion is carried around the walls of Constantinople in its casket, and then to Hagia Sophia, where it is placed on the "throne of mercy," then to the Chrysotriclinium of the Boucoleon Palace, where it is placed on the throne of state. Finally it is given a permanent place in the Chapel of the Pharos, on the right-hand side, facing the east.

From alternative contemporary suggestions of how the image came to be formed—by Jesus drying his face, and by Jesus wiping away the "bloody sweat" of the agony of Gethsemane—it is clear that those who viewed the cloth in 944 had no idea that they were looking at a shroud, or a cloth bearing the image of Christ's entire body. It may be conjectured on the basis of both artistic and literary evidence that this was due to the way the cloth was folded at the time, with only the face visible and the rest of the image unsuspected and inaccessible because of the cloth being pinned taut within a frame.

January 945 Constantine Porphyrogenitus gains Byzantine throne.

He strikes gold solidus to commemorate the bringing of the Mandylion to Constantinople (this carries the front-facing Christ Enthroned likeness).

He also commissions feast-homily on the Mandylion, the "De Imagine Edessena," and institutes August 16 as the official feast day of the Mandylion.

1011 A copy of the Mandylion is brought to Rome about this time, where an altar is consecrated to it by Pope Sergius. This copy becomes subsequently known as the Veronica (from *vera icon*—"true likeness"). In the course of time the legend of the woman Veronica develops from this and development of the Hemorrhissa story.

Circa 1025 "Threnos" or Lamentation scenes appear in art about this time, showing for the first time Christ laid out in death in the attitude visible on the Shroud.

Also in these scenes a large cloth is depicted, consistent with the full size of the Shroud—whereas hitherto burials had been depicted with Christ wrapped "mummy" style.

Someone, perhaps for the purpose of remounting the cloth, appears to have unpinned it from the frame, re-

vealing for the first time since the days of the apostles, the Shroud's full-length figure images.

1036 Mandylion recorded being carried in procession in Constantinople.

1058 Christian Arab writer Abu Nasr Yahya says he saw Mandylion in Hagia Sophia.

These accounts do not suggest the cloth was publicly exhibited on these occasions. A Byzantine hymn suggests it was still regarded as too holy for ordinary gaze.

Circa **1130** British monk-chronicler Ordericus Vitalis records in his "Ecclesiastical History" (Migne, *PL*, 188.690): "Abgar reigned as toparch of Edessa. To him the Lord Jesus sent . . . a most precious cloth, with which he wiped the sweat from his face, and on which shone the Savior's features miraculously reproduced. This displayed to those who gazed on it the likeness and proportions of the body of the Lord." A Latin codex of the same period quotes Christ as sending this message to Abgar: ". . . I send you a cloth on which the image not only of my face but of my whole body has been divinely transformed." (Vati. Lib. Codex 5696, fol. 35).

Direct depictions of the cloth in art, common for the first time in this century, suggest that when remounted still only the face was left visible.

1146 Turkish Moslems capture Edessa. The city's historic churches, including the Hagia Sophia Cathedral, are ruthlessly destroyed. But the Mandylion is safe in Constantinople within the Pharos Chapel.

1201 Nicholas Mesarites, keeper of the relic collection in the Pharos Chapel (see Heisenburg, *Die Palasrevolution des Johannes Komnenos,* [Wurzburg, 1907], p. 30), says collection included "the sindon with the burial linens." The sindon "is of linen, of cheap and easily obtainable material . . . defying decay because it wrapped the mysterious naked dead body after the Passion."

August **1203** Robert de Clari, French crusader in Constantinople, describes seeing at the Church of St. Mary of

Blachernae ". . . the sydoine in which Our Lord had been wrapped, which stood up straight every Friday so that the *figure* of Our Lord could be plainly seen there."
This unique account suggests first time ever public expositions to allay Byzantine fears of the crusaders in their midst.

April 12, 1204 Crusaders sack Constantinople, destroying buildings and church treasures. In the confusion the Mandylion/Sydoine disappears. In de Clari's words:
". . . neither Greek nor Frenchman knew what became of it."
The cloth leaves Constantinople.

Historical gap in which many looted relics found their way to the churches and cathedrals of the West. Reputed "Mandylions" turn up at Rome, Genoa, and Paris, but in no case has a clear claim to being the original been established.

An alternative theory is that the cloth, still folded so that only the face was visible, was acquired by the rich, powerful, and secretive order of the Knights Templars. Certainly, according to late-thirteenth-century rumor, they worshiped at secret chapter meetings a strange "idol" of a man's head with a reddish beard. If this is the case, then the cloth is most likely to have been kept initially with Templar Treasury at Acre. Then . . .
From literary accounts, and from an apparent Templar copy found at England, it would appear that the cloth was still in its frame, visible.

1291 Fall of Acre. Templar Treasury is transferred to Sidon. Then to Cyprus.

1306 Treasury is brought to France by Jacques de Molay, Templar Grand Master, lands at Marseilles and then is moved north to the Temple at Paris.

October 13, 1307 Templars throughout France arrested at dawn on orders of King Philip the Fair. Search is made for the "idol" but none is found. Fiercest struggle is at Paris Temple.
The Shroud is cut from its frame to be smuggled away to safety . . .

March 19, 1314 Grand Master Jacques de Molay and the order's master of Normandy, *Geoffrey de Charnay*, are burnt at the stake in Paris for heresy, after proclaiming the order's innocence.

To the de Charny family?

June 1353 French knight Geoffrey de Charny (relation to the earlier Geoffrey de Charnay uncertain) obtains rent from King John the Good for foundation of collegiate church of Lirey.

June 25, 1355 Geoffrey de Charny created *porte-oriflamme*—bearer of the French royal battle standard.

While apparently making preparations for expositions of the Shroud, at no stage during his lifetime does Geoffrey de Charny appear to have publicly revealed his possession of the Shroud—suggesting some shame attached to the circumstances in which it had been acquired.

May 28, 1356 Inauguration of now completed collegiate church of Lirey. Geoffrey de Charny praised by Henry of Poitiers, bishop of the local see of Troyes.

September 19 Geoffrey de Charny killed by the English at the Battle of Poitiers during last stand, defending his king.

November Geoffrey's widow, Jeanne de Vergy, appeals to regent of France for grants formerly made to her husband to be made out in favor of her infant son, Geoffrey II de Charny.

November 21 Jeanne's appeal granted, but real value uncertain due to France's precarious economic situation.

1357(?) First known expositions of the Shroud, held out full-length by the canons of Lirey. Huge crowds of pilgrims are attracted, and special souvenir medallions struck for these (see example in Cluny Museum, Paris, bearing arms of Geoffrey de Charny and Jeanne de Vergy).

In order to maintain the costly collegiate church, Jeanne de Vergy decides to carry out Geoffrey's intentions by holding first public expositions—for financial gain.

Bishop Henry of Poitiers refuses to believe Shroud could be genuine in possession of so comparatively humble a family. Orders expositions to be stopped.

Shroud is stored away. Jeanne de Vergy subsequently remarried to wealthy nobleman Aymon of Geneva.

1389 Geoffrey II de Charny plans renewed expositions of Shroud. As Pope Clement VII (formerly Robert of Geneva) is close relation, permission is obtained easily via papal legate.

> *To avoid controversy it seems to have been agreed in advance that the cloth should be described only as a "representation" of the Shroud; but as d'Arcis makes clear, it is "noised abroad in private" that it is the true Shroud.*

April Expositions commence, causing wrath of Pierre d'Arcis, Bishop of Troyes, who has not been consulted. D'Arcis appeals to the pope.
Pope Clement VII upholds expositions and commands Bishop d'Arcis to "perpetual silence."
D'Arcis appeals a second time, quoting Henry of Poitiers's claims that the Shroud had been fraudulently produced.

January 6, 1390 Pope Clement again insists d'Arcis keep silent, threatening him with excommunication, and sends a letter the same day to Geoffrey de Charny restating conditions under which expositions could be carried out.

May 22, 1398 Death of Geoffrey II de Charny.

1400 Daughter Margaret de Charny marries Jean de Baufremont, who is later killed at Agincourt, 1415.

June 1418 Margaret de Charny marries Humbert of Villersexel, Count de la Roche, Lord of St. Hippolyte sur Doubs.

July 6 Due to danger from marauding bands, Lirey canons hand over Shroud to Humbert de Villersexel for safekeeping. He receives it in his castle of Montfort near Montbard. Later it is kept at St. Hippolyte sur Doubs, the seat of the counts de la Roche, in the chapel called des Buessarts. According to seventeenth-century chroniclers, at this time public expositions took place each year in a meadow on the banks of the Doubs called the Pré du Seigneur.

(The copy of the Shroud subsequently to be known as the "Besançon Shroud" would seem to have been made about this time.)

1438   Death of Humbert de Villersexel.

May 8, 1443   Canons of Lirey serve notice on Margaret de Charny, requesting her to return the Shroud to them.

May 9   Parlement of Dôle gives judgment on case of Margaret de Charny *v.* Lirey canons.

July 18, 1447   Court of Besançon gives judgment on case of Margaret de Charny *v.* Lirey canons.

1449   Margaret de Charny shows Shroud at Liège in Belgium, an incident recorded by chronicler Zantiflet.
Lacking suitable heirs, Margaret looks for worthy family to safeguard Shroud's future.

September 13, 1452   Margaret de Charny shows Shroud at Germolles (near Mâcon) in a public exposition at the castle.

March 22, 1453   Margaret de Charny, at Geneva, receives from Duke Louis of Savoy castle of Varambon and revenues of estate of Miribel near Lyon for "valuable services."
Margaret decides to give Shroud to House of Savoy.

May 29, 1457   Margaret de Charny is threatened with excommunication if she does not return Shroud to Lirey canons.

May 30, 1459   Letter of excommunication sent. Charles de Noyers, Margaret's half brother, negotiates compensation to Lirey for the loss of the Shroud, which they recognize they will not now recover. The excommunication is lifted.

October 7, 1460   Margaret de Charny dies.

February 6, 1464   Duke Louis of Savoy assigns 50 gold francs to Lirey canons as compensation for the loss of the Shroud.

Good Friday, 1494 Duchess Bianca of Savoy exhibits the Shroud at Vercelli in presence of Rupis, secretary of the Duke of Mantua.

June 11, 1502 The Shroud is deposited in the chapel of Chambéry castle.

April 14, 1503 Exposition of the Shroud at Bourg-en-Bresse for the benefit of Archduke Philip of Flanders. It was shown on an altar in one of the great halls of the duke's palace.

1506 Pope Julius II assigns May 4 as annual Feast of the Holy Shroud. Expositions thereafter are probably held annually on this date.
   Chambéry now designated as the Shroud's permanent home.

August 10, 1509 New reliquary for the Shroud, donated by Margaret of Austria, brought to Chambéry by Laurent de Gorrevod, governor of Bourg-en-Bresse.

June 15, 1516 King Francis I of France arrives in Chambéry to venerate the Shroud after victory at Marignac.

October 28, 1518 Exposition of the Shroud at Chambéry in honor of Cardinal of Aragon takes place on castle walls.

1521 Exposition of Shroud at Chambéry for benefit of Dom Edme, abbot of Clairvaux. Carried by three bishops, it is shown on the castle walls, and then for privileged observers hung over the high altar of the Sainte Chapelle, Chambéry.

December 4, 1532 Fire in the chapel where the Shroud is kept at Chambéry. Removed to safety only just in time, the cloth is found to have been holed and scorched by molten silver.

April 15, 1534 Poor Clare nuns in their convent at Chambéry sew a backing piece of holland cloth onto the Shroud, then sew patches over the most damaged areas.

May 2 Repairs completed, the Shroud is returned.

1535 The Shroud is taken to Piedmont, passing through the Lanzo valley.

May 4 Exhibited in Turin.

1536 Exhibited in Milan.

1537 The Shroud is taken for safety to Vercelli because of French invasions.

March 29 The Shroud is exhibited from the tower of Bellanda, Nice.

1549 The Shroud, again at Vercelli, is kept in the treasury of Sant'Eusebius Cathedral.

November 18, 1553 French troops sack Vercelli. The Shroud saved by one of the canons, Antoine Claude Costa, who hides it in his house.

1560 Exposition of the Shroud from a balcony at Vercelli.

June 3, 1561 The Shroud is returned to Chambéry and deposited in the Church of St. Mary the Egyptian, in the Franciscan convent.

June 4 The Shroud is taken to the Sainte Chapelle in procession, accompanied by four trumpeters, torches, etc.

August 15 Exposition of Shroud in the Sainte Chapelle, Chambéry, the first in a quarter of a century.

1566 Exposition of Shroud for benefit of new duchess of Savoy from Nemours. The father of St. Francis de Sales is present. The Shroud is kept in an iron box at this time as the silver case had been destroyed during the 1532 fire.

September 14, 1578 The Shroud is conveyed to Turin for veneration by St. Charles Borromeo. This is part of a shrewd move by Duke Emmanuel Philibert to transfer his capital to Turin.
    Shroud moved to Turin.

October 10   St. Charles Borromeo, having journeyed on foot from Milan, arrives in Turin, and venerates the Shroud.

1613   Exposition of the Shroud at Turin during which St. Francis de Sales is one of the assistant bishops who hold the cloth before the people.

1639   Exposition of the Shroud at Turin at which St. Jeanne Françoise de Chantal, founder of the Order of the Visitation, is present. This takes place in the duke's residence, now the Palazzo Madama.

1670   Congregation of Indulgences grant plenary indulgence "not for venerating the cloth as the true Shroud of Christ, but rather for meditating on the Passion, especially his Death and Burial."
  This is a tacit cognizance that the Shroud's authenticity is not beyond dispute.

June 1, 1694   Shroud placed in the Royal Chapel of Turin Cathedral, in the special shrine designed for it by Guarino Guarini. On this occasion it is given a new black lining cloth by the Blessed Sebastian Valfré, who also added patches where those of the Poor Clares were becoming inadequate.
  The Shroud is given a new permanent home.

1804   Exposition of the Shroud at Turin for visit of Pope Pius VII.

1815   Exposition of the Shroud at Turin on Pope Pius VII's return to Italy after he had been held captive by Napoleon at Fontainebleau.

1842   Exposition of the Shroud at Turin.

1868   Exposition of the Shroud at Turin. Princess Clotilde of Savoy sews a new red silk lining cloth.

May 25, 1898   Exposition of the Shroud at Turin for eight days on the occasion of Italian kingdom's fiftieth anniversary. A first attempt at photography by Secondo Pia is unsuccessful due to lighting problems.

May 28 Pia makes second, successful attempt to photograph the Shroud as it hangs, under glass, above the high altar of Turin Cathedral.

Midnight Pia discovers "lifelike" image visible when the Shroud is seen in negative.

June 2 The Shroud is returned to its reliquary in the Royal Chapel.

April 21, 1902 Yves Delage, agnostic professor of comparative anatomy at the Sorbonne in Paris, lectures on the authenticity of the Shroud before the French Academy.

May 2–23, 1931 Exposition of the Shroud at Turin for twenty days on the occasion of the marriage of Prince Umberto of Piedmont. A new definitive set of photographs is taken by professional photographer Giuseppe Enrie. The "negative" image is revealed yet more clearly.

September 24–October 15, 1933 Exposition of the Shroud at Turin for the Holy Year, at the request of Pope Pius XI.

1939 The Shroud is taken to the Abbey of Monte Vergine (Avellino) for safety at the outbreak of war.

1946 Cardinal Fossati brings the Shroud back from Monte Vergine to Turin. The monks who have looked after it are given a private showing.

1955 Group Captain Leonard Cheshire, V.C., takes a crippled Scottish girl, Josie Woollam, to Turin in the hope of a cure. She is allowed to hold the rolled up Shroud in her lap, but no cure is reported.

June 16–17, 1969 The Shroud is shown to members of a special scientific commission appointed by Cardinal Pellegrino of Turin. They are allowed to examine it. New photographs in color, black-and-white, and Wood's light, are taken by Giovanni Battista Judica-Cordiglia.

October 1, 1972 Attempt to set fire to the Shroud made by unknown person who broke into the Royal Chapel after climbing over the roof of the Palace. Shroud survives due to asbestos protection within altar shrine.

November 22–23, 1973 The Shroud is exhibited for TV and press purposes in the Hall of the Swiss within the former palace of Turin. Samples of surface matter from the Shroud are taken for analysis by Dr. Max Frei, criminologist from Zurich.

November 24 Members of the commission supervise extraction of threads from areas of the Shroud seeming to bear bloodstains, also two small portions of the linen.

March 23–24, 1977 First U. S. Conference of Research on the Shroud, Albuquerque, New Mexico.

APPENDIX B

MEMORANDUM OF PIERRE D'ARCIS, BISHOP OF TROYES, TO THE AVIGNON POPE CLEMENT VII

(Written late 1389)

The case, Holy Father, stands thus. Some time since in this diocese of Troyes the Dean of a certain collegiate church, to wit, that of Lirey, falsely and deceitfully, being consumed with the passion of avarice, and not from any motive of devotion but only of gain, procured for his church a certain cloth cunningly painted, upon which by a clever sleight of hand was depicted the twofold image of one man, that is to say, the back and front, he falsely declaring and pretending that this was the actual shroud in which our Saviour Jesus Christ was enfolded in the tomb, and upon which the whole likeness of the Saviour had remained thus impressed together

Translated from the Latin by the Rev. Herbert Thurston and published in "The Holy Shroud and the Verdict of History," *The Month*, CI (1903), pages 17–29.

Paris, Bibliothèque Nationale, Collection de Champagne, v. 154, folio 138.

with the wounds which He bore. This story was put about
not only in the kingdom of France, but, so to speak, throughout the world, so that from all parts people came together to
view it. And further to attract the multitude so that money
might cunningly be wrung from them, pretended miracles
were worked, certain men being hired to represent themselves as healed at the moment of the exhibition of the
shroud, which all believed to be the shroud of our Lord. The
Lord Henry of Poitiers, of pious memory, then Bishop of
Troyes, becoming aware of this, and urged by many prudent
persons to take action, as indeed was his duty in the exercise
of his ordinary jurisdiction, set himself earnestly to work to
fathom the truth of this matter. For many theologians and
other wise persons declared that this could not be the real
shroud of our Lord having the Saviour's likeness thus imprinted upon it, since the holy Gospel made no mention of
any such imprint, while, if it had been true, it was quite unlikely that the holy Evangelists would have omitted to record
it, or that the fact should have remained hidden until the
present time. Eventually, after diligent inquiry and examination, he discovered the fraud and how the said cloth had
been cunningly painted, the truth being attested by the artist
who had painted it, to wit, that it was a work of human skill
and not miraculously wrought or bestowed. Accordingly,
after taking mature counsel with wise theologians and men of
the law, seeing that he neither ought nor could allow the
matter to pass, he began to institute formal proceedings
against the said Dean and his accomplices in order to root
out this false persuasion. They, seeing their wickedness discovered, hid away the said cloth so that the Ordinary could
not find it, and they kept it hidden afterwards for thirty-four
years or thereabouts down to the present year. And now
again the present Dean of the said church with fraudulent
intent and for the purpose of gain, suggested, as it is reported, to the Lord Geoffrey de Charny, Knight, and the
temporal lord of the place, to have the said cloth replaced in
the said church, that by a renewal of the pilgrimage the
church might be enriched with the offerings made by the
faithful. Acting upon the Dean's suggestion, who was thus
treading in the footsteps of his predecessor, the Knight went to
the Cardinal de Thury, your Holiness' Nuncio and Legate in
French territory, and suppressing the facts that the said cloth
at the time above referred to was asserted to be the shroud

of our Saviour, and that it bore the Saviour's likeness imprinted upon it, and that the Ordinary had taken action against the canons in order to stamp out the error which had arisen, and that the said cloth for fear of the Ordinary had been hidden away, nay even, it is said, conveyed out of the diocese, he represented to the Cardinal that the said cloth was a picture or figure of the shroud, which many people came to visit out of devotion and which had previously been much venerated and resorted to in that church, but on account of the war and other causes, by the command of the Ordinary, had been placed for a long time in safer keeping, petitioning that he might be allowed to set up in the said church this picture or figure of the shroud which so many out of devotion desired to see, so that it might there be shown to the people and venerated by the faithful. Then the said Lord Cardinal, without entirely approving the petition, but probably acting on the facts before him and so far prudently, granted to the petitioner by Apostolic authority that without asking leave of the Ordinary or of any other person he might set up this picture or figure of the shroud of our Lord in the said church or in any other decent place. And under cover of this written authority the cloth was openly exhibited and shown to the people in the church aforesaid on great holidays, and frequently on feasts and at other times, with the utmost solemnity, even more than when the Body of Christ our Lord is exposed; to wit, by two priests vested in albs with stoles and maniples and using the greatest possible reverence, with lighted torches and upon a lofty platform constructed for this special purpose; and although it is not publicly stated to be the true shroud of Christ, nevertheless this is given out and noised abroad in private, and so it is believed by many, the more so, because, as stated above, it was on the previous occasion declared to be the true shroud of Christ, and by a certain ingenious manner of speech it is now in the said church styled not the *sudarium* but the *sanctuarium*,[1] which to the ears of the common folk, who are not

---

[1] The words *sudarium* and *sanctuarium* in the Latin hardly indicate the ingenious assonance which the writer evidently intended to denounce as a deliberate deception of the people and which local pronunciation may possibly have assisted. Formerly the cloth had been called the *Saint Suaire;* now this was not said, but it was styled the *sanctuaire.* The word *sanctuarium* was one which seems to have been applied to any relic or object of pious veneration, in fact its most common signification was simply "relic."

keen to observe distinctions, sounds much the same thing, and crowds of people resort there as often as it is shown or is expected to be shown, under the belief, or more truly the delusion, that it is the true shroud. Moreover, it is currently reported amongst them that it has been approved by the Apostolic See by means of the letters of the said Lord Cardinal.

Accordingly, most Holy Father, perceiving this great scandal renewed amongst the people and the delusion growing to the peril of souls, observing also that the Dean of the said church did not keep within the terms of the Cardinal's letters, obtained though they were by the suppression of the truth and the suggestion of what was false, as already explained, desiring to meet the danger as well as I could and to root out this false persuasion from the flock committed to me, after consultation with many prudent advisers, I prohibited the said Dean under pain of excommunication, by the very act sufficiently published [eo ipso latae], from exhibiting this cloth to the people until otherwise might be determined.

He, however, refusing obedience and lodging an appeal, in defiance of the prohibition went on with the exhibition as before. Moreover, the knight, maintaining and defending this behaviour, by holding the said cloth with his own hands on a certain solemn feast, and showing it to the people with the observances above described, caused himself, by a royal warrant [salvagardia], to be put in formal possession and occupation of the said cloth and of the right of exhibiting it, and had this notified to me; and so under cover of the appeal as well as of the said royal warrant this delusion is shielded and propagated, to the contempt of the Church, scandal of the people, and peril of souls—all which I am powerless to remedy—nay more, to the defamation of my above-named predecessor who denounced the abuse in his time, and of myself who to the best of my poor ability am also anxious to take such prudent action as I may. But, alas! The scandal is upheld and defended and its supporters cause it to be spread abroad among the people that I am acting through jealousy and cupidity and to obtain possession of the cloth for myself, just as similar reports were circulated before against my predecessor; while, on the other hand, others aver that I move too half-heartedly in the matter and that I make myself a laughing-stock by allowing the abuse to continue. But though I have earnestly and humbly cited the said knight and besought him that he would for a time suspend the exhibition of the said cloth until your Holiness could be consulted and should pronounce upon the matter, he paid no attention, or rather without my knowledge he had had representations made to your Holiness in the same sense as those already made to the said Lord Cardinal, adding that I refused to defer to the said Cardinal's letters, that I disregarded the appeal and went on launching inhibitions and sentences of excommunication against those who exhibited the cloth and against the people who came to venerate it. But with all deference to the author of these representations, my action in thus proceeding against those who exhibited and venerated the cloth was in no wise derogatory to the said Lord Cardinal's letters, obtained though they were surreptitiously. This authorization of his by no means conceded that the cloth could be exposed with publicity or venerated, but only that it might be restored to or lodged in the said church or some other decent place. And because they would not keep to the terms of the Cardinal's permit therefore it was that I proceeded against them according to the ordinary forms of law, as in my duty I am bound, and not without much asking of counsel, with the view of removing the scandal and the said popular delusion, believing that I should be gravely in fault if I connived at such abuses. Moreover, having to look to my own security in this matter, I was compelled, acting always upon the advice of prudent counsellors, to have recourse to the aid of the secular arm, and this more particularly because the said knight in the first instance had begun to place the matter in the hands of the civil authorities by causing himself to be put in formal possession of the right of exhibiting the cloth by the King's warrant, as said above, which seems a sufficiently absurd proceeding. Accordingly I took measures to have the cloth placed in the custody of the King's officers, always with the same end in view, viz., that at least until I could bring the whole story to the notice of your Holiness there might for the time being be an end of these exhibitions. And in this request I prevailed without any difficulty with the court of the King's Parliament when once they were fully informed of the superstitious origin of this shroud, of the use to which it was put, and of the delusion and scandal to which I have called attention. Indeed it is a wonder to all who know the facts of the case that the opposition which hampers me in these proceedings comes from the Church, from which quarter I should have looked for vigorous support, nay, rather have expected punishment if I had shown myself slothful or remiss. However, the knight above mentioned has been beforehand with me, and, having represented the matter as I have explained, has obtained from your Holiness a Brief in which the said Lord Cardinal's letters are substantially confirmed *ex certa scientia* and permission is granted that in spite of all prohibitions and appeals, the said cloth may be shown and exposed for the veneration of the faithful; while, as I hear,—for I have not been able to procure a copy of the said Brief,—perpetual silence is enjoined upon myself.

But whereas the canon law requires me to see that no man be imposed upon by false representations and documents for purposes of gain, and because I am certain that this Brief was obtained by suggestion of what is false and suppression of the truth, and that otherwise it would never have been issued, while I was neither cited nor heard, especially as the resumption ought to stand in my favour that I would not interfere in such a cause without reason, or disturb any man in any practice of devotion which was harmless and free from extravagance, I do most confidently trust that your Holiness will bear with me if in view of the foregoing facts I still oppose the said exposition until I have fuller instructions from your Holiness yourself, now better informed of the truth of the case. I would ask you then, most blessed Father, to vouchsafe to bestow your attention upon the foregoing statement and to take measures that such scandal and delusion and abominable superstition may be put an end to both in fact and seeming, in such wise that this cloth be held neither for *sudarium* nor *sanctuarium*, nor for an image or figure of our Lord's *sudarium*, since our Lord's *sudarium* was nothing of the kind, nor, in fine, under any other ingenious pretext be exhibited to the people or exposed for veneration, but that to express horror of such superstition it be publicly condemned, the surreptitious letters above spoken of being recalled, or more truly declared null and void [for fear that the keen-eyed persecutors and detractors of the Church should rail at the Church's discipline and say that a more prompt and efficacious remedy against scandals and impostures is found in the secular tribunals than in those of ecclesiastical authority].[2] I offer myself here as ready to supply all information sufficient to remove any doubt concerning the facts alleged both from public report and otherwise, in order to exonerate myself and also to discharge my conscience in a matter which I have greatly at heart. Moreover, if health had allowed I should have presented myself personally to your Holiness to state my complaint to the best of my poor ability, for I am convinced that I cannot fully or sufficiently express in writing the grievous nature of the scandal, the contempt brought upon the Church and ecclesiastical jurisdiction, and the danger to souls; still I do what I can, chiefly that I may be guiltless before God, leaving all else to the disposition of your Holiness, whom may the Almighty long preserve, &c.

APPENDIX C

COURT OF CONSTANTINE

PORPHYROGENITUS "STORY OF THE

IMAGE OF EDESSA"

(A.D. 945)

A narrative based on various historical accounts, on the non-man-made holy image of Christ our God, which was sent to Abgar. And how it was translated from Edessa to this most blessed queen of cities, Constantinople.

1. God, the Word, the Coeternal with the Father, was beyond all understanding not only in himself, but also almost the majority, or even all of his works, are obscured by the

---

[2] The words in brackets, though they appear in the Bishop's own draft, were probably not retained in the copy sent to the Pope, as they are marked *Vacat*. Probably the Bishop, on second thoughts, judged them to be too strong.

Official history of the Mandylion, written shortly after the cloth's translation to Constantinople from Edessa. Translated from the Greek by Bernard Slater and boys of Bradford Grammar School, West Yorkshire, assisted by the Reverend John Jackson.

From Migne, *Patrologia cursus completus, series graeca* (Paris, 1857–66), vol. CXIII, cols. 423–54.

same darkness of uncomprehensibility—not only his creations as maker of the universe, but also what he wrought by the primal and unique power of his divinity when he came among us and took our human nature according to the divine purpose. It is, therefore, imperative that anyone who is not ignorant of his own shortcomings and realizes that he can have no knowledge of things that are beyond his powers, must not claim too much and risk his ignorance by contending either that he knows everything or that nothing is beyond his understanding.

Therefore with regard to the impression of God's assumed Human Form—which was depicted without being drawn by the marvelous will of its creator—which the towel received which was then sent to Abgar as a healing charm, but has now been transferred, under God's purpose, from Edessa to this queen of cities to save and guard it so that it may seem to lack no good thing, since it has the undoubted right to rule all, he who hears of and looks at the matter with a respect for religion and a sense of justice, must, I think, make a careful, systematic study of the records, and try to arrive at a genuine knowledge of the ancient story—the reason why by a moist secretion without coloring or painter's art an impression of the face was made in the linen cloth and how the cloth which was made of such a perishable material eventually became indestructible, and all other scientific investigations that the man with the proper approach would make—but with the realization that concessions must be made to the unintelligibility of God's wisdom, since anyone who tries to achieve detailed understanding of everything forces himself into total ignorance and falls to the depths of unintelligibility, and he is in danger not only of failing to grasp the supreme issues, but of appearing not to make any concession in trivial matters, meeting with severe punishment. And so to all who approach the subject with a right faith and a newer interest I say, Come, listen, and I will tell you those things which after making necessary, exhaustive tests of everything, and pursuing a painstaking enquiry into the true facts, from the works of historians, and from people who have come to us from Syria and the secret memories which they said were personal among them, I have succeeded in authenticating.

2. When our Lord, God, and Savior, Jesus Christ, visited us for the purpose of redeeming the human race, there was

widespread peace, as the prophet had foretold, over the earth, plurality of governments had been destroyed and the whole world was held safe as it were by one girdle, the Roman empire, and was subject to one ruler.

By this unification everyone had dealings with everyone else without fear and people seemed to inhabit a world divided into parts but which seemed to be the property of one Lord—just as the whole universe has one creator—and they bowed their neck to the principal slave, and kept the peace with one another. It was also because of this unity that the toparch of Edessa at that time, Abgar, was a friend and acquaintance of the praetor of Egypt, and they exchanged frequent communications through their messengers. Thus, at the same time as the Lord our God, to fulfill the Father's intentions, put before men the teaching of salvation, and by his marvelous and unexpected miracles converted men to faith in Him, it happened that one of Abgar's servants, named Ananias, happened to be traveling through Palestine to Egypt, when he saw Christ in the distance, drawing the people away from error by his words and performing incredible miracles. When he had completed his journey to Egypt and discharged his duties, he returned to his lord. He knew that Abgar was crippled with chronic arthritis and eaten by black leprosy, and that he was in constant pain suffering from this double burden or rather many-sided disease, since he was troubled by the pain in his joints and endured the miseries of leprosy. He was also ashamed at his disfigurement on account of which he would scarcely let himself be seen by men. He was not only bedridden for most of the time but also hid himself away in shame when friends came to visit him. For this reason during his return he (the servant) took pains to get some clearer information from these same men, so that he might have certain news to take to his master, that perhaps even he (the master) might be thought worthy of a cure through that man. Once more he found out from them that our Lord was busy with the same things—raising the dead, giving sight to the blind, making the lame to walk, and healing every form of sickness.

3. With this knowledge then and realizing that our Lord had clearly done these things, he returned and informed Abgar and spread the news of what he had seen and heard among more people. For this reason, since he had performed an incidental service greater than his main task and had

brought good news to Abgar in person, he was considered worthy of a fitting reception, and he was considered to be one of his most loyal servants. For since the sickness always treats the promise of a cure as a great prize and the story and the hope of cure sets the man on, it persuades him to send someone off in search of this man who has been brought to his notice. Abgar first decided to summon by letter the person who was reputed to be able to cure such illnesses. The letter he wrote to our Lord was soon heard of everywhere and its contents were as follows:

4. "Abgar the Toparch of Edessa sends his greetings to Jesus the Savior who has come to light as a good physician in the city of Jerusalem.

"Your deeds have come to my notice and your healings performed without either medicine or herbs. For as rumor has it, you make the blind see, the lame walk, you cure lepers and drive out unclean spirits and demons, you heal those who are tortured by chronic illnesses, and you raise the dead. Having heard all these deeds of yours, I have thought of two possible explanations: either that you are God and have come down from heaven and do these things, or that you do these things because you are the Son of God. For this reason I have written to you to ask you to take the trouble to come to me and cure me of my disease. For I have also heard that the Jews murmur against you and want to harm you. I have a very small city, but it is stately and will be sufficient for us both to live in peace."

5. Since, then, Ananias was the person who had received clear tokens of Jesus' goodwill towards his master, and also happened to know the route and had knowledge of the artist's craft, he was sent by Abgar to deliver this letter to Jesus. Abgar also told him that if he was not able to persuade Jesus to return to him by means of the letter, he was to bring back to him a portrait accurately drawn of Jesus' appearance so that he might be informed as it were by a shadow, not only through word of mouth but also through sight as well what he was like who had done these fantastic miracles.

When Ananias, who had been sent, reached Judea, he found our Lord in the open air talking to a crowd of people who had collected and performing some extraordinary miracles. Since he was not able to approach Jesus because of the people who came from different places for different needs, he sat on a rock which did not protrude far from the ground and which was quite near to the place where Jesus was talking. Our Savior could easily be distinguished in the crowd as he stood out from the rest, and immediately Ananias focused his eyes on him, held a piece of paper in his hand and began to draw a likeness of him.

6. Jesus realized what was happening by his divine inspiration, and so he summoned Thomas and said, "Go to that place and bring me that man who is sitting on the rock drawing me, and bring the letter which he has brought from home, so that he may fulfill the command of the man who sent him."

Thomas went and, recognizing Ananias by what Jesus had said he would find him doing, he brought him to Jesus. Before he took the letter from him, Christ told him the reason for his coming to him and the purport of the letter. He then took it and, having read it, gave him another letter for Abgar as follows:

7. "Blessed are you, Abgar, in that you believed in me without having actually seen me. For it has been written about me that those who have not seen me do not believe in me, so that those who have not seen me may believe and live. About your letter in which you asked me to come to you —it is necessary for me to fulfill all that I was sent here to fulfill, and, once I have done that, to return to my Father who sent me here. When I have returned to him, I will send to you one of my disciples to cure your suffering and to give you and your household eternal life and peace. He will also provide your city with a sufficient defence to keep all your enemies from taking it."

8. Christ entrusted this letter to Ananias, and knew that the man was anxious to bring to completion the other command of his master, that he should take a likeness of Jesus' face to Abgar. The Savior then washed his face in water, wiped off the moisture that was left on the towel that was given to him, and in some divine and inexpressible manner had his own likeness impressed on it. This towel he gave to Ananias and instructed him to hand it over to Abgar so that the latter might have some consolation for his longing and disease.

When he was returning with these things, Ananias then

hurried to the town of Hierapolis, which is called Memmich in the Saracen and Mabbog in the Syrian language. He lodged outside this city at a place where a heap of tiles which had been recently prepared was lying, and here Ananias hid that sacred piece of cloth. About midnight, a great fire appeared covering so much ground that it seemed in the town that everything round about was on fire.

They were terrified for their own lives, left the city, and searched for the conflagration which they had seen. There they found Ananias, and arrested him on the grounds that he had committed the crime. They asked about the matter, inquired who he was, where he was going, and from where he had come.

9. Because Ananias was quite at a loss at the unusual nature of this accusation, he told them where he was from, where he was coming from, and what he was carrying. He told how he had hidden his bundle among the tiles, from where the flame had indeed seemed to emanate. The Hieropolitans at once wanted to find out whether this statement was true, and so they searched the spot and found there not only what Ananias had placed there, but also, in one of the tiles nearby, another copy of the likeness of the divine face. Unexpectedly and incomprehensibly the divine image had been transferred to the tile from the cloth without being drawn. On seeing this, the people were filled with confusion and amazement because of this and also, since they could nowhere find a fire burning but the flame seemed to be emitted by the luster on the face [of Jesus] they retained the tile on which the divine image had been stamped, as a sacred and highly valued treasure. They guessed from what they had seen that it was some divine potency. The original copy, and the bearer of it, they were afraid to retain, and sent to Abgar. Up to this time, the image on the tile has been kept safe and revered by the inhabitants of this township—the unpainted copy of the unpainted portrait, the copy not made by human hands. Ananias completed the remainder of his journey and declared to his master all that had occurred on route, giving him also the salutary tokens which he had brought.

10. This is the generally received story about the divine portrait of our Savior in the cloth. However, there is another

story about this which is neither incredible nor short of reliable witnesses.

Therefore I will give this also so that no one may suspect
that the first opinion is correct through ignorance of the second. It would not be at all surprising if the facts had often
been distorted in view of the time that has elapsed. The chief
point, that the Savior's face was impressed on the cloth by
some miracle, is agreed by all. There is, however, some disa-
greement about the circumstances, notably the time. Yet it
does not affect the truth whether the event in fact occurred
before or after the time which is stated. The alternative version of the story is as follows:

11. They say that when Christ was about to go voluntarily
to death he was seen to reveal his human weakness, feel anguish, and pray. According to the Evangelist, sweat dropped
from him like drops of blood. Then they say he took this
piece of cloth which we see now from one of the disciples
and wiped off the drops of sweat on it. At once the still-visi-
ble impression of that divine face was produced. Jesus gave
the cloth to Thomas, and instructed him that after Jesus had
ascended into heaven, he should send Thaddaeus with it to
Abgar, thereby fulfilling the promise he had made by letter.
After our Lord Jesus Christ had ascended into heaven,
Thomas gave the divine portrait of Christ's face to Thaddaeus and sent him to Abgar.

12. When Thaddaeus had reached Edessa, he first lodged
with one of the Jews who were living there; this man was
called Tobias. Before talking to Abgar, the disciple of Christ
wished to make himself known to Abgar by his actions. He
therefore cured those who were ill in the city calling only the
name of Christ. Therefore, talk about Christ became widespread (as happens in such situations; when things happen
unexpectedly, there are always plenty of people to announce
them) and the rumors of the arrival of one of Christ's disciples reached the ears of Abgar by one of his nobles, named
Abdu.

Abgar at once presumed, from the hopes he had formed,
that this was the man whom Jesus had promised in his letter
that he would send to him. He learned more perfectly about
Thaddaeus from Abdu, and decided to have him brought to
him. Tobias therefore went and told this to the apostle.
Thaddaeus replied that he had been sent to him by the

power of the Lord and next day went to see Abgar. When he was about to appear before him, he placed the portrait on his own forehead like a sign and so entered.

Abgar saw him coming in from a distance, and thought he saw a light shining from his face which no eye could stand, which the portrait Thaddaeus was wearing produced.

Abgar was dumbfounded by the unbearable glow of the brightness, and, as though forgetting the ailments he had and the long paralysis of his legs, he at once got up from his bed and compelled himself to run. In making his paralyzed limbs go to meet Thaddaeus, he felt the same feeling, though in a different way, as those who saw that face flashing with lightning on Mount Tabor.

13. And so, receiving the likeness from the apostle and placing it reverently on his head, and applying it to his lips, and not depriving the rest of the parts of his body of such a touch, immediately he felt all the parts being marvelously strengthened and taking a turn for the better; his leprosy cleansed and gone, but a trace of it still remained on his forehead. Having been instructed then by the apostle more clearly of the doctrine of truth, and concerning the amazing miracles by Christ and his divine passion and burial and resurrection from the dead and his taking up into heaven, and having confessed that Christ was the true God, he asked about the likeness portrayed on the linen cloth. For when he had carefully inspected it, he saw that it did not consist of earthly colors, and he was astounded at its power, by which he had miraculously risen from his bed, and become numbered among the healthy. At this, Thaddaeus explained about the time of the agony, and that the likeness was due to sweat, not pigments. He said he had come by the word of the Lord, and went through all that has been revealed in the previous part of our account.

14. When then after the laying on of hands in the name of Jesus Christ by Thaddaeus, the pain had vanished and his loosened limbs were as it were drawn together, and his deformity disappeared and everything now tended to health, Abgar was possessed by complete wonder, and said, "Truly you are a genuine disciple of Jesus the Son of God, who cured without drugs and herbs. And I am overcome by such great love for him, and faith in him, that did I not fear the superiority of the power of the Romans, who do not tolerate

their subjects taking up arms against one another, I would perhaps have waged war against the Jews who crucified the Lord, and subdued them. But as it is, since I have been told his was voluntary passion, and since I am persuaded that had he not willed it the wicked would not have prevailed against him, I take no further action.

"I ask to be thought worthy of divine baptism, and with all my household to enter into this fellowship, and to devote myself to the Lord Christ."

Having first performed therefore many miracles and having healed all from their sicknesses, among whom was the man who first brought the report about him to Abgar and whom he freed from his gout—the apostle of the Lord brought Abgar to the holy font. And having performed the customary rites for him, he baptized Abgar and his wife and children, and all in his house. And Abgar went forth from this divine water of cleansing completely pure and healthy, and even the remaining small traces of leprosy on his forehead vanished at once.

15. Henceforward the ruler totally honored and reverenced such a likeness of the Lord's appearance and added this to the other marks of honor. A statue of one of the notable Greek gods has been erected before the public gate of the city by the ancient citizens and settlers of Edessa to which everyone wishing to enter the city had to offer worship and customary prayers. Only then could he enter into the roads and streets of the city. Abgar then destroyed this statue and consigned it to oblivion, and in its place set up this likeness of our Lord Jesus Christ not made by hand, fastening it to a board and embellishing it with the gold which is now to be seen, inscribing these words on the gold: "Christ the God, he who hopes in thee is never disappointed."

And he laid down that everyone who intended to come through that gate, should—in place of that former worthless and useless statue—pay fitting reverence and due worship and honor to the very wondrous miracle-working image of Christ, and only then enter the city of Edessa. And such a monument to and offering of his piety was preserved as long as Abgar and his son were alive, his son succeeding to his father's kingdom and his piety. But their son and grandson succeeded to his father's and grandfather's kingdom but did not inherit their piety, but spurned their piety and deserted to demons and idols. Therefore, as intending to pay their due to demons, he wished just as his grandfather had consigned that idolatrous statue to oblivion so he would bring the same condemnation on the image of the Lord also. But this treacherous move was balked of his prey. For the bishop of the region, perceiving this beforehand, showed as much forethought as possible, and, since the place where the image lay had the appearance of a semispherical cylinder, he lit a lamp in front of the image, and placed a tile on top.

Then he blocked the approach from the outside with mortar and baked bricks and reduced the wall to a level in appearance. And because the hated image was not seen, this impious man desisted from his attempt. For the following reason, I think the priest decided to place the tile in front of the image namely that there might be no rot from the dampness of the building or the wetness of the mortar in the receptacle of the image which might increase the damage done by lapse of time.

16. Then a long interval of time elapsed and the erection of this sacred image and its concealment both disappeared from men's memories. When then Chosroes, king of the Persians, in his time was ravaging the cities of Asia and hurried to Edessa too and in front of it fixed a rampart and moved up every sort of machine and prepared every suitable instrument for the taking of the city and constructed every kind of machine for heaving missiles, violently shaking walls, and breaking through gates, the Edessenes, being in such great danger, considered among themselves all possible means for resisting the hostile array and sent embassies to the Roman generals to seek aid.

Halio, however, who was at that time the commander of the Roman forces, was himself distressed by the enemy, and was unable to send help to Edessa, but he did attempt to cheer their spirits with a letter, reminding them of the letter from the Lord and of the true declaration which it contained, because of which rumor and belief had it that the city was impregnable. Meanwhile, however, the Persians as well as the open attack were in addition planning surprise attacks. At a distance from the city they began to dig and made cunning preparations to get inside the city by tunneling underground; but when they were actually within the walls, still

underground, just like underwater divers their presence was
revealed to the defenders for this reason. . . . The copper
utensils, which were hung up all over the house where a
coppersmith lived, rang as the Persians were burrowing underground and carrying earth out. Therefore, the citizens, in
their helplessness, and reduced to the depths of despair,
turned for refuge to God, and with heartfelt anguish and
tears, they prayed fervently to him. And so it was in the
course of that night there appeared to the bishop (Eulalius it
was) a well-dressed, awe-inspiring figure of a woman, larger
than human, who advised him to take the divinely created
image of Christ, and with it to entreat that the Lord would
give a complete demonstration of his marvelous acts. The
bishop replied that he had no idea whether the image existed
at all, or, if so, whether they or anyone else had it. Then the
apparition in woman's form said that such an image lay hidden in the place above the city gates in a way which she
described.

17. The bishop was convinced by the clearness of the vision which appeared to him, and therefore at dawn he went
prayerfully to the spot, made a thorough search, and found
this sacred image intact, and the lamp which had not been
put out over so many years. On the piece of tile which had
been placed in front of the lamp to protect it he found that
there had been engraved another likeness of the image which
has by chance been kept safe at Edessa up to the present
time. And so he took in his hands the sacred likeness of
Christ, God in human form, and with rising hopes he walked
over that place where, because of the rattling of the copper-
ware, the Persians had been detected by the noise of the
bronze vessels in the act of trying to dig their way. The citizens began to dig from inside, and when the two sides came
within a short distance of each other they dripped oil from
that lamp into the fire which they had prepared for use
against the enemy, and by letting it fall onto the Persians
who were in the tunnel, killed them all. Next, after their deliverance from this stratagem, they tried a similar form of attack against the siege equipment outside the walls, and at
one stroke burned them down, killing many of the enemy
who manned them. As morale by this time was once more
high, they had also been firing frequent volleys of stones
from the walls, and because of this it so happened that the

commander of the accursed army had fallen, along with many others. This was not all; also, the fire which had been lit outside by the Persians for use against the defenders, and which was fed by an immeasurable quantity of wood from olive trees and trees of all other kinds that had been cut down, was turned against the men who had kindled it by the divine [power] of the sacred image, the defender's ally. For when Eulalius brought out the image in his hands from its hiding place in the upper wall, and with it made his way through the city, suddenly as often occurs in that region, a violent wind arose and turned the flame on those who were lighting the fire, and it pursued them and burnt them up, just as once happened to the Chaldeans.

18. This story is not an unattested yarn, which I am spinning to entertain or deceive. Three patriarchs together, Job of Alexandria, Christopher of Antioch, and Basil of Jerusalem, have recorded it and have acknowledged that it is true in their correspondence with the emperor Theophilus, who has been a violator of sacred images. When they were demonstrating at length the sanctity and respect due to sacred images, they also made a special point of mentioning this. It is possible for anyone who wishes to read that long letter for himself to find out all about it. But if anyone is well-versed in Evagrius' *Church History,* he will know what that writer has to say, in his fourth book, about this sacred image.

19. He records how, among other things Chosroes did this, wishing to openly prove wrong the lie that the city was impregnable, which was common talk among the Christians. He had a huge, or rather immeasurable, quantity of logs collected according to orders in a short time because of the manpower of his army. He fixed them in the ground in a double wall around the city and poured earth into the space in between. On this he built another wall to face that of the city. This was higher than the walls of Edessa, and now, as never before, he intended to throw missiles at the defenders from a higher position. As they saw this construction by means of which they expected the enemy to walk into the town as if over level ground rising up like a mountain over against their walls, the men of Edessa felt helpless; but nevertheless they made counterpreparations as best they could by trying to dig a trench in front of the recently built enemy wall, so that if they could set on fire the stakes in front of the

mound, they might be able to scoop out the earth from underneath into the trench and that thus that great wall which had risen up like something in a dream could be quickly demolished and would cave in. They managed to dig the trench, but failed utterly in their object of setting the timber on fire, since the fire was able to take a firm hold only of some material which they had laid down but not of the wood because the earth inside was packed tight, and the wood was still green. They brought the sacred image into that trench which they had just dug. With it, they purified some water and sprinkled this on the fire and on the timber, making the fire become effective. Because divine power helped them as they did this in faith, the water became like oil on the fire and kindled the flames more and caused it to consume anything in its path. So it was at this point that the Persian king, abandoning hope of storming the city and learning of the source of the offender's relief, proceeded to make peace and returned to his own country.

20. He too, however, was not long in benefiting from the favor of this sacred image which was now the support of his enemies and destroyer of his own people. His daughter was possessed of an evil spirit. She became unnaturally disturbed and cried out continually through the spirit's activity within her, saying that unless the miraculous image was brought from Edessa, the spirit confined within her could not be freed. The king heard this and reflected upon the events of the siege, for he had indeed noticed the sudden remarkable strength and courage of the Edessenes. He wrote immediately to the chief man of the city, and to Eulalius the bishop, and to the citizens themselves, begging that this sacred and most potent image should be sent to him in all haste. He mentioned his daughter's suffering as the reason for this request, which he begged them, in every possible way, not to disregard. But the Edessenes considered how untrustworthy were the Persian ways, and they suspected that the Persian king wanted by some trick to deprive them of their strength. They were wary of letting their protectress and patron go, and also of breaking the state of peace on such a pretext as this. So they made a sagacious plan, one that was of considerable benefit to themselves.

They made a new image, in every way like the old one, as near perfect a reproduction as possible, grafting with men's

materials as close a resemblance as they could to something
not man-made. This copy they sent to the king who had
asked for it. When the party bringing the image entered Persian territory, the demon became inspired, and through the
king's daughter cried out that it would soon come out and
change its abode thanks to the power of that which was coming, but only if the image called for went back and did not
approach the king's land nor the Persian city. The demon in
addition to this required and entreated many other things of
the king. The king promised and the demon came out of the
girl and the king's child was then restored to good health.
Chosroes (the king) either as a fulfillment of the spirit's
demands and confirmation of his own promise, or through fear
of the power of the approaching image, because of his own
loathsome and abominable behavior, sent messengers to
order the image's return to the city from which it came. And
he offered gifts at his own expense to those who had sent it.

21. So there was among the Edessenes this valuable property, this inexhaustible source of wealth, the original image,
no copy, eternally winning veneration from them and offering protection in return. Then all the best and most beautiful
treasures began to flow from everywhere into this royal city
[i.e., Constantinople] and it was divinely decreed that this
sacred image should be stored here along with the other
treasures. The Roman [i.e. Byzantine] who was master of
the Roman Empire was keen to gain possession of this by his
own efforts and enrich the royal city. So a number of times
he sent to Edessa and asked that this image should be sent to
him together with the letter written in the Lord's hand. He
promised to give them something in return—namely two hundred Moslem captives and twelve thousand silver pieces in
coin. But the people of Edessa said it was not profitable for
them to trade the guardian and protector of their native city
for silver and mortal men.

22. He then pressed his request on them further, but again
and again they fended him off. At last, in the six thousand
four hundred and fifty-second year from the creation of the
world, the emir of Edessa sent requesting assurance from the
king by a secret letter sealed with a golden seal for secrecy
that Roman armies would not come as enemies to attack
these four cities—i.e., Rochas (which is what the barbarians
called Edessa), Chara, Sarate, and Samosata. Nor should

they plunder the territories around these cities nor enslave the inhabitants of them. But two hundred Moslems taken from kindred peoples should be released to him and the promised amount of silver should be paid; then he would hand over the image which they were asking for and the letter written by Christ.

23. The emperor, in his eagerness for such a boon, gave in to all the proffered terms. He dispatched Abraham, bishop of Samosata, dear to God, who at this point of time was visiting them, to receive the sacred image and the letter of our Lord Jesus Christ. Both the emperor who sent and the bishop who obliged him had qualms, lest some trick were played on them in the transaction, and there were handed to him, instead of the genuine divine article, the copy made for the Persian affair. He received on his request, as earnest of good faith, both these and yet another copy which was worshiped in the Nestorian church, and, as it seemed, was copied from the original long ago. These were given back—only the one which was the true article was retained.

24. But this happened later. Meanwhile rebellion arose among the faithful of Edessa, and the city was in great turmoil as they would not allow their most precious possession to be taken away, which brought them protection against harm. Eventually the Moslem emir managed, by persuading some, using force against others, and terrifying others with threats of death, to get the image handed over. Then there was a sudden outbreak of thunder and lightning with torrential rain, as if by design or arrangement, just as the image and the letter of Christ were about to leave the city of Edessa. Once more those who had clung to these things before were stirred again. They maintained that God was showing by these events that it was not in accordance with Divine Will that these most holy objects should be transferred. But as the Moslem emir, in whom rested absolute authority, judged it necessary to stand by their original agreements and fulfill their promise, the very precious image and the letter written by Christ were taken from the city and brought to this.

25. The journey in the course of time brought the bearers of the sacred objects to the banks of the Euphrates. There arose once more an uproar just as violent as before, the Edes-

senes saying that unless there appeared a sign from God, come what may, they would not give up the effective cause of their safety. So to those who were full of hesitation and tempted God a sign was given—for the boat in which they had determined to cross the Euphrates was still moored to the Syrian bank, as only the bishops had yet boarded it, bearing the sacred image and the letter, while the tossing of the water held back those involved in the dispute. Suddenly, without any rowers, helmsman, or even anyone towing, it set off and, guided merely by the will of God, reached the opposite bank. This miracle filled all the onlookers with stunned amazement and induced them willingly to carry out their mission.

26. The bearers of the sacred objects next reached Samosata. There were the bishops of Samosata and Edessa with his principal priest and certain other very devout Christians, and with them a servant of the emir who took his name from Rome. When they had already spent some days there and many miraculous things had happened, they continued their journey. Countless miracles again happened by agency of the holy image and the letter of Christ while en route. Blind men were unexpectedly made to see, the lame were made well again, those who had long been bedridden leapt up, and those with withered hands were made whole again. In short, all diseases and sicknesses were dispelled. And those who were healed glorified God and praised his wondrous deeds.

27. Already having completed most of the journey they soon came to the monastery of the Holy Mother of God, called the monastery of Eusebius, which happens to be situated in the Optimatan Province.

In the church of this monastery the casket holding the wonder-working image was deposited with due reverence and religious ceremony, and many people who came there with a pure intention were cured of their diseases. There came also here a man troubled by an evil spirit, whom the evil spirit used as an instrument, and uttered bountiful praises to the image and letter through him. For previously, similarly possessed people said to the Lord, "We know who you are, O Holy one of Israel," and he finally uttered these words as if in prophecy. "Constantinople take the glory and joy, and you Constantine Porphyrogenitus, your kingdom." When these words had been uttered, the man was made whole and immediately freed from the attack of the evil spirit. There are many who bear witness to this utterance. For as the emperor had sent the chief men of his council to meet and honor the desired object and many of the royal bodyguard came with them, it happened that both the magistrates and nobles and some of the lower rank heard and witnessed it. Since the utterance was soon proved true, there is just cause for wondering from where the evil spirit received its gift of prophecy. For those who have turned aside from the divine glory and have dealings with darkness instead of light are not believed to possess this gift of their own nature. For clearly, just as the divine power used Balaam as the agent of his prophecy at that time, and on various occasions often those unworthy of the gift, entirely in accordance with a wise and ingenious plan, so in this case the power inside the divine image made use of the evil spirit and foretold because of this events which were soon to happen. Since events in the meantime turned out thus, it is perhaps not unreasonable to mention them. But let us proceed to describe the events which followed.

28. On August 15, while the kings were celebrating the customary Feast of the Assumption of the Ever-Virgin Mother of God in the church sacred to her at Blachernae, the bearers of these sacred items arrived during the late evening, and the casket containing the image and letter was deposited within the upper oratory of this holy church. The kings drew near and hailed it from outside with reverent adoration. Then with the honor of an armed escort and many lights they took it aboard the royal galley and reached the palace with it. They set it up there in the holy chapel which is called Pharos [the cloak]—perhaps because it is embellished as splendidly as a fine garment. The next day, which was the sixteenth of the month, having again hailed it and done reverence to it with pious reverence, the priests and the younger kings (for the old Emperor had been left at home on account of his weak disposition) with psalms and hymns and ample lights traversed the road down to the sea, and when they had placed it in the royal galley, they sailed along close to the city, so that in some way it might give protection to the city by its sea voyage, and anchored outside the west wall of the city. The kings, the elder statesmen, the patriarch, and the whole assembly of the church all disembarked and, continuing on foot with a suitable escort, escorted the vessel guard-

ing the most holy and precious relics like a second ark, or even more precious than that. They walked round the outside of the walls as far as the Golden Gate, and then entered the city with high psalmody, hymns, and spiritual songs and boundless light from torches, and, gathering together a procession of the whole people, they completed their journey through the city center; they thought that because of this the city would receive holiness and greater strength and would thus be kept safe and remain impregnable forever. Everybody who had opportunity ran up to see the sight, and great waves of people gathered and crowded together. Then a man who had been paralyzed in his feet and weak for many years, supported by his servants, stood up to see the divine image as it went past. In some marvelous way he was healed at the sight, and when he realized that the ankles of his legs had become firm, he ran up on his own two feet and kissed the container of the image and he glorified God and told of the miracle which had just been done on him. Since all who were present had seen him and had listened to his words, they gave praise to Almighty God, who can at any time perform such amazing miracles.

29. It is impossible to describe in words all the weeping for joy and the intercession, prayers, and thanksgivings to God from the whole city as the divine image and the holy letter passed through the midst of the city since the sight begs description. It is far better to witness such exceptional events than to hear about them, since words are often unequal to the importance of the occasion. When the leaders of the procession arrived at the square outside the Augusteum, they turned a little to the left from the direct road and came to the famous Church of the Wisdom of God, they went inside the sanctuary and laid the image and the letter on the throne of mercy.

30. Here the whole assembly of the church worshiped and performed the requisite acts of honor, and then those who were taking part in the procession came out of there again with the sacred burden and went to the palace. They placed the image for the time being in what they call the Chrysotriclinium, on the emperor's throne, from which they usually give decisions on the most important matters of state. They

not unreasonably thought that the emperor's throne also would be completely hallowed, and all who sat on it would most likely receive a share of justice and goodness. The usual sort of earnest prayer was made, and then after this was finished the divine image was taken up again from there, consecrated and dedicated in the aforementioned Chapel of the Pharos on the right side towards the east, for the glory of the faithful, for the protection of the emperor, and to ensure the safety of the whole state and the Christian community.

31. O Holy Image of the Likeness of the Unchanging Father! O likeness of the likeness of the Person of the Father! O sacred and all-praiseworthy token of the archetypal glory of Christ, our Lord! I speak of you in faith just as if you were alive. Save and guard for ever him who piously and mercifully rules us and who celebrates in grand manner the memory of your coming; whom by your presence you have raised to his father's and grandfather's throne. Keep his children safe for the succession of their life and let their rule last for ever. Guarantee a state of peace for the country. Keep this queen of cities impregnable; and grant that we may please your archetype, Christ our Lord, and be admitted into his heavenly kingdom, while we give praise and sing of his glory. For he is worthy of glory and worship for ever and ever. Amen.

APPENDIX D

SAMPLES TAKEN FROM THE TURIN SHROUD

NOVEMBER 24, 1973

FOR PROFESSOR G. RAES

ACTUAL DIMENSIONS	DESCRIPTION
————	One 12mm. weft thread from bottom right-hand edge Character: *No image*

One 13mm. warp thread from bottom right-hand edge
Character: *No image*

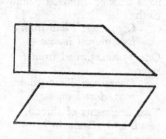

One 40mm. × 13mm. sample cut from bottom right-hand edge (piece I of Raes's report)
Character: *No image*

One approximately 40mm.× 10mm. sample cut from the side strip (piece II of Raes's report)
Character: *No image*

FOR PROFESSORS MARI and RIZZATTI
(*representing PROFESSOR FRACHE*)

One 28mm. thread from bottom right-hand edge
Character: *No image*

One 8mm. thread corresponding to bloodstain seeming to be from scourging
Character: *Scourge mark*

One 4mm. thread and 6.5mm. thread, being originally joined, from apparent scourge mark above (Reddish tint of blood observed on snapping to be only on surface of thread; interior perfectly white)
Character: *Scourge mark*

One 19.5mm. thread from area of blood flows across small of back
Character: *Flow across small of back, dorsal image*

Two 12mm. threads from bloodstain that appears to have trickled from foot onto cloth

> Character: *Flow from foot, dorsal image*

One 17mm. thread from same

> Character: *Flow from foot, dorsal image*

Two fragments of thread, 7mm. and 16mm. in length respectively, from same

> Character: *Flow from foot, dorsal image*

One 13mm. thread from image of bloodstained right foot

> Character: *Bloodstain of right foot, dorsal image*

FOR PROFESSORS FILOGAMO and ZINA

One 13mm. thread from image of bloodstained right foot (taken parallel to above)

> Character: *Bloodstain of right foot, dorsal image*

One 18.5mm. thread from same

> Character: *Bloodstain of right foot, dorsal image*

KEY:
samples seeming to bear image
samples without image

APPENDIX E

PLANT SPECIES OF POLLEN SAMPLES
FROM THE SHROUD

(as identified by DR. MAX FREI)

At the International Congress on the Turin Shroud, October 7, 1978, Dr. Max Frei released for the first time the full list of the plant species whose pollens he had found on the Shroud. At the same time he publicly affirmed his support for the author's theory that the Shroud is one and the same as the former Mandylion of Edessa/Urfa.

This paperback edition was too far advanced toward publication for more than cursory updating of the main text, but essentially the historical arguments advanced in this book are substantially strengthened by Max Frei's findings. Although the full implications have yet to be studied in detail, it is quite clear that the Shroud has been in Palestine. Frei is also certain that the Shroud has been in the area he describes as Anatolian steppe, which he qualifies as a phytogeographical term for the region of the towns of Bitlis, Diyarbakir, Mardin, Urfa, Gaziantep, and Malatya. Urfa is of course the modern Turkish name for the former Parthian and Byzantine city of Edessa.

The list as given below is a direct translation from the Italian, in which it was published for the Turin Congress.

SPECIES	DESCRIPTION AND GENERAL DISTRIBUTION	LIKELY ORIGIN IN CASE OF SHROUD
1. *Anabis aphylla* L.	Desert plant (halophyte). Distribution southeast Persia, Arabia, Crimea, southern Palestine, Morocco.	Jerusalem
2. *Alnus glutinosa* Vill.	Europe, western Asia, Siberia, Japan.	France or Italy
3. *Althae officinalis* L.	Asian plant, widely cultivated, indigenous to most temperate countries.	France, Italy, or Jerusalem

SPECIES	DESCRIPTION AND GENERAL DISTRIBUTION	LIKELY ORIGIN IN CASE OF SHROUD
4. *Acacia albida* Del.	Desert plant very common in the Jordan valley and around the Dead Sea.	Jerusalem
5. *Artemisia herba -alba* Asso.	Semidesert plant, prevalent east of Jerusalem. Regions: Iran, Syria, Arabia, North Africa, Sinai, reaching south of France and Spain.	Jerusalem or Urfa
6. *Atraphaxis spinosa* L.	Plant which grows in rocky places in the Irano-Turanian region.	Urfa
7. *Capparis* spp.	Plant growing on cliffs, walls, and in semidesert regions. Distribution: Iran, Mesopotamia, Anatolia, eastern Mediterranean.	Jerusalem or Urfa
8. *Carduus personata* Jacq.	Mesophytic plant. Region: southeast Europe.	France or Italy
9. *Carpinus betulus* L.	Mesophytic tree. Region: central and southeast Europe.	France or Italy
10. *Cedrus libani* Lk.	Originating from the mountains of the southeast Mediterranean, nowadays widely distributed around Europe.	France, Italy, Istanbul, or Jerusalem
11. *Corylus avellana* L.	Hazelnut. Distribution: Europe, western Asia.	France, Italy, or Istanbul
12. *Cupressus sempervirens* L.	Cypress. Originating in eastern Mediterranean basin, often cultivated.	France, Italy, Istanbul, or Jerusalem
13. *Echinops glaberrimus* DC.	Rocky areas. North African plant.	Jerusalem
14. *Epimedium pubigerum* DC.	Woodland plant from Bulgaria and Turkey.	Istanbul
15. *Fagonia mollis* Del.	Desert plant. Distribution: Sahara, Arabia. Frequently found in the Jordan valley.	Jerusalem
16. *Fagus sylvatica* L.	Beech. Mountains, Mediterranean Europe.	France or Italy

17. *Glaucium grandiflorum* B+H — Plant native to the steppes. Irano-Turanian region. The farthest south it can be found is Israel. — Urfa or Jerusalem

18. *Gundelia turnefortii* L. — Plant native to the steppes and rocky or salty areas. Irano-Turanian region. — Urfa or Jerusalem

19. *Haloxilon persicum* Bg. — Desert plant (halophyte). Israel/Irano-Turanian region. — Jerusalem

20. *Haplophyllum tuberculatum* Juss. — Desert plant. Sahara, Arabia. — Jerusalem or Urfa

21. *Helianthemum vesicarium* Boiss. — Plant native to the steppes and rocky semidesert regions, Iran to as far as Morocco. — Jerusalem

22. *Hyoscyamus aureus* L. — Cliff plant, found on old walls, ruins, and nowadays on the walls of the ancient citadel of Jerusalem. East Mediterranean, Irano-Turanian region. — Jerusalem

23. *Hyoscyamus reticulatus* L. — Plant native to the steppes, fields, and ruins. Irano-Turanian region. — Jerusalem or Urfa

24. *Ixiolirion montanum* Herb. — Lily found from Central Asia to Lebanon, Syria, and Palestine. Natural and cultivated steppes. — Jerusalem or Urfa

25. *Juniperus oxycedrus* L. — Mediterranean as far as the Caucasus and Persia. — Jerusalem or Istanbul

26. *Laurus nobilis* L. — Indigenous and cultivated in all Mediterranean countries. — Italy, Istanbul, or Jerusalem

27. *Linum mucronatum* Bert. — Plant native to limestone steppes, and not found in Europe. Irano-Turanian region. — Jerusalem or Urfa

28. *Lythrum salicaria* L. — Plant found in marshy areas, rice fields. Distribution: Euro-Asiatic and North America. — France, Italy, or Istanbul

29. *Oligomeris subulata* (Del.) Boiss. — Desert plant which grows in sand and limestone from Morocco to Persia. — Jerusalem

SPECIES	DESCRIPTION AND GENERAL DISTRIBUTION	LIKELY ORIGIN IN CASE OF SHROUD
30. *Onosma orientalis* L.	A cliff plant, often found on ruins, to be found today on the walls of the ancient citadel of Jerusalem. Iran, Iraq, Syria, Turkey, Lebanon, Palestine.	Jerusalem
31. *Oryza sativa* L.	Rice. Originating in tropical countries, cultivated where temperature and irrigation allow.	Italy
32. *Paliurus spina-christi* Mill.	Plant found growing from western Asia to the Mediterranean.	Jerusalem or Istanbul
33. *Peganum harmala* L.	Desert plant. Distribution from southwest Asia to North Africa and southern Europe.	Jerusalem or Urfa
34. *Platanus orientalis* L.	Plane tree. Originating in the Balkans, western Asia, and Himalayas, cultivated in parks. Represented by hairs from the fruit.	France, Italy, Istanbul, Jerusalem, or Urfa
35. *Poterium spinosum* L.	Often prevalent in dry areas. Eastern and mid-Mediterranean as far west as Sardinia.	Jerusalem or Istanbul
36. *Prosopis farcta* Macbr.	Plant found frequently around the Dead Sea and in the Irano-Turanian region.	Jerusalem or Urfa
37. *Amygdalus arabica* Oliv.	Rocky areas, particularly Irano-Turanian region.	Jerusalem or Urfa
38. *Pteranthus dichotomus* Forsk.	Plant native to sandy or salt deserts. Distribution: Irano-Turanian region, Mediterranean, Sudan.	Jerusalem or Urfa
39. *Reaumuria hirtella* J. et Sp.	Plant native to salty areas, often predominant. Sahara, Arabia, Irano-Turanian region.	Jerusalem or Urfa
40. *Ricinus communis* L.	Castor-oil plant. Cultivated in all hot countries.	Italy, Jerusalem, Urfa, or Istanbul

41.	*Roemeria hybrida* (L.) DC.	Plant native to the steppes, Irano-Turanian region. To be found as far as central Europe, but very rare.	Jerusalem, Istanbul, or Urfa
42.	*Scabiosa prolifera* L.	Dry regions from Turkey to Palestine.	Jerusalem or Urfa
43.	*Scirpus triquetrus* L.	Plant native to marshy areas, rice fields. Distribution: Asia, Africa, Europe, Australia.	France, Italy, Istanbul, or Jerusalem
44.	*Secale* spp.	Cultivated rye.	France or Italy
45.	*Silene conoidea* L.	Native to the steppes, today often an ornamental(?) (*segetale*) plant. Distribution: Irano-Turanian region, Mediterranean.	Urfa or Jerusalem
46.	*Suaeda aegyptica* Zoh.	Desert plant (halophyte). Sahara/Arabian regions.	Jerusalem
47.	*Tamarix nilotica* Bunge.	Bush often prevalent in salty areas, Sahara/Arabia regions.	Jerusalem
48.	*Taxus baccata* L.	Plant widely distributed throughout Europe, Asia, and North America.	France, Italy, or Istanbul
49.	*Zygophyllum dumosum* Boiss.	One of the frutices most frequently found in the desert around the Dead Sea.	Jerusalem

Note by Dr. Max Frei: Some pollens are still missing from the list, as they have yet to be identified; others which have been identified but were lost or destroyed during preparation have been omitted because it would be impossible to prove them.

Note by the author: Max Frei's "Irano-Turanian" defines a specific botanical region. According to Davis, *Flora of Turkey* (Edinburgh, 1965), this "reaches from Inner Anatolia southwards to Palestine and eastwards to Mongolia. . . . The following regions belong to it: Central Anatolia, East Anatolia, Syrian Desert, North Iraq, Iran, W. Pakistan, parts of the Aralo-Caspian Deserts, Western Turi Shan."

At the Turin Congress Dr. Frei pointed out that he had

been careful to consider the possibility of distant transportation in the case of the pollens found on the Shroud. In his judgment the spectrum of pollens from Palestine and Turkey could not be explained by storms and accidental contamination. Experimental research using viscous plates showed that 95 per cent of pollen collected was produced by plants growing within an area of a few hundred meters.

NOTES AND REFERENCES

Introduction

1. Memorandum of Pierre d'Arcis, Bishop of Troyes, to Pope Clement VII, Paris, Bibliothèque Nationale, Collection de Champagne, v. 154, folio 138. Translated from the Latin by the Rev. Herbert Thurston, S.J., and published in "The Holy Shroud and the Verdict of History" *The Month*, CI (1903), pp. 17–29. (See Appendix B.)

2. Canon Ulysse Chevalier, *Etude critique sur l'origine du Saint Suaire de Lirey-Chambéry-Turin* (Paris: A. Picard, 1900); *Le Saint Suaire de Turin, est-il l'original ou une copie?* (Chambéry: Menard, 1899); *Le Saint Suaire de Turin: Histoire d'une relique* (Paris: A. Picard, 1902).

3. Rev. Herbert Thurston, "The Holy Shroud as a Scientific Problem," *The Month*, CI (1903), pp. 162–78; "What in Truth Was the Holy Shroud?" *The Month*, CLV (1930), pp. 160–64. See also note 1 above.

4. Erwin Panofsky, *Early Netherlandish Painting: Its Origins and Character* (Cambridge, Mass.: Harvard University Press, 1953), I, p. 304, n. 3 referring to p. 18 of text.

5. Laurence Bright, *The Tablet*, May 25, 1974.

6. Kurt Berna, *Das Linnen* (Stuttgart, 1957); English edition: John Reban, *Inquest of Jesus Christ: Did He Die on the Cross?* (London: Leslie Frewin, 1967). Berna and Reban are anagrams of Naber, the "publisher" of Berna's books in Stuttgart; Hans Naber may be Berna's real name.

7. Giulio Ricci, *L'uomo della Sindone* (Rome, 1965).

8. Peter M. Rinaldi, *It Is the Lord: A Study of the Shroud of Christ* (New York, 1972).

9. Maurus Green, "Enshrouded in Silence," *Ampleforth Journal*, LXXIV (1969), pp. 319–45.

10. Dr. David Willis, "Did He Die on the Cross?" *Ampleforth Journal*, LXXIV (1969), pp. 27–39; "False Prophet and the Holy Shroud," *The Tablet*, June 13, 1970; "The Holy Shroud on T.V.," *The Tablet*, December 8, 1973.

PART I   The Shroud as Understood up to 1973

Chapter I   The Shroud on View

1. "Istud equidem palam omnes vidimus (tunc enim aderam) et obstupuimus." Ph. Pingone, *Sindon evangelica* (Augustae Taurinorum, 1581 [1st edition 1578]).
2. For a graphic account of the repair work see L. Bouchage, *Le Saint Suaire de Chambéry à Sainte-Claire en Ville* (*avril–mai 1534*) (Chambéry, 1891), pp. 21–26.
3. It has been suggested that these marks were derived from a fire in Besançon in 1349, some holding that the Turin Shroud was kept in Besançon Cathedral from shortly after the Fourth Crusade (1204) until 1349. There is in fact no reliable evidence to support this theory, the so-called Besançon Shroud, destroyed in the French Revolution, having been a mere sixteenth-century copy of that of Turin.

Chapter II   The Camera Reveals

1. Secondo Pia, "Memoria sulla riproduzione fotografica della santissima Sindone" (1907), appended to an article by his son, Giuseppe Pia, published in *Sindon,* April 1960. (*Sindon* is the official journal of the Centro Internazionale di Sindonologia, Via San Domenico 28, Torino, Italy). For the best description in English see John Walsh, *The Shroud* (New York: Random House, and London: W. H. Allen, 1963), to which I am indebted for much of the material in this chapter.
2. Translation from Walsh, op. cit. (British edition), p. 23.
3. Giuseppe Enrie, *La Santa Sindone rivelata dalla fotografia* (Turin, 1938). Translation from Walsh, op. cit., p. 98.
4. Translation from *The Keys,* 1974.
5. Preface to Paul Vignon, *Au souffle de l'esprit créateur* (1946).
6. See Vignon, *The Shroud of Christ,* trans. from the French (London, 1902), pl. VI.
7. Joseph Blinzler, *Das Turiner Grablinnen und die Wissenschaft* (Ettal, 1952).
8. See Henri Verbist, *Le Saint Suaire de Turin devant la science* (Brussels and Paris: Editions Universitaires, 1954), plate between pp. 80 and 81.

Chapter III   The Shroud and Medical Opinion

1. Paul Vignon, *The Shroud of Christ* (London, 1902).
2. Translation from John Walsh, *The Shroud* (London: W. H. Allen, 1963).
3. Pierre Barbet, *A Doctor at Calvary,* trans. from the French (New York, 1953).
4. Moedder's theories are to be found in the following articles: "Die Todesursache bei der Kreuzigung," in *Stimmen der Zeit,*

CXLIV (1949), pp. 50–59; "Die neueste medizinische Forschungen über die Todesurache bei der Kreuzigung Jesu Christi," in *Der Gottesfreund*, III (1950), pp. 40–51; "La causa di morte nell' crocifissione in alcuni esperimenti," S.S.R.M., 1951, pp. 28–31.

5. Giovanni Judica-Cordiglia, *La Sindone* (Padua, 1961).
6. See note 10 to the Introduction.
7. Dr. Anthony Sava, "The Wound in the Side of Christ," *Catholic Biblical Quarterly*, XIX, no. 3, (July 1957), pp. 343–46.
8. Dr. Robert Bucklin, "The Medical Aspects of the Crucifixion of Christ," *Sindon*, December 1961, pp. 5–11.
9. Leo Vala's work is reviewed in two articles, one appearing in the British journal *Amateur Photographer*, March 8, 1967, the other in *British Journal of Photography*, March 24, 1967. Each article was written by the respective journal's editor.
10. Robert K. Wilcox, *Shroud* (New York: Macmillan, 1977), p. 136.
11. Bucklin, op. cit., p. 7.
12. From unpublished notes written by Dr. Willis shortly before his death.
13. Ibid.
14. Vignon, *The Shroud of Christ*, p. 30.
15. Willis's unpublished notes.
16. E. A. Wuenschel, "The Shroud of Turin and the Burial of Christ," *Catholic Biblical Quarterly*, 7 (1945), pp. 405–37; 8 (1946), pp. 135–78.
17. Judica-Cordiglia, op. cit.
18. Barbet, op. cit., pp. 102–4.
19. Bucklin, op. cit., p. 9.
20. Willis's unpublished notes.
21. Barbet, op. cit.

Chapter IV   The Shroud and New Testament Archaeology

1. H. Gressman, "Festschrifte" for K. Budde, appendix to the *Zeitschrift für die alttestamentliche Wissenschaft*, 34 (1920), pp. 60–68.
2. H. Daniel-Rops, *Daily Life in Palestine at the Time of Christ* (London: Weidenfeld, 1962).
3. *Dictionary of Greek and Roman Antiquities*, ed. William Smith (London, 1851).
4. A. Pauly, G. Wissowa, and W. Kroll, eds., *Real-Encyclopaedie der klassischen Altertumwissenschaft*, (Stuttgart, 1893), entries under "Hasta," "Lancea," and "Pilum."
5. Vasilius Tzaferis, "Jewish Tombs at and near Giv'at ha-Mivtar, Jerusalem," *Israel Exploration Journal*, 20 (1970).
6. Nicu Haas, "Anthropological Observations on the Skeletal Remains from Giv'at ha-Mivtar," *Israel Exploration Journal*, 1970, p. 58.

7. Christofari, *Le Christ dans son vrai Linceul*.
8. Herbert Thurston, "The Holy Shroud and the Verdict of History," *The Month*, CI (1903), p. 19.

Chapter V   The Shroud and the Recorded Burial of Jesus

1. Edmund Wilson, *The Scrolls from the Dead Sea* (London: W. H. Allen, 1955), p. 60.
2. "In the Gospels there is no mention of the washing of the bloodstained body of Jesus; but there is no doubt that it was first performed." P. Germanus a Corde Iesu, "Passionis D.N.I.C. praelectiones historicae," 3 (1936), p. 491. "After the Sacred Body stained with the Precious Blood had been washed clean it was wrapped in linen bands. . . ." M. J. Lagrange, O.P., *The Gospel of Jesus Christ* (London, 1938), vol. 2, p. 278. "Until proof to the contrary is forthcoming, we shall think that before being wrapped in the shroud the bloodstained body of the divine Crucified was washed." F. M. Braun, O.P., *La sépulture de Jésus*. All quoted in Alfred O'Rahilly, "The Burial of Christ," *Irish Ecclesiastical Record*, 59 (1941).
3. The argument chiefly centers on the apparent permissible washing of the dead on the Sabbath, prescribed in the Mishnah, *Shabbath* 23:5: "They may make ready [on the Sabbath] all that is needful for the dead and anoint it and wash it, provided they do not move any member of it. . . . They may bind up the chin, not in order to raise it but that it may not sink lower. . . . They may not close a corpse's eyes on the Sabbath" (*Mishnah*, trans. Herbert Danby [Oxford University Press, 1954], p. 120). It seems clear that it would have been permissible to wash and anoint the corpse on the Sabbath, but not to buy the aromatic oils—the equivalent of our scented soap. These could only be bought after six P.M. on the Saturday (as the Mishnah 23:4 instructs and Mark 16:1 indicates was done). But by then it would have been too dark to start, which in fact would have been the case even if everything had been already prepared. I owe these remarks to Dr. John Robinson, who states, "I entirely agree that the body was not washed."
4. Père Benoit, O.P., *Passion et résurrection du Seigneur* (Paris, 1966), pp. 286–88.
5. Kathleen M. Kenyon, *Jerusalem: Excavating 3,000 Years of History* (London: Thames and Hudson, 1967).
6. L. E. Cox Evans, "The Holy Sepulchre," *Palestine Exploration Quarterly*, 100 (1968), pp. 112–36.
7. This translation is based on the Jerusalem Bible, but substitutes the original Greek words for the various items of grave linen. It also deletes the words "on the ground" which occur twice in the Jerusalem translation but which cannot be justified from the original Greek.

PART II The Shroud Under the Microscope

Chapter VI The Shroud and the Turin Commission

1. For the information in this and succeeding chapters I am indebted to the report of the Turin Commission on the Holy Shroud: *La S. Sindone: Ricerche e studi della commissione di esperti nominata dall'Archivescovo di Torino, Card. Michele Pellegrino, nel 1969,* a supplement to the *Rivista diocesana torinese,* January 1976.

2. The map was drawn up on Cartesian co-ordinates, and recommended as a work of future reference. So far, however, I have been unable to obtain a copy, despite several enquiries.

Chapter VII The Shroud as a Textile

1. I owe this description to Fr. David Sox, who had the opportunity of examining the samples in Professor Raes's laboratory.

2. I owe this information to British textile expert Elizabeth Crowfoot.

3. G. Raes, "Appendix B—Rapport d'Analise," *La S. Sindone,* supplement to *Rivista diocesana torinese,* January 1976, p. 82.

4. "Tex." is the most universally accepted of several systems for measuring the fineness of yarns. To a specialist the figures indicate that the Shroud thread is indeed very fine.

5. A yarn has Z twist if the spirals conform in direction of slope with the central position of the letter Z.

6. *Mishnah,* trans. Herbert Danby (Oxford University Press, 1954), Division I Zera'im, Tractate 4 Kila-im, 8:1 and 9:1; Division II Mo'ed, Tractate 7 Betzah, 1:10; Division IV Nezikîn, Tractate 5 Makkoth, 3:8–9; Division VI Tohorôth, Tractate 5 Parah, 12:9, and Tractate 12 Uktzin, 2:6.

Chapter VIII Is There Actual Blood on the Shroud?

1. Turin Commission on the Holy Shroud, *La S. Sindone,* supplement to *Rivista diocesana torinese,* January 1976, pp. 49–54.

2. Ibid., pp. 55–57.

3. Ibid., p. 65.

Chapter IX A Criminologist and the Shroud

1. Information in this chapter has been derived from personal interviews with Dr. Frei at his home in Zurich in August 1976, followed by a two-week tour with him on location in Turkey and Israel in October 1976. I am also indebted to his "Note a seguito dei primi studi sui prelievi di polvere aderente al lenzuolo della S. Sindone," *Sindon,* April 1976.

2. From a report to British film producer David Rolfe, January 1977.

3. From a press release signed in Zurich, March 8, 1976.

PART III Investigating the Shroud's History

Chapter X Where Was the Shroud Before the Fourteenth Century?

1. The pioneer book on this subject is that of Willard Libby, *Radiocarbon Dating* (Chicago: University of Chicago Press, 1955). The whole subject has since undergone considerable development and sophistication—for a good general guide see David M. Browne, *Principles and Practice in Modern Archeology* (London: Hodder & Stoughton, 1975).
2. Turin Commission on the Holy Shroud, *La S. Sindone*, supplement to *Rivista diocesana torinese*, January 1976, pp. 31–38.
3. Their knowledge was nearly twenty years out of date—see Chapter XXIV.
4. Memorandum of Pierre d'Arcis, Bishop of Troyes, to Pope Clement VII, trans. Rev. Herbert Thurston, S.J., in "The Holy Shroud and the Verdict of History," *The Month*, CI (1903), pp. 17–29. (See Appendix B.)
5. Ibid., p. 22.
6. Ibid.
7. See for instance a receipt of July 6, 1418, quoted in U. Chevalier, *Etude critique sur l'origine de Saint Suaire de Lirey-Chambéry-Turin* (Paris: A. Picard, 1900), pièce justificative Q: "Ouquel est la figure ou representation du Suaire Nostre Seigneur Jésucrist. . . ."
8. For a history of the legal appeals see Chapter XXI of this book; also M. Perret, "Essai sur l'histoire du S. Suaire du XIVe. au XVIe. siècle," *Mémoires de L'Académie des Sciences, Belles Lettres et Arts de Savoie*, IV (1960), pp. 77–90.
9. Père Anselme, *Histoire Généalogique, 1726–33*, vol. VIII, pp. 201–3.
10. A. Piaget, "Le livre Messire Geoffroi de Charni," *Romania*, t. 26 (1897), pp. 394–411.
11. Werner Bulst, *The Shroud of Turin*, trans. S. McKenna and J. J. Galvin, (Milwaukee: Bruce Publishing Company, 1957).
12. Froissart, *Les Chroniques*, (J. A. C. Buchon, 1835), vol. I, p. 350.

Chapter XI Pre-Fourteenth-Century "Shrouds" That Led Nowhere

1. Maurus Green, "Enshrouded in Silence," *Ampleforth Journal*, LXXIV (1969), pp. 319–45.
2. "Now the Lord, when he had given the sindon to the servant of the priest, went to James and appeared to him. . . ." St. Jerome, *De vir. Illust.*, ch. ii.

3. M. and J. O. Wardrop and F. C. Conybear, "The Life of St. Nino," from *Studia biblica et ecclesiastica* (Oxford, 1900), vol. V.
4. Translation by Alfred O'Rahilly, "The Burial of Christ," *Irish Ecclesiastical Record*, 59 (1941), p. 59, from Migne, *Patrologia latina*, vol. 80, 689.
5. From T. Tobler, *Itineraria Hierosolymitana et descriptiones Terrae Sanctae* (Geneva, 1879).
6. St. Bede, *De locis sanctis: Adamni Abbatis Hiliensis*, Book III, *De locis sanctis, ex relatione Arculfi Episcopi Galli*, X and XI Acta Sanctorum Ordinis Benedicti, IV, p. 456ff.
7. J. Francez, S.J., *Un pseudo linceul du Christ* (Paris, 1935).
8. Ibid., pp. 5–7.
9. Robert de Clari, *The Conquest of Constantinople*, trans. from the Old French by E. H. McNeal (New York: Columbia University Press, 1936). The original French word *figure* has been substituted for "features" which occurs in McNeal's translation.
10. H. Thurston, "The Holy Shroud and the Verdict of History," *The Month*, CI (1903), pp. 17–29.
11. Ibid.

Chapter XII   The Shroud Face and the "Familiar" Christ Likeness in Art

1. F. W. Farrar, *The Life of Christ Represented in Art* (London, 1901), p. 84.
2. Justin Martyr: "He appeared without beauty as the Scripture proclaimed." *Dial c. Tryph.* 14, 36, 85, 88; Clement of Alexandria: "not displaying the beauty of the flesh, but manifesting the beauty of the soul in his beneficence, and that of the flesh in his immortality." *Paedagogus*, III, p. 1.
3. St. Jerome, *In Matt.* 1:8.
4. The letter is not found in the writings of Eusebius but was quoted in the Acts of the Second Council of Nicaea (A.D. 787), from the Acts of the Second Council of Constantinople (A.D. 756). It is given in Migne, *Patrologia latina*, vol. 20, 1546.
5. St. Augustine, *De Trinitate*, VIII, 4, 5, in Migne, *Patrologia latina*, vol. 42, 1801.
6. Otto Pacht, "The Avignon Diptych and Its Eastern Ancestry," from *De Artibus Opuscula*, XL, *Essays in Honor of Erwin Panofsky* (New York, 1961), pp. 402–17.
7. John Beckwith, *Early Christian and Byzantine Art*, Pelican History of Art (London: Penguin Books, 1970), p. 123.
8. Paul Vignon, *Le Saint Suaire de Turin devant la science, l'archéologie, l'histoire, l'iconographie, la logique* (Paris, 1939).
9. Edward A. Wuenschel, *Self-Portrait of Christ: The Holy Shroud of Turin* (Esopus, New York, 1954).

*Chapter XIII   The Shroud and the Tradition of Christ's Face
Impressed on Cloth*

1. Rev. Adrien Parvilliers, S.J., *La dévotion des prédestinés, ou
les stations de Jérusalem et du Calvaire pour servir d'entretien
sur le passion de Notre Seigneur J.C.* This work appeared in 14
editions between 1696 and 1892.
2. Influential colleagues, among them Fr. Peter Rinaldi, have repeatedly drawn a blank when they have made enquiries in
Rome. In my own case a friendly correspondence with the
British apostolic delegate, Archbishop Bruno Heim, terminated
abruptly when I merely enquired whom in the Vatican I could
contact to ask even for a photograph.
3. Joseph Wilpert, *Römische Mosaiken und Malereien*, II, 2
(1924), pp. 1,123ff.
4. Gervase of Tilbury, *Otia imperialia*, III, p. 25, from *Scriptores
rerum brunsvicensium*, ed., G. Leibnitz (Hanover, 1707), I,
p. 968.
5. Juliana of Norwich, *Revelations of Divine Love*, trans. James
Walsh, S.J. (London: Burns & Oates, 1961), chap. 10, pp. 62,
63.
6. See Robert Brentano, *Rome Before Avignon: A Social History
of Thirteenth-Century Rome* (London: Longmans, 1974) for
a description of this procession. See also Matthew Paris, *Chronica majora*, an 16, iii, p. 7 RS; also Innocent III, *Opera omnia*,
IV, from Migne *Patrologia latina*, vol. 217 (Paris, 1855), cols.
345–50.
7. From "De Gestis Henrici II et Ricardi I," *Mon. Germ. Hist.
Script.*, 27, p. 131.
8. *Ordo Romanus*, XI, 8, Mabillon *Mus. ital.*, ii., 122.
9. Peter Mallius, *Descriptio basilicae vaticanae*, XXV, ed. De.
Rossi, Inscript. christ, II, 1,218, n. 90.
10. C. Tischendorf, *Evangelia apocrypha*, ed. 2 (Leipzig, 1876),
pp. 456–57; trans. M. R. James, *The Apocryphal New Testament* (Oxford University Press, 1924), pp. 157–58.
11. Alexander Roberts and James Donaldson, eds., *The Ante-
Nicene Fathers* (Grand Rapids, Mich.: Eerdmans, 1951), vol.
VIII, pp. 472–76.
12. Macarius of Magnesia, *Apocritus*, ed. C. Blondel (published
posthumously by P. Foucart, Paris, 1876), p. 1; trans. T. W.
Crafer (London: SPCK, 1919). See also T. W. Crafer, "Macarius
Magnesius: A Neglected Apologist," *Journal of Theological
Studies*, VIII (1906–7), pp. 401–23, 546–71.
13. Eusebius, *History of the Church*, trans. G. A. Williamson (Penguin Books, 1965), bk. 7, p. 18.
14. See F. W. Farrar, *The Life of Christ Represented in Art* (London, 1901), p. 82.

*Chapter XIV Were Shroud and Mandylion One
and the Same Thing?*

1. Sir Steven Runciman, "Some Remarks on the Image of Edessa," *Cambridge Historical Journal*, III (1929–31), pp. 238–52.

2. Kurt Weitzmann, "The Mandylion and Constantine Porphyrogennetos," *Cahiers archéologiques*, XI (1960).

3. Runciman, op. cit., p. 244.

4. André Grabar, "La Sainte Face de Laon et le Mandylion dans l'art orthodoxe," *Seminarium Kondakovianum* (Prague, 1935), p. 16 (translated from the French by the author).

5. John Beckwith, *Early Christian and Byzantine Art,* Pelican History of Art (London: Penguin Books, 1970).

6. Grabar, op. cit.

7. Acta Thaddaei 3, from *Acta apostolorum apocrypha,* ed. R. A. Lipsius (Leipzig, 1891), I, p. 274; trans. in Alexander Roberts and James Donaldson, eds., *The Ante-Nicene Fathers* (Grand Rapids, Mich.: Eerdmans, 1951), vol. VIII, pp. 558–59.

8. Germanos, "Sermon Before Leo the Isaurian," in Migne, *Patrologia graeca,* vol. 110, 920.

9. Court of Constantine Porphyrogenitus, "Narratio de imagine edessena," in Migne, *Patrologia graeca,* vol. 113, paragraphs 1 and 13. (See Appendix C.)

10. Symeon Magister, "De Const. Porph. et Romano Lecapeno," sec. 50, p. 491 of Ms. and 748 of *Corpus scriptorum historiae byzantinae* (Bonn, 1878).

11. Court of Constantine Porphyrogenitus, op. cit., cols. 423–54.

12. Ibid., paragraph 10.

13. Symeon Magister, op. cit.

14. Roberts and Donaldson, op. cit., p. 558.

15. Ibid., n. 4.

16. The actual word used in the Acta Thaddaei is *tetradiplon.* I owe valuable information on this to Dr. John Robinson of Trinity College, Cambridge, and to G. W. H. Lampe, Professor of Divinity at Cambridge, editor of the *Lexicon of Patristic Greek.* The word is not even in the Liddell and Scott Greek lexicon and from the *Lexicon of Patristic Greek* appears to be used only in this passage in all literature. It seems to mean doubled, then redoubled, then doubled again—i.e., doubled three times, which has the effect of "doubling in four" producing 4×2 folds. The word does not appear to be a translation into Greek from a Syriac source word, and seems to reflect the character of the Mandylion as the author saw it. From the allusions to the synagogue, hours of prayer, Sabbath day, etc., he would appear to have been a sixth-century Jewish Christian writing in Greek. He may well have been a citizen of Edessa, which had a substantial Jewish community.

17. "Fastening it to a board and embellishing it with the gold

which is now to be seen. . . ." Court of Constantine Porphyrogenitus, op. cit., paragraph 15.

18. Turin Commission on the Holy Shroud, *La S. Sindone,* supplement to *Rivista diocesana torinese,* January 1976, p. 20.

PART IV   Towards a History—The Shroud and
the Mandylion

Chapter XV   To the Earliest Christian City—
A Mysterious "Portrait"

1. J. B. Segal, *Edessa the Blessed City* (Oxford, 1970), p. 109. By far the best modern authority on Edessa. I am deeply indebted to Professor Segal for much valuable advice and assistance.

2. "The Aramaic of Edessa was more than a mere local dialect: it was the medium of commerce throughout the Euphrates valley, while the Aramaic of Palmyra and of Palestine hardly differed from it more than the Lowland Scots differ from the English." F. C. Burkitt, *Early Eastern Christianity,* 1904.

3. Eusebius, *History of the Church,* trans. G. A. Williamson (London: Penguin Books, 1965), bk 1, 13, pp. 65–70.

4. The principal Syriac texts are: "The Doctrine of Addai," published by Dr. W. Cureton in *Ancient Syriac Documents Relative to the Earliest Establishment of Christianity in Edessa,* 1864, from two manuscripts from the Nitrian collection, one of the fifth and the other of the sixth century; *The Doctrine of Addai the Apostle,* trans. G. Phillips and Wright, 1876, from a manuscript then in the Imperial Library of St. Petersburg.

5. Court of Constantine Porphyrogenitus, "Narratio de imagine edessena," in Migne, *Patrologia graeca,* vol. 113, paragraphs 12–13.

6. Eusebius, op. cit., p. 68.

7. *The Doctrine of Addai the Apostle,* trans. Phillips and Wright.

8. There is an interesting cross reference to this character in the *Annals* of the great Roman historian Tacitus, who records how certain Parthian tributary states, which would include Edessa, became aggrieved at the insolence of Artabanus III, King of the Parthians. The states therefore organized a "secret Parthian mission to Rome . . . supported by Abdu, a eunuch (for among orientals that condition, far from being despised is actually a source of power)" and "other leading men." The Emperor Tiberius agreed to help the plotters, but Artabanus learned of the plot and "acted prudently. Abdu, invited with ostensible friendliness to dinner, was disabled by a slow poison." Although Tiberius eventually succeeded in helping the rebel Parthians overthrow Artabanus, that is the last we hear

of Abdu. Tacitus records these events as taking place in A.D. 35 by our reckoning, consistent with the time of Abgar V and the reputed Christian mission. Tacitus, *Annals*, trans. Michael Grant (London: Penguin Books, 1956), VI, 31.

9. "Shavida and Ebednebo, chiefs of the priests of this city, with Piroz and Dancu their companions, when they saw the signs which he did, ran and threw down the altars upon which they sacrificed before Nebo and Bel their gods except the great altar which was in the middle of the city." *The Doctrine of Addai the Apostle*, trans. Phillips and Wright. This is historically accurate. Nebu and Bel were the chief gods of Edessa, the former representing the sun and the latter the moon.

10. "The Teaching of Addaeus the Apostle," translated in Alexander Roberts and James Donaldson, eds., *The Ante-Nicene Fathers* (Grand Rapids, Mich.: Eerdmans, 1951), vol. VIII, p. 665.

11. Rev. John Wilkinson, *Egeria's Travels*, (London: SPCK, 1972).

12. Sir Steven Runciman, "Some Remarks on the Image of Edessa," *Cambridge Historical Journal*, III (1929–31).

13. Court of Constantine Porphyrogenitus, op. cit., paragraphs 15, 17.

14. Segal, op. cit., p. 185, n. 3.

15. M. A. R. Colledge, *The Parthians* (New York: Praeger, 1967), chap. 7, "Architecture."

16. Vasilius Tzaferis, "Jewish Tombs at and near Giv'at ha-Mivtar, Jerusalem," *Israel Exploration Journal*, 20 (1970), p. 26.

17. Numerous examples are illustrated in the works by Colledge and Segal quoted above.

18. Parthians head the list of those described in Acts 2:5–12 as living in Jerusalem and hearing the disciples at Pentecost—resulting in a reported three thousand conversions to Christianity. Hugh J. Schonfield, in his translation of the New Testament, *The Authentic New Testament* (London: Dobson, 1956), p. 193, actually substitutes "Edessa" for the name Judaea. He notes: "Both context and sense show that the reading 'Judaea' here must be wrong. On the evidence of an underlying Semitic source for this section, I have assumed a scribal misreading of the original 'Hadditha' [Edessa] which comes the most suitably geographically between Mesopotamia and Cappadocia." See also Jean Daniélou, "Christianity as a Jewish Sect," in *The Crucible of Christianity*, ed. Arnold Toynbee (London: Thames and Hudson, 1969), p. 277.

19. If this inscription was indeed written in the first century, it presumes recognition of Jesus as a "god" from the very earliest years, consistent with St. Thomas's outburst of John 20:28. The halo at this period presents no difficulty—many examples of Parthian gods feature this device, adopted from Helenistic

art, which had percolated into the Parthian region during the Seleucid conquests.

20. Colledge, op. cit., p. 109.

Chapter XVI   The "Portrait" Is Found— "Not Made by Hands"

1. Most authors, following Werner Kümmel, have dated the earliest Gospels to around A.D. 70. This view has very recently been challenged by Dr. John Robinson's *Redating the New Testament* (Philadelphia: Westminster Press, 1977). Dating considerations apart, gospel writers may well have lost all touch with what happened to the Shroud because of Edessa's remoteness from mainstream Christianity.

2. John Wilkinson, *Egeria's Travels* (London: SPCK, 1972).

3. Evagrius, Ecclesiastical History, original text in Migne, *Patrologia graeca*, vol. 86, 2, 2748–49; translation from Bohn's Ecclesiastical Library (1854).

4. Procopius of Caesarea, *Buildings* II, chap. 7, translation from Loeb edition (London: Heinemann, 1940), p. 143.

5. Ibid., p. 145.

6. See E. Kitzinger, "The Cult of Images before Iconoclasm," *Dumbarton Oaks Papers*, VIII (1954).

7. Titus Tobler and Augustus Moliner, "De Locis sanctis quae perambulavit Antoninus Martyr," from *Itinera hierosolymitana et descriptiones Terrae Sanctae*, Publications de la Société de l'Orient Latin (Geneva, 1879), vol. XLIV, p. 116.

8. Edward Gibbon, *The Decline and Fall of the Roman Empire*, chap. 49.

9. See André Grabar, *Byzantium from the Death of Theodosius to the Rise of Islam* (London: Thames and Hudson, 1966), p. 186, fig. 201.

10. See Otto Pacht, "The Avignon Diptych and Its Eastern Ancestry," *De Artibus Opuscula*, XL, *Essays in Honor of Erwin Panofsky* (New York, 1961), pp. 402–17, fig. 18.

11. Ibid., figs. 14 and 15.

12. See Walter Oakeshott, *The Mosaics of Rome* (London: Thames and Hudson, 1967), p. 70 and pl. VIII.

13. Hartmann Grisar, *Kapella Sancta Sanctorum* (1908), pp. 40, 41, 53; *Encyclopedia Cattolica* (Vatican City), entry and illustration under "Acheropita."

14. For a complete study of this see James D. Breckenridge, *The Numismatic Iconography of Justinian II*, Numismatic Notes and Monographs (New York: The American Numismatic Society, 1959).

15. Rev. Christopher P. Kelley, "Canterbury's First Ikon," *Sobornost*, 1976.

16. André Grabar, "Une hymne Syriaque sur l'architecture de la Cathédrale d'Edesse," from *L'art de la fin de l'antiquité et du*

moyen âge (Collège de France Fondation Schlumberger pour des études Byzantines, 1968); original text thirteenth-century *Codex vaticanus syriacus*, 95, fol. 49–50.

17. Translation of Syriac hymn, or *sougitha*, from J. B. Segal, *Edessa the Blessed City* (Oxford, 1970), p. 189.

18. Tenth-century Greek text as published in E. von Dobschutz, *Christusbilder: Untersuchungen zur christlichen Legende* (Leipzig, 1899), pp. 110–14.

19. Gibbon, loc. cit.

Chapter XVII   The Cloth Leaves Edessa

1. For the most definitive background, see Steven Runciman, *The Emperor Romanus Lecapenus and His Reign* (Cambridge, 1963).

2. John of Damascus, "De imaginibus oratorio," chap. 27, in Migne, *Patrologia graeca*, vol. 94, 1261; "De Fide Orthodoxa," 4, 16, in ibid., 1173.

3. Theodore of Studium, in Migne, *Patrologia graeca*, vol. 177, vol. 64, 1288.

4. H. C. Bowen, *Ali ibn Iza* (Cambridge, 1928).

5. "The Edessans owed part of the taxes which they had to pay and had nothing with which to pay it. A crafty man . . . advised the collector of taxes 'If you take the portrait [i.e., the Mandylion] they will sell their children and themselves rather than allow it [to be removed]. When [he] did this the Edessans were in consternation. . . . They came to the noble Athanasius and asked him to give them the 5,000 dinars of the taxes and to take the portrait to his place until they repaid him. He gladly took the portrait and gave the gold. Then he brought a clever painter and asked him to paint one like it. When the work was finished and there was a portrait as exactly as possible like [the original] because the painter had dulled the paints of the portrait so that they would appear old, the Edessans after a time returned the gold and asked him for the portrait. He gave them the one that had been made recently and kept the old one in his place. After a while he revealed the affair to the faithful [the Jacobites/Monophysites] and built the wonderful shrine of the Baptistery. He completed it at expense great beyond reckoning because he knew that the genuine portrait . . . had remained in his place. After several years he brought it and put it in the baptistery." Text from Michael the Syrian, translated in J. B. Segal, *Edessa the Blessed City* (Oxford, 1970), p. 214.

6. Court of Constantine Porphyrogenitus, "Narratio de imagine edessena," in Migne, *Patrologia graeca*, vol. 113, paragraph 24.

7. J. B. Chabot, "Anonymi auctoris Chronicon ad annum Christi 1234 pertinens," *Corpus scriptorum christianorum orientalium*,

81–82, Scr. Syri 36–37, 1953, quoted and translated in Segal, op. cit., p. 253.

8. Court of Constantine Porphyrogenitus, op. cit., paragraphs 28, 29.

9. Ibid., paragraph 27.

10. See Warwick Wroth British Museum coin catalogue, 1908, pl. LIII, no. 7. See also, in particular A. Blanchet, "L'influence artistique de Constantin Porphyrogénète," *Mélanges Grégoire: Annales de l'Institut de Philologie et d'Histoire Orientales et Slaves,* IX (1949), pp. 97–104, in which Blanchet specifically advances the theory that this coin was issued to commemorate the coming of the Mandylion. The coin carries alongside the portrait of Christ the inscription "Rex Regnantium."

11. For a special study of this icon, see Kurt Weitzmann, "The Mandylion and Constantine Porphyrogennetos," *Cahiers Archéologiques,* XI (1960).

Chapter XVIII   The Full-length Figure Comes to Light

1. Robert de Clari, *The Conquest of Constantinople,* trans. E. H. McNeal (New York: Columbia University Press, 1936).

2. Ibid.

3. ". . . then John carrying the Holy Mandylion," from Michael Glykas, *Annals* IV, ed. Bonn (1170); chronicle reference for the year 1036.

4. See G. Graf, *Geschichte der christlichen arabischen Literatur,* II (1944–53), pp. 259–60.

5. Translation from Pauline Johnstone, *The Byzantine Tradition in Church Embroidery,* (London, 1967), p. 54.

6. E. von Dobschütz, *Christusbilder* (Leipzig, 1889), p. 134**, appendix entitled "Der ältere lateinische Abgartext."

7. Translation from Maurus Green, "Enshrouded in Silence," *Ampleforth Journal,* LXXIV (1969), p. 333.

8. Ordericus Vitalis, *Historia ecclesiastica,* part III, bk. IX, 8, "De Gestis Balduini Edessae principatum obtinet."

9. Vatican Library Codex No. 5696, fol. 35, published in P. Savio, *Ricerche storiche sulla Santa Sindone* (Turin, 1957), footnote 31, p. 340; translation by Maurus Green.

10. Gervase of Tilbury, *Otia Imperialia,* III, from *Scriptores rerum brunsvicensium,* ed. G. Leibnitz (Hanover, 1707), I, pp. 966–67; translation by Maurus Green.

11. Kurt Weitzmann, "The Origins of the Threnos," *De Artibus Opuscula,* XL, *Essays in Honor of Erwin Panofsky* (New York, 1961), pp. 476ff. and plates 161–66.

12. Ibid., fig. 15, p. 165.

13. G. Schlumberger, *Mélanges* (Paris, 1895), pl XI; see also Dora Iliopoulou-Rogan, "Sur une fresque de la période des Paléologues," *Byzantion,* XLI (1971), pp. 109–21; and A. Banck,

Byzantine Art in the Collections of the U.S.S.R. (Sovietsky Khudoznik, Leningrad-Moscow, 1965), pls. 186–89.

14. Ilona Bercovits, *Illuminated Manuscripts in Hungary*, (Dublin: Irish University Press, 1969), plate III.

15. For general background see Gabriel Millet, *Broderies religieuses de style byzantin* (Paris, 1947).

16. Ibid., plate CLXXVI/2.

17. Ibid., plate CLXXVI/1.

18. See Carlo Bertelli, "The Image of Pity in Santa Croce in Jerusalemme," *Essays in the History of Art Presented to Rudolf Wittkower* (London: Phaidon, 1967), pp. 40–55; also E. Mâle, *L'art religieux de la fin du moyen âge en France* (1931), pp. 98–103, "Le Pathétique."

19. Principally a Mandylion icon of 1650 from the church of the Prophet Elijah, Jaroslav. The Hann icon is also of the seventeenth century. These are undoubtedly based on earlier Byzantine examples now lost to us.

20. The earliest Grail romance is the *Perceval,* or *Conte del Graal* by Chrétien de Troyes, a Northern French poet of the late twelfth century. To the perplexity of students of Grail literature, Chrétien's source is unknown, the only clue being a statement by him that he found the tale in a book given to him by Philip, Count of Flanders, to whom the work is dedicated. Chrétien left his work unfinished, and what is most strange is that other writers who ostensibly complete his poem reveal knowledge of other, widely differing versions of the story, some obviously dating earlier than the time of Chrétien. Chrétien's patron was Henri, Count of Champagne, nephew of Henri of Blois, the Bishop of Winchester who commissioned the Shroud-figure style frescoes in the Holy Sepulcher Chapel, Winchester Cathedral, England. The Knights Templars (see next chapter) began in the Champagne region and under the same patronage. There are many diverse elements which need further exploration.

21. See Geoffrey Ashe, *King Arthur's Avalon*, (London: Collins, 1957), chap. 7, for a fascinating account of these.

22. Dobschutz, op. cit., p. 134.

23. ". . . after I had three times made my obeisance to the Emperor with my face upon the ground I lifted my head and behold! The man who just before I had seen sitting on a moderately elevated seat had now changed his raiment and was sitting on the level of the ceiling. How it was done I could not imagine, unless he was lifted up by some sort of device as we use for raising the timbers of a wine-press. . . ." F. A. Wright, trans., *The Works of Liutprand of Cremona* (London, 1930), pp. 207, 208.

24. J. J. Chifflet, *De linteis sepulchralibus Christi crisis historica*

(1624), in Blasius Ugolinus, *Thesaurus antiquitatum sacrarum*, 33 (1767).

25. Quaresimus, *Terrae Sanctae elucidata*, (Venice, 1881–82).

26. André Grabar, "La Sainte Face de Laon et le Mandylion dans l'art orthodoxe," *Seminarium Kondakovianum* (Prague, 1935), p. 29.

27. Ibid., plate VI, 2. The fresco is from the church of Poganovo.

28. Jacopo Grimaldi, *Opusculum de sacrosancto Veronicae sudario Salvatoris Nostri Jesu Christi; . . .* (Rome, 1620). Grimaldi attributes the umbella to the time of Pope John VII (A.D. 705–7), as does E. Müntz, "Une broderie inédite exécutée pour le Pape Jean VII," *Revue de l'art chrétien*, 1900, pp. 18–21. This view is not shared by modern experts such as Walter Oakeshott and Pauline Johnstone. With Joseph Wilpert (*Römische Mosaiken und Malereien*, II, 2 [1924], pp. 1,123ff.), I would attribute it to the time of Celestine III. The close affinity of the figure to that of the Pray manuscript (Bercovits, op. cit.), definitely datable to ca. 1192, is especially significant.

29. William of Tyre, "Historia rerum in partibus transmarinis gestarum," XX, 25 from Migne, *Patrologia latina*, vol. 201, 804; translation by Maurus Green.

30. William of Tyre, *Historiae*, bk. 20, chap. 23, p. 985, in *Recueil des historiens des croisades* (Paris, 1844); translation by Maurus Green.

31. Comte Riant, *Exuviae sacrae constantinopolitanuae* (Geneva, 1878), II 208. The document is actually a forgery, purporting to be a letter from the Byzantine Emperor Alexius Comnenus to Robert of Flanders, and concocted at the time for propaganda purposes. This need not invalidate its description of relics in the imperial collection.

32. ". . . sudarium quod fuit super caput eius." Ibid., p. 211.

33. ". . . et in alia capsula est mantile quod visui domini applicatum imaginem vultus eius retinuit." Ibid.

34. "Likblaejur med Sveitaduk." Ibid., p. 214.

35. Greek text in A. Heisenberg, *Nicholas Mesarites—Die Palasrevolution des Johannes Comnenos* (Wurzburg, 1907), p. 30.

36. Robert de Clari, op. cit., p. 104.

37. Ibid., p. 112. The original French *figure* has been substituted for Neale's translation "features." While *figure* in modern French means face, dictionaries of Old French suggest that at the time of Robert de Clari it did mean figure, as in modern English.

38. For good general background on this see Ernle Bradford, *The Great Betrayal: Constantinople 1204* (Hodder and Stoughton, 1967).

39. Edward Gibbon, *The Decline and Fall of the Roman Empire*, chap. 60.

Chapter XIX 1204 to the 1350s—The Missing Years

1. Translation from W. R. Lethaby and H. Swainson, *Sancta Sophia* (1894), p. 287.
2. Pauline Johnstone, *The Byzantine Tradition in Church Embroidery* (London, 1967), p. 26.
3. Steven Runciman, "Some Remarks on the Image of Edessa," *Cambridge Historical Journal,* III (1929–31).
4. Baldwin had earlier surrendered the relics to Venetian moneylenders who were his creditors, and St. Louis actually bought the relics from them. But he insisted that Baldwin should sign an official document transferring possession. This was the Chrysobull, or Golden Bull in which the *toellam* was mentioned. The text is quoted in Riant, *Exuviae sacrae constantinopolitanuae* (Geneva, 1878), II, pp. 135ff.
5. For a very journalistic claim for this having been the Mandylion, see an excellently illustrated article, "Is This the Face of Christ?" by Conrad Allen, *Weekend Telegraph* (England), December 23, 1964. See also Carlo Bertelli, "Storia e vicende dell'immagine edessena," Paragone, no. 217, *Arte* 1968, pp. 3–33.
6. The list is quoted in Riant, op. cit.
7. For general background to the Knights Templars see C. G. Addison, *History of the Knights Templars* (1842); Desmond Seward, *The Monks of War: The Military Religious Orders* (London: Eyre Methuen, 1972); E. J. Martin, *The Trial of the Templars,* (London, 1928); G. Mollat, *The Popes at Avignon, 1305–1378* (London: Nelson, 1963), important chapter on the "Trial of the Templars," pp. 229–46. For source documents see M. Michelet, *Procès des Templiers* (Paris 1841–51), 2 vols.
8. Michelet, op. cit., II, p. 279.
9. From the Inquisition's *Articles Against Singular Persons,* translated in Martin, op. cit.
10. Deposition of Jean Taillefer, in Michelet, op. cit., I, p. 190. He went on to say that he could not describe it more particularly, except that he thought it was of a reddish color.
11. From the patois version of the king's instructions, quoted in G. Lizerand, *Dossier de l'affaire des Templiers* (Paris, 1923), pp. 24–28.
12. *Procès,* I, p. 399.
13. *Procès,* II, p. 364. Raoul de Gizy was preceptor for the Province of Champagne.
14. Robert of Oteringham, senior of the order of Minorites (Franciscans), from Addison, op. cit., p. 272.
15. G. Legman, *The Guilt of the Templars* (New York: Basic Books, 1968).
16. It is specifically forbidden by the Koran.

17. See on this point Sir H. C. Lea, *History of the Inquisition in the Middle Ages* (New York, 1887), vol. III.

18. Wolfram von Eschenbach, *Parzival*.

19. From the Inquisition's *Articles Against Singular Persons*, articles 56–57.

20. Lea, op. cit., p. 283.

21. For sources see Comte Riant, *Archives de l'Orient latin*, vol. II, part 14, "Etudes sur les derniers temps du royaume de Jérusalem," pp. 388–89. Translation by the author. A *mihrab* is a Moslem prayer niche.

22. Ibid.

23. Hugh de Peraud, visitor general of the order, described one "idol" as having been supported by two feet at the front and two feet at the back. These may well have been to enable a similar copy on a plaque to stand on an altar.

24. "the natural size of a man's head" from a deposition by Templar Jean Taillefer, *Procès*, I, p. 190.

25. V. Godfrey-White, "The Knights of the Temple," unpublished manuscript. I am deeply indebted to Miss Godfrey-White for much assistance with this chapter.

26. See E. Gilson, *The Mystical Theology of St. Bernard*, trans. A. C. Downes (London: Secker and Warburg, 1948). St. Bernard was founder of the Abbey of Clairvaux, and one of the four Latin fathers of the Church. He was one of the most influential men of his age.

27. Dom. John Mabillon, *Life and Works of St. Bernard*, trans. and ed. Samuel J. Eales (London, 1896), vol. IV, "Cantica Conticorum—Sermons on the Song of Solomon," sermon XII.

28. Ibid., sermon XIII.

29. Godfrey-White, op. cit., chap. VII, "The Gift of the White Mantle and the Vision of the Sacred Face."

30. Rule 17 of the Templar Order.

31. For a description of this see H. V. Morton, *A Stranger in Spain* (London: Methuen, 1955).

32. *Articles Against Singular Persons*, articles 58–61, "That they bound or touched the head of the said Idols with a Cord wherewith they girt themselves on their shirts, or next the Skin. That at their reception, the aforesaid little Cords, or others of their length, were delivered to every brother. That they did this in honor of the Idol. That they enjoined them to gird themselves with the said little Cords, as is said above, and to wear them continually."

33. Heinrich Finke, *Papsttum und Untergang des Templerordens* (Münster, 1907), II, p. 334.

34. *Chronicles of St. Denis*, art. III, quoted in de Puy, *Histoire de l'Ordre Militaire des Templiers* (1713), I, p. 25.

35. Inventory of Edward II quoted in appendix to T. H. Baylis,

The Temple Church and Chapel of St. Anne (Geo. Philip & Son, 1895).

36. The torture of the Templars by the Inquisition is not simply an inference. Templar Bernard de Vado told the papal commissioners, "So greatly was I tortured, so long was I held before a burning fire, that the flesh of my heels were burned away; and these two bones, which I now show to you, these came away from my feet. Look and see if they be not missing from my body." Raynouard, *Monuments historiques relatifs a la condemnation des Templiers* (Paris, 1813), p. 73.

The grand master on October 24 and 25, 1307, ten days after capture, confessed his own guilt and that of the order. He even issued an instruction to all Templars under his own seal, directing them to confess to the crimes of which they were charged. But in the presence of the pope's representatives all Templars including Grand Master de Molay solemnly revoked what they had confessed; in the words of the knight Aimery de Villiers de Duc: "I confessed to some things because of the torture inflicted on me by Guillaume de Marcilly and Hugues de la Celle, knights of the king; but they were not true. Yesterday, when I saw fifty-four of my brethren going in carts to the stake because they would not confess to the sins imputed to us, I thought that I should never be able to withstand the fear of the fire. I know in my heart that I would confess to anything; I would confess that I had killed God, if they asked me." Langlois, *Revue des deux mondes,* vol. CIII (1891), p. 411.

Chapter XX Found Once More—As the Shroud

1. There is a possibility that Geoffrey de Charnay was an uncle of the Geoffrey de Charny of Lirey. A television writer, Henry Lincoln, has produced a genealogy showing a Geoffrey de Joinville, de Charnay, de Briquenay as a brother of Margaret de Joinville, who would have been mother of Geoffrey de Charny of Lirey if his father was, indeed, Jean de Charny. But this must remain theory until it can be positively shown that Geoffrey de Joinville/de Charnay was indeed one and the same as Geoffrey de Charnay the Templar.

2. Père Anselme, *Histoire généalogique,* VIII, pp. 201–3.

3. Preserved in the archives of the department of Aube, rack G822.

4. Archives of the department of Aube, records of Lirey, 96, reproduced in Ulysse Chevalier, *Autour des origines du Suaire de Lirey* (Paris: Picard, 1903), doc. E, pp. 29–30.

5. A. Forgeais, *Collection des plombs historiés trouvés dans la Seine* (Paris, 1862–66), IV, p. 105.

6. M. Perret, "Essai sur l'histoire du S. Suaire du XIVe. au XVIe. siècle," *Mémoires de l'Académie des Sciences, Belles Lettres et Arts de Savoie,* IV, (1960), pp. 61, 62.

7. There is a late text copied in the seventeenth century by J. J. Chifflet, (*De linteis sepulchralibus Christi crisis historica* [1624], in Blasius Ugolinus, *Thesaurus antiquitatum sacrarum*, 33 [1767]), which claims that the Shroud had been given to Geoffrey by King Philip VI of France. But the text refers to Geoffrey as "Count" de Charny, a title which was not created until a century after his death. Moreover it is inconceivable that a king of France should have given such a priceless relic to one of his knights, however brave, or that the gift, if it occurred, was not recorded.

8. D'Arcis memorandum quoted in Herbert Thurston, "The Holy Shroud and the Verdict of History," *The Month*, CI (1903), p. 26.

9. Froissart, *Les Chroniques*, (J. A. C. Buchon, 1835), vol. I, "Eclat de la chevalerie," p. 202, quoting Geoffrey de Charny.

10. Ibid., p. 205.

11. The "Ordre de l'Etoile," or "Ordre de Notre Dame de la Noble Maison." François Menestrier, *De la chevalerie ancienne et moderne* (Paris, 1683), p. 179; Dacier, "Recherches historiques sur l'établissement et l'extinction de l'ordre de l'Etoile," in *Mémoires de l'Académie des Inscriptions et Belles Lettres*, XXXIX (1777), p. 662. It is worth noting that the Templars, imprisoned in the Abbey of St. Genevieve in 1310, composed a moving prayer: "Que Marie, l'Etoile de la mer, nous conduise au port de salut." Fr. Aymeri of Limoges, referred to in Albert Ollivier, *Les Templiers* (Paris: Editions du Seuil, 1958), p. 171.

12. Léopold Pannier, *La noble maison de saint Ouen, la villa clipiacum et l'Ordre de l'Etoile* (Paris, 1872).

13. Arch. Nat., JJ77, no. 395.

14. Cornelius Zantiflet, *Chronicon*, col. 254.

15. Perret, op. cit., p. 57.

16. P. A. Eschbach, *Le Saint Suaire de Notre Seigneur Vénéré à Turin* (Turin, 1913), p. 34, n. 1.

17. "Icelle église estoit venue en telle ruine que le dicte Sainct Suaire seurement ne se pourroit guerder en icelluy lieu." Margaret de Charny's argument for not returning the Shroud to the Lirey canons in 1447.

18. Aube Arr. de Troyes, cant. de Bouilly, Arch. Nat., JJ74, no. 357.

19. Froissart, *Oeuvres*, Glossary Index volume XX, p. 545.

20. This and all the subsequent references to the d'Arcis memorandum are derived from Herbert Thurston's translation, op. cit.

21. Ibid., p. 23.

22. Ibid.

23. Ibid., p. 25.

Chapter XXI Years of Gradual Acceptance

1. U. Chevalier, *Etude Critique sur l'origine de Saint Suaire de Lirey-Chambéry-Turin* (Paris: Picard, 1900), pièce justificative Q.

2. L'abbé Loge, *Histoire du comté de la Roche et de Saint Hippolyte, sa capitale* (1888).

3. Jules Gauthier, *Notes iconographiques sur le Saint Suaire de Besançon* (Académie des Sciences, Belles-Lettres et Arts de Besançon, 1883).

4. For a particularly valuable work on this see William H. Forsyth, *The Entombment of Christ: French Sculpture of the Fifteenth and Sixteenth Centuries* (Cambridge: Harvard University Press, 1970).

5. For the most authoritative account of the legal battle, with sources, see M. Perret, "Essai sur l'histoire du S. Suaire du XIVe. au XVIe. siècle," *Mémoires de l'Académie des Sciences, Belles Lettres et Arts de Savoie*, IV (1960), pp. 77–82.

6. Archives of the department of Côte-d'Or, B8440.

7. See B. Secret, "La Savoie franciscaine," *Le rosier de saint François*, Chambéry, Nov. 1942, p. 208; G. Pérouse, "Dépenses de voyage de Louis, duc de Savoie, dans la Bresse et le Dauphiné en 1451 et 1452," *Mémoires et documents publiés par la société Savoisienne d'Histoire et d'Archéologie* XLII (1903), p. xxxvff.

8. S. Guichenon, *Histoire généalogique de la royale maison de Savoie*, (Turin, new ed. 1778), vol. II, p. 186.

9. U. Chevalier, *Le Saint Suaire de Turin: Histoire d'une relique* (Paris: A. Picard, 1902), p. 16.

10. Sixtus IV, *De sanguine Christi* (1473), from U. Chevalier, Etude critique . . . , pièce justificative C.

11. L. Celier, *St. Charles Borromée* (1538–1583) (Paris: V. Lecoffre, 1923), pp. 184–85.

12. Translation from *The Keys*, 1974. The original Italian has the papal "we," which I have transformed into the singular for better appreciation of a specifically personal statement by Pope Paul.

PART V The Shroud—A Paranormal Phenomenon?

Chapter XXII The Continuing Research

1. I am indebted to information given to me about this project at the conference, and to an interview with Dr. Jackson.

2. John P. Jackson, Eric J. Jumper, and Kenneth E. Stevenson, eds., "The Three Dimension Image on Jesus' Burial Cloth," paper read at the Albuquerque conference, March 23, 1977.

3. A. P. Bender, "Beliefs, Rites, and Customs of the Jews Con-

nected with Death, Burial, and Mourning," part IV, *Jewish Quarterly Review*, VII (1895), pp. 101–3. Bender quotes the practice from J. G. Frazer, *Journal of the Anthropological Institute*, XV, p. 71, who in turn quotes Bodenschatz, *Kirchliche verfassung der heutigen Juden*, IV, p. 174, and Gubernatis, *Usi funebri*, p. 50. Archaeological evidence for the practice is lacking due to Jewish corpses being put in ossuaries after decomposition. But it is by no means unlikely.

4. Walter C. McCrone, "Dating Methods of the Shroud and Chemistry of Its Image and Stains," paper read at the Albuquerque conference, March 23, 1977.

5. Ibid.

Chapter XXIII   The 1978 Exposition

1. At the time of going to press Dr. Ray Rogers is working on these samples.

2. Ricci believes this to have been a facecloth interposed between the Shroud and Jesus' body, and points to various marks which he believes match up with the Shroud. As with so much of Ricci's work, the evidence is very thin.

3. The technique uses a Van de Graaff accelerator. For further information, see "Accelerator Technique Improves Radioisotope Dating," *Physics Today*, December 1977.

4. Ideally, fresh samples should be taken to supplement those cut off for Professor Raes in 1973. One of the two Raes samples is from the side-strip, which *may* not be of the same date as the main Shroud.

Chapter XXIV   The Last Miracle

1. See Paul Vignon, *The Shroud of Christ* (London, 1902).

2. Giovanni Judica-Cordiglia, *La Sindone* (Padua, 1961).

3. I am particularly indebted to Dr. David Gledhill of the Department of Botany, Bristol University, for much patience in finding many examples in the University's collection.

4. Jean Volckringer, *Le problème des empreintes devant la science* (Paris: Libraire du Carmel, 1942).

5. Geoffrey Ashe, "What Sort of Picture?" *Sindon*, 1966, pp. 15–19.

6. John Hersey, *Hiroshima* (Penguin Books, 1946), pp. 104–5 (reprinted from *The New Yorker*, August 1946). Italics added.

7. For a detailed explanation of this see Sheila Ostrander and Lynn Schroeder, *Psychic Discoveries Behind the Iron Curtain* (London: Abacus, 1970).